Ciarcia's Circuit Cellar

BY STEVE CIARCIA

"BOOKS OF INTEREST TO COMPUTER PEOPLE"

A DIVISION OF BYTE PUBLICATIONS, INC.

70 Main St., • Peterborough, N.H. 03458 • (603) 924-7217

The author of the programs provided with this book has carefully reviewed them to ensure their performance in accordance with the specifications described in the book. Neither the author nor BYTE Publications Inc however, makes any warranties whatever concerning the programs. They assume no responsibility or liability of any kind for errors in the programs or for the consequences of any such errors. The programs are the sole property of the author and have been registered with the United States Copyright Office.

Copyright © 1979 BYTE Publications Inc. All Rights Reserved. BYTE and PAPERBYTE are Trademarks of BYTE Publications Inc. No part of this book may be translated or reproduced in any form without the prior written consent of BYTE Publications Inc.

Library of Congress Cataloging in Publication Data

Ciarcia, Steve.
    Ciarcia's Circuit Cellar.

    Articles written by the author for a BYTE magazine column, Ciarcia's Circuit Cellar, which began in Nov. 1977.
    Includes bibliographies.
    1. Minicomputers—Collected works. I. Title.
II. Title: Circuit Cellar.
TK788.3.C58   621.3819.5   78-20920
ISBN 0-931718-07-4

Printed in the United States of America

This book is dedicated to my two Scottish terriers,
Brenda and Whiskey
who kept the late night vigil slaving over a
hot computer with me.

Table of Contents

Preface   vii

No Power for Your Interfaces? (October 1978 BYTE)   1
    Discussion of DC-to-DC conversion with various methods to achieve voltage multiplication. A specific dual voltage converter is detailed for construction.

Memory Mapped IO (November 1977 BYTE)   7
    Tutorial defining both classical input/output (IO) decoding and memory mapped methods.

Try an 8 Channel DVM Cocktail (December 1977 BYTE)   13
    Construction of an 8 channel 3½ digit DC digital voltmeter interface.

Add More Zing to the Cocktail (January 1978 BYTE)   25
    Further enhancements to the digital voltmeter that increase its capability to include AC and DC inputs and fully programmable range selection.

A Penny Pinching Address State Analyzer (February 1978 BYTE)   35
    Simple interface which provides dynamic display of the microprocessor address bus during program execution.

Program Your Next EROM in BASIC (March 1978 BYTE)   39
    An interface to program a 2708 EROM from a BASIC interpreter.

Control the World (September 1977 BYTE)   47
    A tutorial on digital to analog conversion with a design provided for a 4 channel self-refreshing 8 bit digital to analog converter interface, with application examples.

Tune In and Turn On, Part 1 (April 1978 BYTE)   61
Tune In and Turn On, Part 2 (May 1978 BYTE)   71
    Two part article which discusses the various methods for carrier current remote control and which provides a functional design for a 10 channel *AC wireless remote control system*.

Talk to Me (June 1978 BYTE)   77
    Discussion of the requirements for recording digitized speech and implemented by constructing a 200,000 sample per second analog to digital converter.

Build a Keyboard Function Decoder (July 1978 BYTE)   89
    Simple circuit which decodes keyboard control codes.

Let Your Fingers Do the Talking, Part 1 (August 1978 BYTE)   95
Let Your Fingers Do the Talking, Part 2 (September 1978 BYTE)   105
    A design for a 16 by 16 resolution noncontact touch input system which can be attached over a video screen. Part 2 discusses software applications.

Come Upstairs and Be Respectable (May 1977 BYTE)   109
    Design for an asynchronous communications interface to allow remote terminal location.

I've Got You in My Scanner (November 1978 BYTE)   115
    Using the components and knowledge of previous articles and adding a stepper motor, a pseudo "radar" is constructed to track luminous targets.

About the Author   123

Preface

I have briefly alluded to my fantasy life in several articles. Not unlike most of the other people in the world who often feel caught up in the ridiculous, no, just silly demands that are made on us in the name of Reality, I prize the little corners of my imagination that allow me to tune out occasionally. If you're like me you know what a lifesaving device it is to be able to find yourself in the middle of an impossibly stalemated business meeting and to ponder the wonders of leisure time, Escape.

("Hello, Walter Mitty? This is Steve Ciarcia. I've booked passage for two to India and we leave immediately. Charge? No charge. I've made the whole thing up, so it's on the house.")

For me, leisure time (grip yourselves, sports freaks and needlepoint enthusiasts) involves soldering, circuit design, and other electronics related activities, or electro-funk as my wife calls it.

My association with BYTE magazine has produced an almost too good situation blending work with the ordinarily hard to justify leisure time pursuits of my past two decades (I wired the bottom step of my mother's house when I was 10 so I could turn the television off and look asleep when she came up to check on me). In sort of a Mittyesque arabesque I have been able to turn work into fun by writing for BYTE. To those who want to stop reading and smack me right now, I don't blame you: but then, why stop with me? Think of all those guys who spend their lives drawing cartoons for *Playboy*? Or what about the ones who photograph for it? Do they know about your pain as a Teflon tensile tester (my wife held that position one summer during college)? No, I say! So why single me out for your anger? ("Hi, Hef? This is Steve Ciarcia calling. Listen Hef, I have this 35mm camera that I've learned to use really well taking pictures for my articles in BYTE magazine, and I started thinking that I'd like to change from circuit photography to more, shall we say, human interest stuff. . . . No, I don't have any European cut shirts but I do have an Artificial Intelligence T-shirt, yeah, just like the one I saw David Ahl wearing last year.")

All my life I've spent experimenting, building, and just "fiddling" in electronics. In fact, mine was not a childhood measured in developmental milestones as per Dr. Spock. I plotted my maturation in terms of the number of basements I had filled with junk. My family moved a lot and I managed to fill eight of them.

Then my parents started hinting that they wanted basement privileges. Fortunately this was about the time I decided to combine matrimonial bliss with owning my own basement. Dispensing with our first basement rather quickly, we then spent five years in a pleasant little house. One day I realized that my expanding electronics collection was creating a bulge in my basement wall. A difficult decision was made — we would move again. Altough my wife said she was rather fond of the upstairs (I never saw much of it myself), she too wanted to get further into the woods. The real estate agents were skeptical when I said I wanted a big cellar and wasn't particular what went on top of it. When they found what I wanted my wife was skeptical. Like a pig in mud though, I knew as soon as I saw the 2500 square feet of concrete basement that this was home.

Well, I could go on, but it won't help to introduce the articles that follow, and I should be a bit more serious about explaining the philosophy behind the articles I write. I don't sit down each month and try to decide what to put into a column. It's rather just a case of documenting what has happened to me in the previous month's time. As far as my personal experiences go, the true accounts are often more humorous than any fictional introductions I could invent.

The real purpose behind "Ciarcia's Circuit Cellar" is to involve, educate, and motivate the reader. It might also further the credibility of the discussion if I explain exactly how I arrived at the topic. Beyond that of course, it is to provide a timely and cost effective design which will aid the personal computer enthusiast and enhance his or her system. The ultimate aim is to widen the interest group to include more nontechnical computer enthusiasts who will become interested and possibly even motivated to construct some of the less complicated construction articles. The actual "Ciarcia's Circuit Cellar" column started in November of 1977. All entries under this column heading up to this time have been included in this anthology. Five additional articles were written for BYTE prior to this time. One has become the subject of a recently published book and two of the others are included here because their topics are still of a timely nature.

The articles reprinted here encompass a considerable latitude. Rather than separate them into logical categories such as digital to analog converters and analog to digital converters, I have maintained a more or less chronological categorization. Often times previous articles are referenced in the later writings. The earliest writings were more tutorial in nature while the later ones became more application oriented. It is necessary to gain a strong understanding of the component parts of these interfaces in the first series of articles to fully utilize the technical presentations of later works.

In addition, a number of articles were written suggesting designs which created sophisticated test gear out of the personal computer. Address state analyzers and multiplexed analog measuring systems are not to be taken lightly, especially when a $39 interface can replace thousands of dollars of expensive meters. These, as most of my other articles, were aimed at illustrating the truly wide open area of hardware and software microcomputer applications.

Above it all, though, is a desire to enjoy owning a personal computer. Now that I have an even larger basement (my 11th to date) I have to start filling it up some way and it would be sacriligious not to wire and completely computer-control the whole house.

If you have an idea for a project to build or have comments about any of my articles, please write (enclose a stamped, self-addressed envelope) and tell me about it. I'm always interested in hearing from readers who have such brainstorms.

Finally, my thanks to Dr. Russell Reiss for contributing ideas which have led to many of my articles.

Steve Ciarcia
POB 582
Glastonbury CT 06033

September 1, 1978

No Power For Your Interfaces?

Build a 5 W DC to DC Converter

Recently I attended a local computer club meeting where we discussed the question of power supplies. Many people were remarking that, while they enjoyed building the projects in my articles, often their power supplies were not compatible with the multiple voltages I required. Many of the newer single board computers that some members owned contained only a hefty +5 V supply and a note that the user should add additional supplies if the basic board is expanded.

This is not an industry copout by any means. The newest digital designs from companies like Intel are made to run on +5 V and this is considered an advance in technology. The 8080A processor requires +12, +5 and -5 V for operation, while the new 8085 uses only a single +5 V supply. As long as all other components such as universal asynchronous receiver-transmitters (UARTs), programmable memories, erasable read only memories (EROMs) and read only memories (ROMs) in the computer are all +5 V, we can eliminate additional power supplies and save money. Computer manufacturers have done just that.

This situation does not cause any problems as long as the user stays with the basic unit, or expands it using single +5 V supply devices. Erasable read only memories such as the Intel 2716 and programmable peripheral interfaces such as the 8255 are designed specifically for this application.

The problem arises when the single supply computer tries to be communications compatible with the rest of the world, or when a bipolar analog interface is added. The RS-232C interface generally requires + and -12 V potentials, and digital to analog converters such as the Motorola 1408L8, which run on +5 and -12 to -15 V.

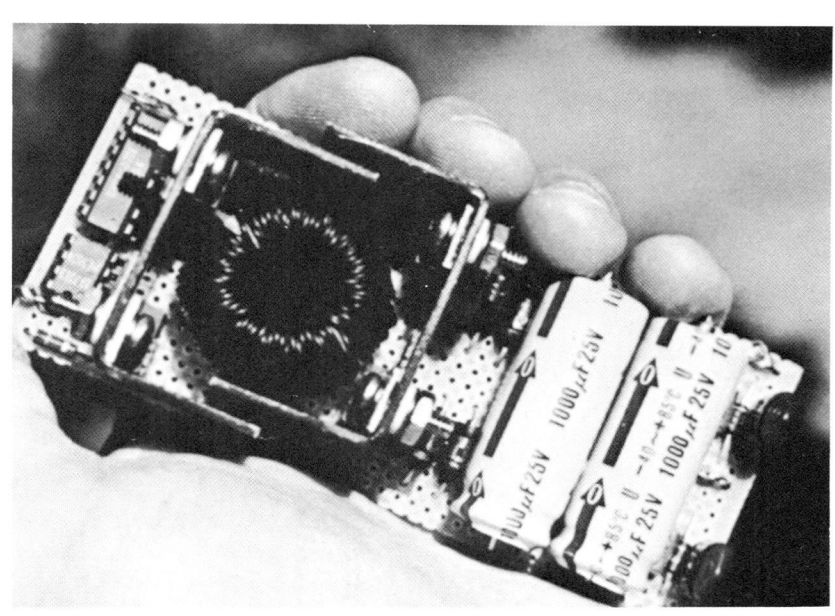

Photo 1: 5 W DC to DC converter, which produces 0.2 A at +12 and -12 VDC from a 5 VDC source. The circuit uses a special custom wound toroidal transformer (see figures 5a and 5b). Note: the prototype shown uses 1000 µF 25 V capacitors, which were later replaced with 100 µF 25 V versions.

The Whole World Isn't TTL Compatible

What is the experimenter to do when a -15 V supply is needed and the computer has only +5 V, or when one wishes to tie an RS-232 terminal into a system? Obviously the answer is to add an additional power supply or two—but, what kind?

Power supply requirements should be based on load requirements. If 0.5 A at +15 V is needed to power a particular interface, then perhaps a 1 A traditional transformer-rectifier-filter-regulator design is in order. More often than not, though, the interface might use one or two dual supply

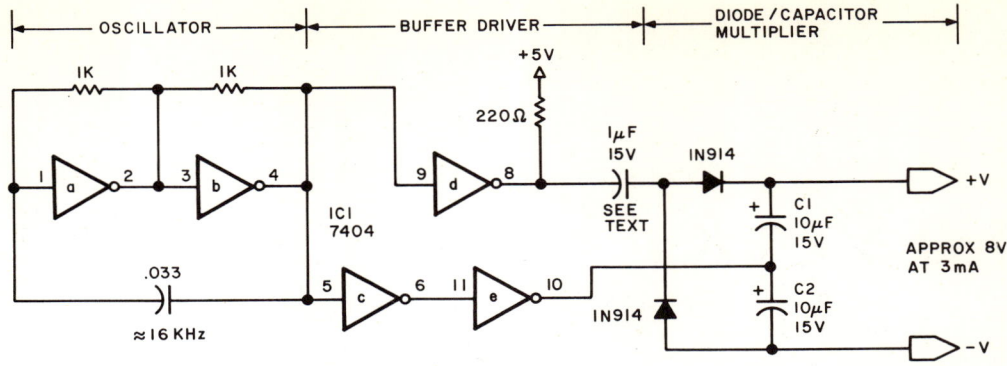

Figure 1: Typical DC to DC converter, a device used to convert one DC voltage into another. The oscillator section supplies a train of square waves to the buffer drivers. On the first half cycle, capacitor C1 is charged to approximately 4 V, and on the second half cycle, C2 is charged to -4 V. The voltage across the two capacitors is twice the input voltage, or approximately 8 V (open circuit). The 1 mF capacitor between IC1d and the two diodes isolates the circuit so that the 8 V can be referenced to ground.

integrated circuits and require only 50 mA, or if the interface is designed with CMOS circuitry, the current requirement could be 5 mA or less. While the 60 Hz transformer design may be more than adequate, the volume and weight of the low frequency magnetics is bulky and may not fit easily within the present enclosure.

The DC to DC Converter

In an application that requires higher voltage at low current, the DC to DC converter is the natural choice for the designer. As its name implies, it converts one DC voltage to another, usually a higher one. All DC to DC converters incorporate oscillator sections to provide AC either to drive transformers or to drive diode-capacitor voltage multipliers. The converters operate at high frequencies to reduce transformer weight. We'll explore the particulars later.

A DC to DC converter need not be low power, but the designs and applications presented here are specifically for low current and limited space applications. The majority of the circuits occupy less than 2 square inches (12.9 square cm).

A DC to DC converter draws its power from some major power bus, such as a +5 V or +12 V computer supply, and converts this source voltage to a higher level of either the same or reversed polarity. The simplest configuration is shown in figure 1. IC1a and IC1b form the oscillator which is common to all DC to DC converters. IC1c, IC1d and IC1e are buffers with the outputs of IC1d and IC1e 180 degrees out of phase,

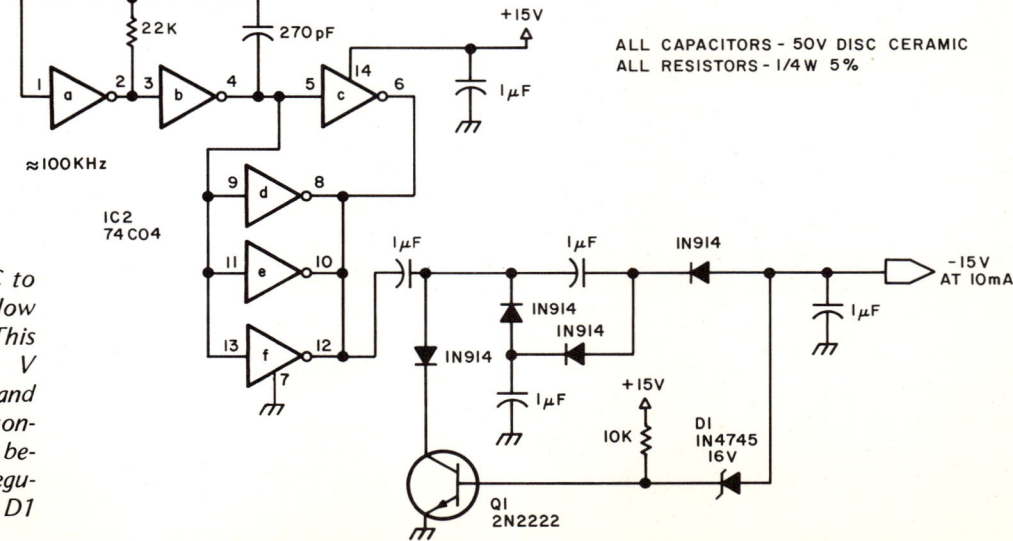

Figure 2: A CMOS DC to DC converter used for low current applications. This circuit produces -15 V from a +15 V source and provides a relatively constant output voltage because of the shunt regulator formed by diodes D1 and Q1.

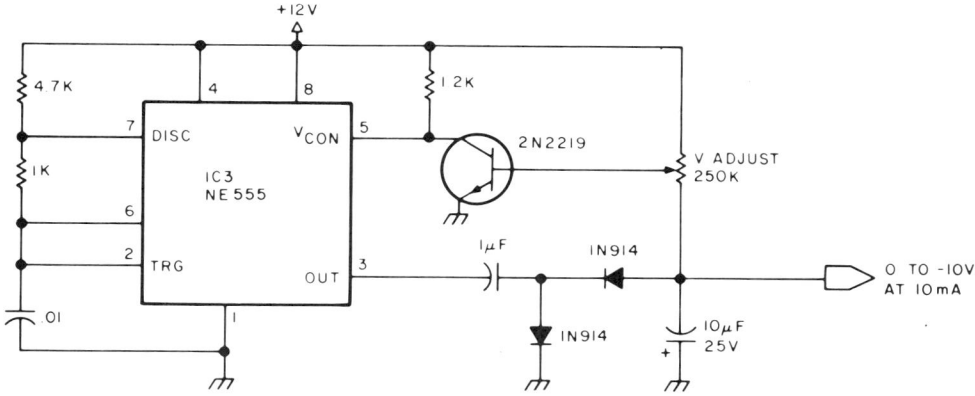

Figure 3: A variable output DC to DC converter capable of producing 0 to -10 V.

simulating a pseudo AC signal to the voltage multiplier. During the first half cycle, the capacitor, C1, is charged to approximately 4 V, and during the second half cycle, C2 is oppositely charged. The voltage across the two capacitors is twice the input voltage, or approximately 8 V (open circuit). If this circuit were not isolated from the drivers (IC1d and IC1e), neither +V nor -V line can be grounded or the multiplier section will be shorted out. The 1 mF 15 V capacitor between pin 8 and the junction of the two IN914 diodes provides isolation and allows the -V lead to be grounded. The output is then approximately 8 V, referenced to ground.

Inverting Supplies

Most often DC to DC supplies are used where a negative voltage is required to power a bipolar linear interface or a dual supply large scale integrated circuit such as a keyboard encoder.

Figures 2 and 3 are examples of converters which would be suitable for these low current applications. Figure 2 produces -15 V from a +15 V source and provides a relatively constant output voltage because of the shunt regulator formed by the diode, D1, and the transistor, Q1. Changing the zener diode, D1, to 13 V makes the output -12 V instead of -15 V. The circuit outlined in figure 3 uses the voltage control input of an NE555 timer circuit to produce a variable output of 0 to -10 V.

Dual Voltage Converters

In most cases single voltage converters use diode steering and charged capacitor voltage multiplication. Transformers or other inductive devices must be incorporated if dual outputs are a requirement. Figure 4 is a very simple ±15 V converter which is powered from a +5 V supply.

Type	Function	+5 V	-5 V	-12 V	+12 V
Ay-5-1013A	UART	20 mA		18 mA	
2708	1 K x 8 EROM	10 mA	45 mA		65 mA
2716 (Intel)	2 K x 8 EROM	100 mA			
2716 (TI)	2 K x 8 EROM	22 mA		12 mA	45 mA
MC1408L8	8 bit digital to analog converter	8 mA		20 mA	
LM301	op amp			3 mA	3 mA
LM741	op amp			2.8 mA	2.8 mA
MM5559	33 bit serial to parallel converter	10 mA		20 mA	

Table 1: Worst case current requirements for a variety of integrated circuits.

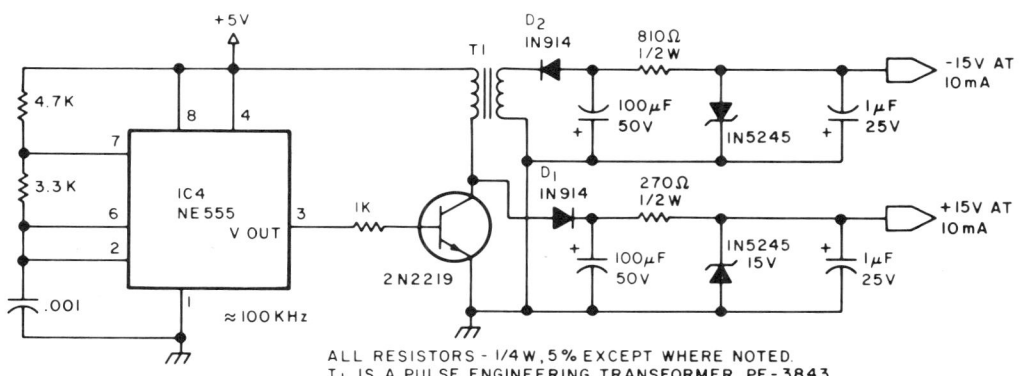

Figure 4: Low current dual voltage output DC to DC converter which supplies -15 and -15 V from a +5 V input.

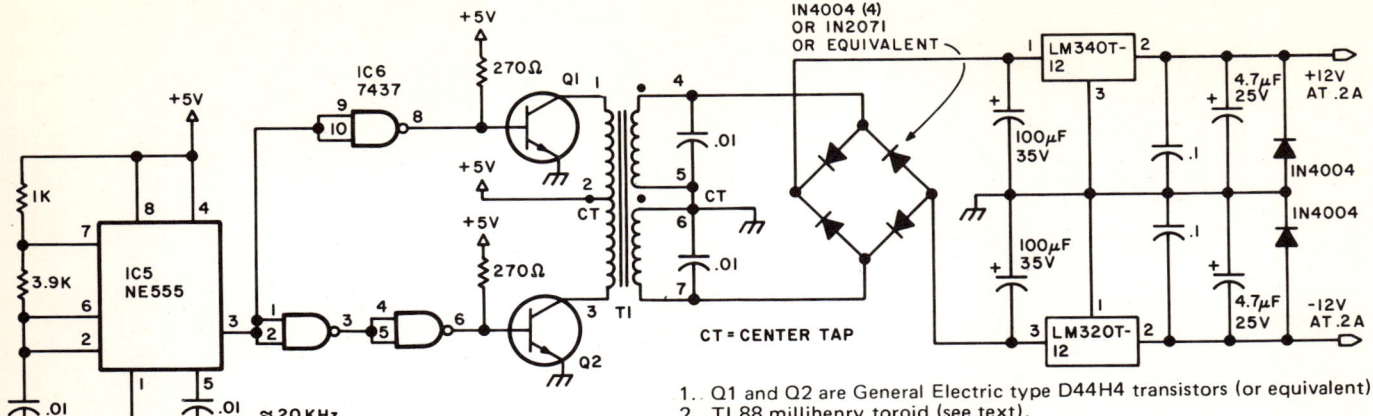

1. Q1 and Q2 are General Electric type D44H4 transistors (or equivalent).
2. T1 88 millihenry toroid (see text).
3. All resistors ¼ W 5%.
4. All capacitors are 100 V ceramic unless otherwise marked.

Figure 5a: 5 W DC to DC converter pictured in photo 1, which produces 0.2 A at +12 and -12 V from a 5 V source. See figure 5b for details of winding a toroidal transformer for this circuit.

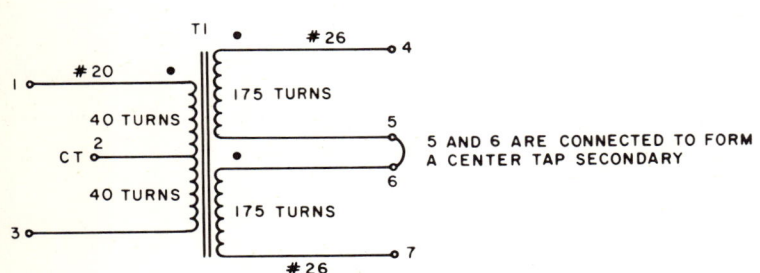

1. Use enamel or Fomvar coated wire for each winding.
2. Be careful when winding not to scratch protective insulation.
3. Primary consists of 80 turns of #20 wire with center tap.
4. Secondaries can be wound as two #26 wire, 175 turn windings or as a single 350 turn winding with center tap.
5. For toroid source see text.
6. Use sandpaper or similar material to remove insulation from terminal wires before soldering.

Figure 5b: Toroid winding details for the custom transformer used in the circuit of figure 5a (see photos 2 thru 5).

Number	Type	+5 V	Gnd
IC1	7404	14	7
IC2	74C04	14	7
IC3	555	8	1
IC4	555	8	1
IC5	555	8	1
IC6	7437	14	7

Table 2: Power wiring table for figures 1 thru 5.

A 100 kHz oscillator switches a transistor on and off, inducing a current into the primary of transformer, T1. The voltage produced at the secondary is rectified and regulated to -15 V.

As with all inductive devices which are pulsed, a high voltage spike is reflected back to the collector of the transistor. Rather than shunting this voltage, as would be the case when we put a diode across a coil, D1 routes this spike to a filter and regulator combination to provide a +15 V output.

Building a DC to DC Converter

One of the first things to determine after deciding to use a DC to DC converter in your system is just how much current it must provide. Table 1 lists the typical voltages and operating current requirements (worst case) of a sampling of devices.

It should be apparent from this listing that EROMs are power-hungry devices and will use more than the 10 mA that the converters discussed thus far can supply. For this reason the unit described in figure 5 is designed to produce a full 200 mA at ±12 V.

This design uses a push/pull inverter technique to create AC which drives transformer, T1. T1 is a toroid transformer and its doughnut shape is quite unlike the more

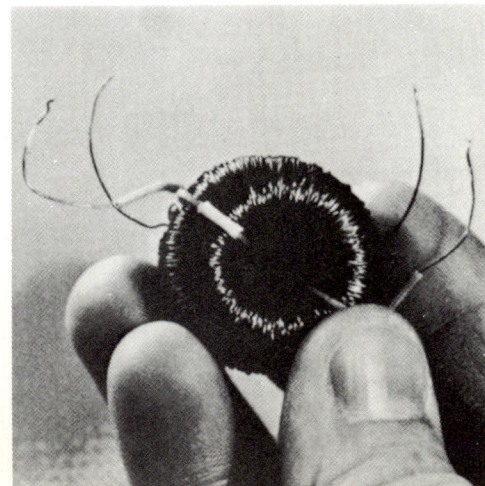

Photo 2: Surplus 88 millihenry toroidal transformer rewound with two secondaries of 175 turns of #26 wire each (after first unwinding the existing two windings of approximately 350 turns each). The unit is used in the circuit of figure 5a.

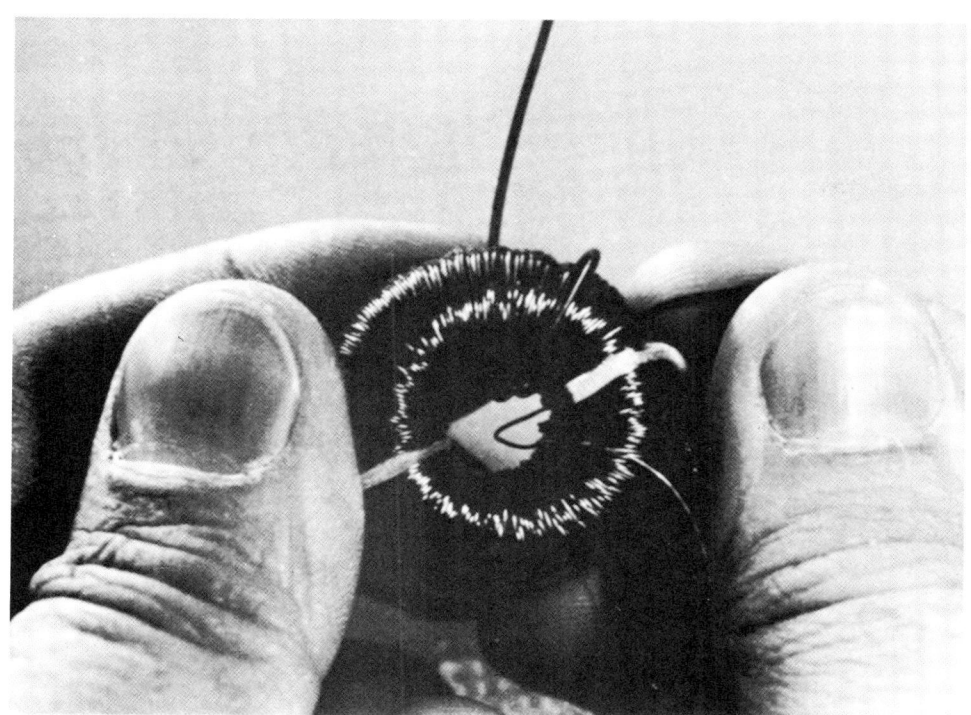

Photo 3: Adding the primary winding, step 1: wind 40 turns of #20 wire evenly around the toroid.

common rectangular filament transformers. The shape and style of the toroid are specifically designed for high frequency operation, which is the main attribute of this inverter design. Heavy magnetic cores are necessary only for low frequencies such as 60 Hz. Since this converter's switching speed is 20 kHz, relatively little magnetic material is necessary, and high power output can be obtained.

The toroid in this design is a surplus 88 millihenry toroid, frequently advertised in the amateur radio magazines. A source I have found is: M Weinschenker, POB 353, Irwin PA 15642. Order 88 millihenry unpotted toroids.

There are two ways to wind this toroid. Since it presently contains two windings of approximately 350 turns each, adding a primary sounds most logical. In reality though, 180 turns of #20 wire couldn't possibly fit in the remaining space, and the number of windings seems to vary from source to source. To obtain a properly wound toroid, it is best to first completely unwind the toroid and then rewind two 175 turn secondaries. The rewound toroid looks like photo 2. Since inductors exhibit an output polarity that is important when tying two secondaries in series, it is advisable to mark the starting lead on each coil and wind each in the same direction. It is not catas-

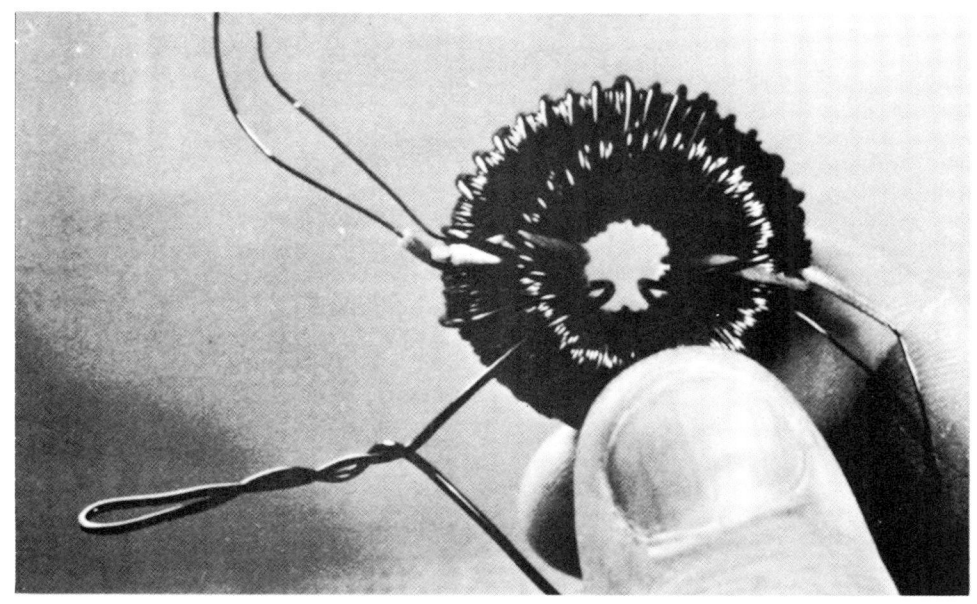

Photo 4: Adding the primary winding, step 2: make a loop for the center tap and continue with 40 additional turns.

Photo 5: The completed transformer. The ends of all enameled wires should be cleaned of insulation before soldering.

trophic if you don't. Polarity can be determined empirically later.

The primary is wound with #20 wire over the two secondaries as in photo 3, and should be distributed evenly around the toroid. When 40 turns have been wound, make a loop in the wire so that it will stick out (as shown in photo 4) and then continue winding the next 40 turns in the same direction. The complete toroid should look like photo 5.

The design outlined in figure 5a is a DC inverter. The NE555 20 kHz oscillator sources the high current 7437 buffers which are necessary to drive the push/pull transistor combination of Q1 and Q2. The continuous on/off action of the transistors produces an alternating current of 20 kHz in the primary winding of the toroid. This in turn induces a voltage proportional to the ratio of the primary to secondary turns, times the primary input voltage into the secondary winding. With approximately 4 V into the primary (taking into account the collector to emitter voltage drop, V_{CE}, transistors Q1 and Q2), 18 to 20 V should be present on each secondary.

The output of the toroid is treated as it would be in a traditional DC regulator design. The two secondaries are connected in series (terminals 4 and 5 connected) to produce 45 V between terminals 3 and 6. If a low voltage is obtained instead of 45 V, then the secondaries are out of phase and the terminals of one of the coils should be reversed. The two terminals which are connected at this point are the center tap and should be grounded.

Four diodes and two capacitors function as the full wave rectifier and filter input to a pair of 3 terminal voltage regulators. The result is a well-regulated + and −12 V supply with output current in excess of 200 mA on each. Overall conversion efficiency is better than 50%.

One note to keep in mind when testing this device: since the output is 5 W with 50% efficiency, the continuous input current to the converter will be approximately 2 A (at 5 V). Peak current will be higher at each clock transition. Use a supply with sufficient current capabilities or it will degrade the performance of the converter and possibly not even work. ∎

Memory Mapped IO

I don't want to get into a fight over which microprocessor chip is better. They all have their favorable and unfavorable features. But, if you look a little closer, you may find that some of these extra features can be added with very little expense.

I was speaking with a fellow computer nut recently, and he was arguing about the merits of the 6800 versus the 8080. I really didn't care to continue the conversation nor to justify why I had an 8080 and Z-80. But, when he said that one reason was that the 6800 had memory mapped IO and the 8080 didn't, I knew he didn't know what it was.

This of course made me curious, and I approached a number of 8080 users to ask if they knew what memory mapped IO was. They assured me that they did, and that it was in fact one of the main features of the 6800. But such a feature is hardly exclusive to the 6800!

First of all, memory mapped IO means simply that a portion of memory address space has been reserved for interfacing with external devices. A byte of data is stored into a memory location, as always, but this storage unit, rather than being made up of 1024 bit programmable memory chips, is an

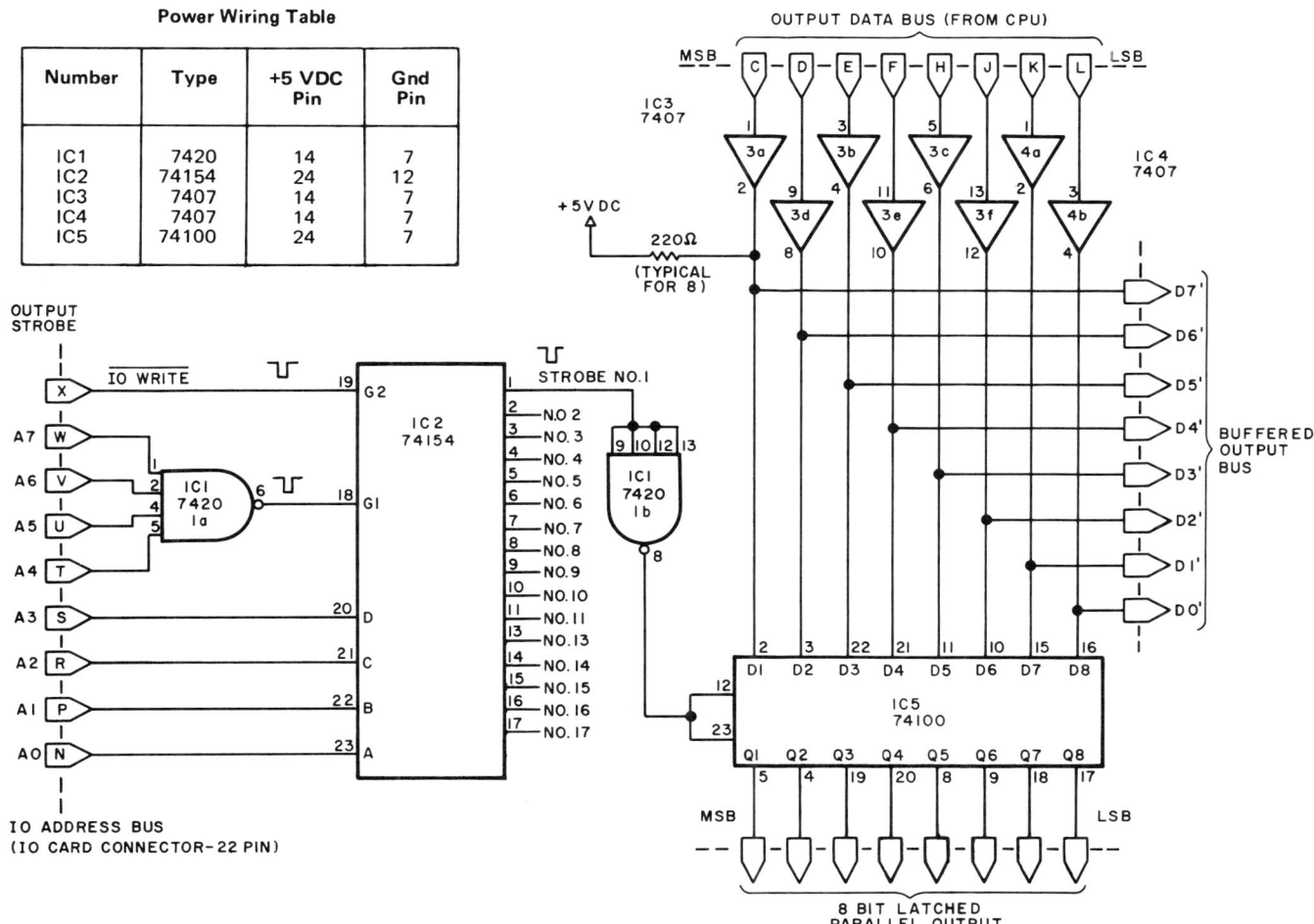

Figure 1: A schematic diagram for a direct addressed output port decoding circuit. The port assignments as diagrammed are from octal codes 360 to 377. The bus pin assignments are for the Digital Group bus system, but the Altair (S-100) bus is logically equivalent.

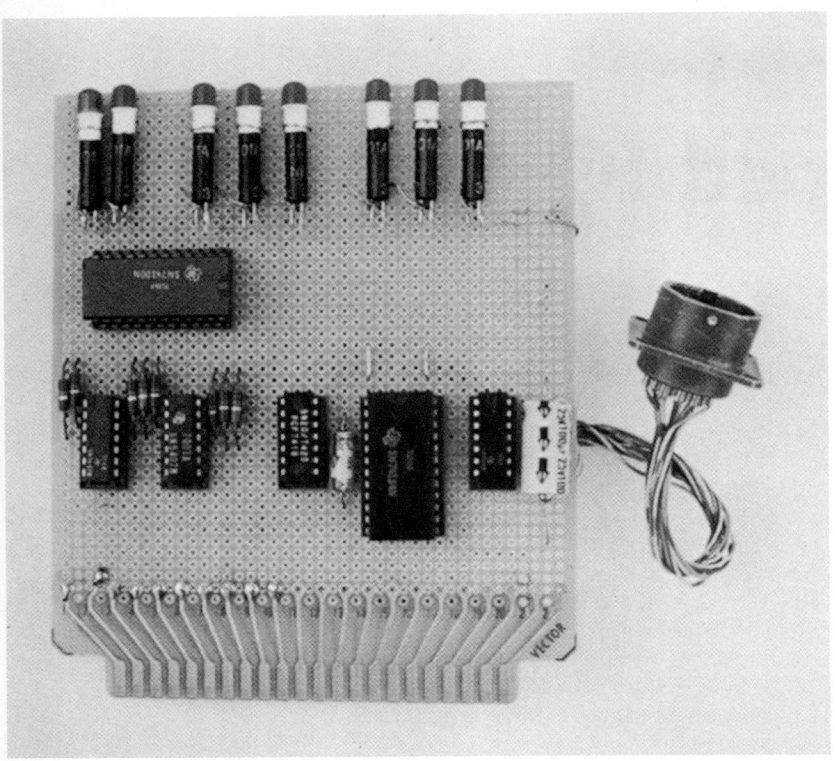

Photo 1: A realization of the hardware circuit shown in figure 1 with the addition of eight lights connected to the outputs of IC5. The connector attaches to bus lines for the author's other front end projects.

Photo 2: A prototype for the circuit shown in figure 2.

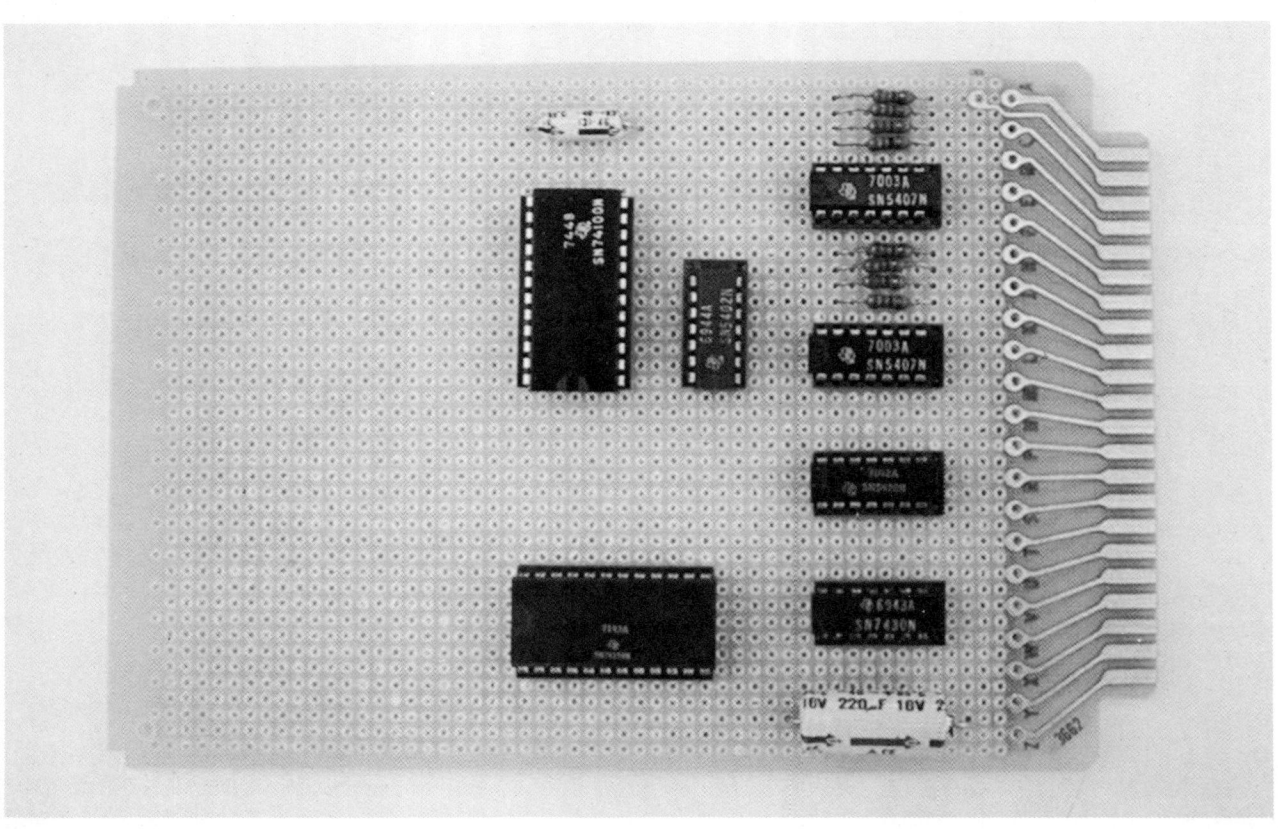

8 bit storage register such as a 74100. This type of procedure provides access to the data byte through the "back door," or output lines of the 74100. If you have followed me to this point, you can see that the concept of memory mapped IO is applicable to any microprocessor that directly addresses memory! I don't know of too many processors which operate without this ability, so we'll just have to conclude that any microprocessor can be wired to provide memory mapped IO, including the 8080.

Look no further! It's a bird...it's a plane...no, it's Superchip! It looks like an 8080, acts like an 8080 and, while not trying to steal Motorola's thunder, has memory mapped IO! The name of this new chip? Well, it's the plain old 8080 with an *intelligent user*.

Why should I consider memory mapped IO?

The 8080 directly addresses 64 K bytes of memory and 512 IO ports (256 in and 256 out). The only way data can arrive at an output port is by being passed through the accumulator and routed to a particular port by a 2 byte output instruction. Similarly, a 2 byte instruction directs input data to the accumulator. Additional programming is necessary to store this input byte in memory.

Obviously, if the data path went to a memory location instead of an output port, a broader range of instructions would be available. The 8080 (like most computers) has some very powerful instructions when it comes to memory operations. For the 8080 these include MOV, MVI, STAX and STA instructions which, by definition, are added to the output data manipulation repertoire with memory mapped IO.

Often the best way to approach a new subject is to analyze the present method. Figure 1 illustrates the basic design of an 8080 output "port." To emphasize simplicity I've used 74100 latches for this example rather than the more complex ports such as the Motorola 6820 peripheral interface adapter. This configuration provides 16 output strobes, starting with the octal output port address 360 and ending with octal 377. Integrated circuits 1 and 2 decode the address bus and, when provided with an output strobe during an output instruction, load the present contents of the data bus into an 8 bit storage register (IC5). ICs 3 and 4 provide buffering and allow more 74100s to be attached to the buffered ouput bus lines for multiple ports. The pin designations are for the Digital Group bus system, but the Altair (S-100) bus is logically equivalent.

Converting an output system to memory mapped IO (illustrated in figure 2) requires the addition of two more integrated circuits, ICs 6 and 7, to decode the additional eight lines associated with memory addressing. With the decoding arrangement illustrated

Power Wiring Table

Number	Type	+5 VDC Pin	Gnd Pin
IC1	7420	14	7
IC2	74154	24	12
IC3	7407	14	7
IC4	7407	14	7
IC5	74100	24	7
IC6	7402	14	7
IC7	7420	14	7

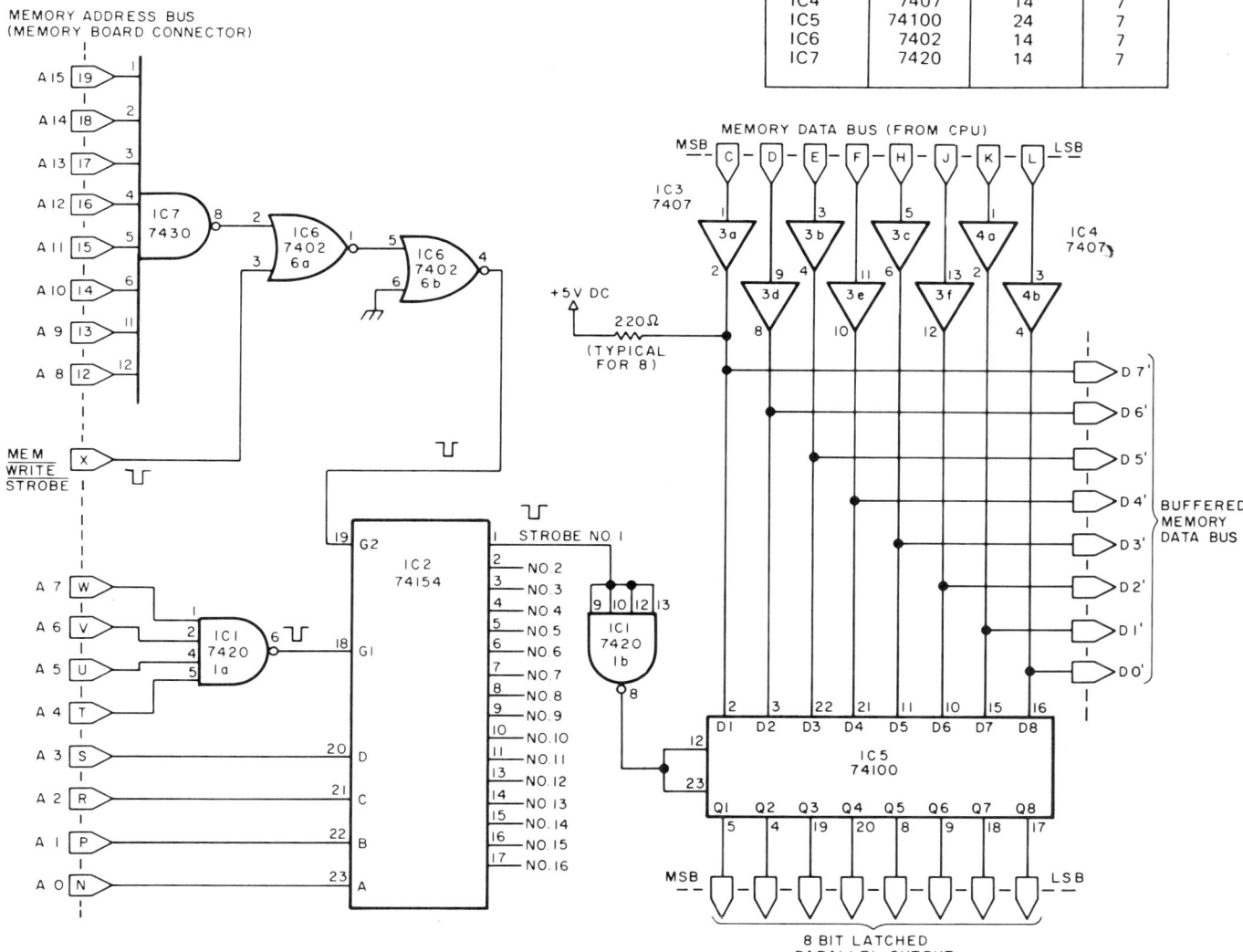

Figure 2: A schematic diagram for a memory addressed output port decoding circuit. The port assignments in this case are from split field octal memory addresses 377/360 to 377/377. Here again, the bus pin assignments are for the Digital Group bus.

Example 1: Output the contents of the B register to port r.

- **8080 Direct IO**
  ```
  MOV B, A    ; Move the contents of the B register to the accumulator
  OUT r       ; Output the accumulator to port #r
              ; Total bytes    3
              ; Total states   15
  ```

- **Memory Mapped IO**
  ```
  LXI HL      ; Set memory pointer HL
  MOV M, B    ; Move B register to memory location HL
              ; Total bytes    4
              ; Total states   17
  ```

For simple data manipulations like this, the direct IO technique, which is familiar to all 8080 users, occupies less memory space.

Example 2: With two 8 bit digital to analog convertors attached to output registers, generate two sawtooth waveforms 180° out of phase.

- **8080 Direct IO**
  ```
           LXI BC      ; Load initial values into B and C (000, 200 octal)
  CONTINUE INC B       ; Increment the B value
           MOV B, A    ; Move the contents of the B register to the accumulator
           OUT 1       ; Output the accumulator to port 1 (1st sawtooth)
           INC C       ; Increment the C value
           MOV C, A    ; Move the contents of the C register to the accumulator
           OUT 2       ; Output the accumulator to port 2 (2nd sawtooth)
           JMP CONTINUE
                  Total bytes    14
                  Total states   60 (one pass)
  ```

- **Memory Mapped IO**
  ```
           LXI HL      ; Load initial values into H and L (000, 200 octal)
  CONTINUE INC H       ; Increment the H value
           INC L       ; Increment the L value
           SHLD ADDR   ; Store H and L in two consecutive memory locations
                         wired as output registers.
           JMP CONTINUE
                  Total bytes    11
                  Total states   46 (one pass)
  ```

in figure 2, the 16 output (memory) locations will be from split octal addresses 377/360 to 377/377.

Now let's compare a couple of simple programs written using each method (see examples 1 and 2). It can be easily seen that the extra instructions which operate on memory can greatly improve the output speed of the 8080. This extra speed, though not necessary when driving a device such as a 110 bps Teletype, can be a saving grace in a computer music or graphics application. In fact, many video display drivers utilize this technique.

Summary

There are certain advantages to converting 8080 peripherals to mapped versus direct IO. Among the major points to consider are the following:

- More IO ports are available. The full 64 K bytes of addressable memory space can be set up for IO. It is not inconceivable that a video graphics display will use 8 K bytes of memory. This, of course, means that the 8 K bytes are decoded to provide 8192 IO port assignments.

- Once the H and L registers have been loaded and provide a memory pointer, memory output is by 1 byte instructions (such as MOV and STAX).

- By not always having to pass through the accumulator, outputs are faster.

- 16 bit IO capability through the use of LHLD and SHLD instructions.

Now, should you consider changing your 8080 system to memory IO? Frankly, if you are the type of person who will never write an assembly language program and is content to stick with high level languages such as extended BASIC, don't even consider it. If the software packages supplied by the computer manufacturers have worked consistently for you to this point, don't tempt fate. The majority of the systems sold, including Altair, IMSAI, DGS and so on, use 8080 IO instructions to all their peripherals. But many video systems bought as plug-in boards for the Altair (S-100) bus have memory mapped IO designs.

Delving into memory mapped IO should be reserved for people willing to use assembly language and prepared to modify standard software if required. In future editions I intend to investigate computer music applications where fast memory mapped 8080 (Z-80) IO will become a necessity. But, for the meantime, you should at least know what it is.■

Photo 1: ICs on ICE. Pictured are all the components necessary to build the 8 channel 3½ digit computer controlled voltmeter described in this article.

On a Test Equipment Diet?

Try an 8 Channel DVM Cocktail

About three weeks ago, I was testing a new 8 bit analog to digital converter which I had just built for an upcoming magazine article: this one, in fact. It was a high speed successive approximation analog to digital converter which performed 200,000 conversions a second, and it worked fine. I had intended to use it for some speech digitization experiments. During the testing phase, however, I became exasperated from continually moving my digital voltmeter (DVM) probes around the circuit to take readings and having to stop to make the same calculations repeatedly. To speed the process up, I wrote a BASIC program which would do the number crunching, provided I typed in the voltage values correctly. More often, though, all I wanted was to monitor a few voltage levels simultaneously.

After stringing my two DVMs, an analog volt-ohm meter (VOM), and my oscilloscope all over the bench to aid in my testing, I concluded that there must be a better way. It's old hat to use one channel of a dual trace scope to troubleshoot the other trace, so it was natural to consider using the analog to digital converter to monitor itself. While the thought was momentarily gratifying, the low resolution inherent with eight bits and clumsy binary conversion made me reconsider.

While thinking over this dilemma I was leaning back in my reclining desk chair with one elbow on my computer and my feet up on my printer. I realized that I should move some of the junk so that I'd have more room in the basement. I concluded that what I needed were eight DVMs. This insane desire was quickly eradicated and replaced by a more economically sound idea. I had designed a 4 channel 8 bit digital to analog converter to run with BASIC. It was only natural to design a multichannel analog to digital converter which also interfaced to BASIC.

12 bit analog to digital converters and 3½ digit DVM chips come in a variety of configurations. Converters which specifically state that they are 12 bit converter modules can have either binary or binary coded decimal (BCD) outputs, but are almost universally parallel binary output devices. The end of conversion signal results in immediate data output. The computer just has to scan the data lines and translate

---

Motorola MC14433 3½ Digit Analog to Digital Converter Specifications:

Accuracy: ± 0.05% of reading ± 1 count
Two voltage ranges: 1.999 V and 199.9 mV
Up to 25 conversions per second
Input impedance > 1000 megohms
Auto zero
Single positive voltage reference
Auto polarity
Drives CMOS or low power Schottky loads
On chip system clock
Over, under, and auto ranging signals available

them into meaningful notation. Chips which are specifically referred to as 3½ or 4½ digit DVM large scale integrated circuit (LSI) chips do not have this luxury. In general, their output is a combination of serial and parallel, one digit at a time. Interfacing to a parallel output analog to digital converter would be far easier with regard to the computer software, but as is generally the case, one never gets something for nothing. 12 bit parallel analog to digital converters are expensive. Most are designed to cover high speed data acquisition applications. Speed (1000 to 100 K conversions per second) costs money.

This leaves us with the 3½ digit DVM LSI chips. They run very slowly by comparison (1 to 50 conversions a second), but cost an order of magnitude less. Software to perform the serial to parallel conversions is a bit more involved, but once it's written, who cares?

One of the latest chips to hit the market is the Motorola MC14433, a 3½ digit low power complementary MOS analog to digital converter. Its specifications (relative to computer applications) are listed in the box on the previous page.

The MC14433 is a modified dual ramp integrating analog to digital converter. This is outlined in figure 1.

The conversion sequence is divided into two integration periods: unknown and reference. During the V_{in} or unknown input integration sequence, the unknown voltage is applied to an integrator with a defined integration time constant for a predetermined time limit. The result is that the voltage level at the output of the integrator will be a function of the unknown voltage input. More positive input voltages will result in higher levels at the integrator output.

During the second cycle of the integration sequence, V_{in} is replaced at the input of the integrator with a negative 2.000 V reference. The output of the integrator starts to move toward zero while the digital circuitry in the chip keeps track of the time it takes to make it to zero again. The time difference between the two integration sequences is then a function of their voltage difference. Since the integration time constants are the same for both periods, if 2.000 V were the unknown applied voltage, t_2 would be equal to t_1. The unknown voltage is equivalent to the ratio of the periods, times the voltage reference, V_{ref}. This is also known as a ratiometric converter. Quite a mouthful. The full scale range of the converter is determined by the level of V_{ref}. Changing V_{ref} to .200 V will make the same 1999 count represent a 199.9 mV full scale. (Obviously, V_{ref} could be set to any value within the voltage limitations of the chip. But, remember, full scale will still be 1999 counts even if it represents 2.463 V, if for example that were V_{ref}.)

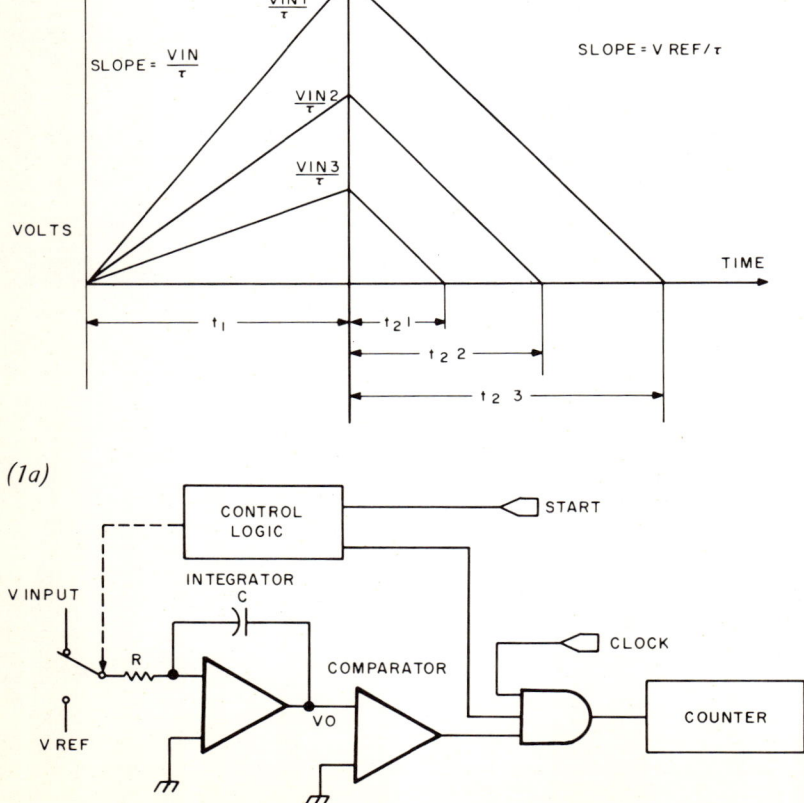

Figure 1: A simplified functional representation of the Motorola MC14433 3½ digit analog to digital converter. 1a shows a block diagram of the device; 1b shows the two integration periods used to convert the input voltage to a 3½ digit decimal number. During time t_1, the unknown voltage (V_{in}) is applied to an integrator having a predefined integration time constant (τ) for a preset time. During t_2 a known negative voltage is presented to the integrator. The time needed for the integrator to return to the 0 level is therefore a function of the unknown voltage. A digital counter keeps track of this time, from which V_{in} can be calculated.

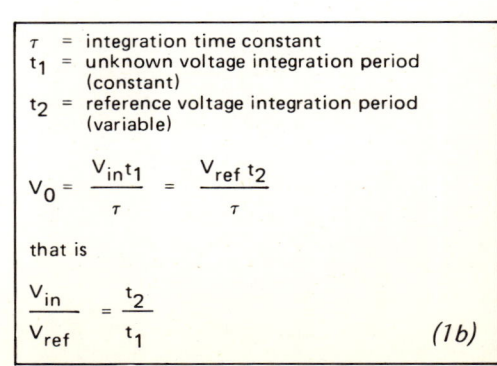

τ = integration time constant
t_1 = unknown voltage integration period (constant)
t_2 = reference voltage integration period (variable)

$$V_0 = \frac{V_{in} t_1}{\tau} = \frac{V_{ref} t_2}{\tau}$$

that is

$$\frac{V_{in}}{V_{ref}} = \frac{t_2}{t_1}$$

(1b)

Making a DVM Chip Computer Compatible

There are more bus configurations than I know what to do with lately, so I set up this interface to run from decoded input and output ports. Whether they be memory mapped IO or not, we do not care, as long as the outputs are latched and the inputs can be driven by low power Schottky TTL devices.

To fully utilize this eight channel 3½ digit DVM, we must design the correct hardware interface and write a universal software driver.

Hardware and Data Format

Figure 2 details the schematic of the 8 channel interface board. IC1 is the MC14433 DVM chip. With the values chosen, it will perform approximately 25 conversions a second. Reducing the 68 K resistor between pins 10 and 11 to about 27 K will increase this to about 50 conversions per second. This is an out of specification condition and, though probably successful, is dependent on individual parts.

Each output pin of IC1 has the power to drive one LS TTL load. Since all input ports are not necessarily low power, we provide IC3 and IC4 as buffers. They are 74LS04s and while they are capable of driving regular TTL, they do invert the output data of the DVM. Any driver program must complement the BCD and digit data it receives from this interface before using it.

IC2 is a MC1403 precision voltage reference chip and supplies the V_{ref} input. This IC will vary only 7 mV over a range of 0° to 70°C from its nominal 2.5 V output. While a zener diode might also supply an adequate reference voltage, the temperature drift characteristics of the average zener would negate the value of a 3½ digit converter if used beyond a 5 or 10°C temperature variation. A precision voltage integrated circuit is an absolute must if this circuit is to be used for practical applications.

IC5 is a 7474 which is used here as a set-reset flip flop. The end conversion signal from IC1 sets it, and an output bit from the computer resets it after reading the output data.

IC6 is an 8 input CMOS multiplexer. Its address lines are tied directly to a latched

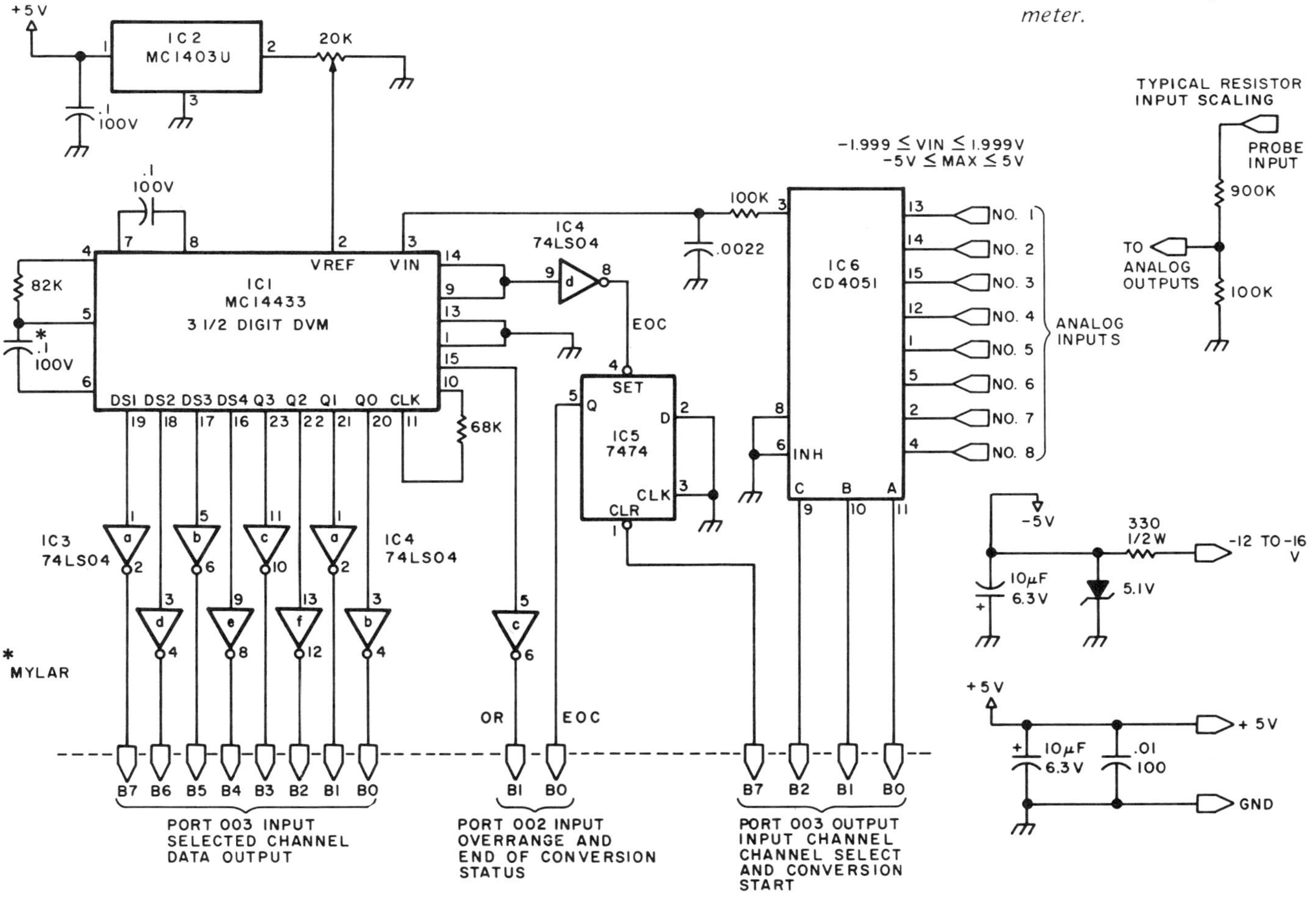

Figure 2: Circuit for the 8 channel 3½ digit voltmeter.

output port. The usual conversion sequence is to set the channel information to the multiplexer, clear the EOC flip flop and wait for an end of conversion signal. More on this later.

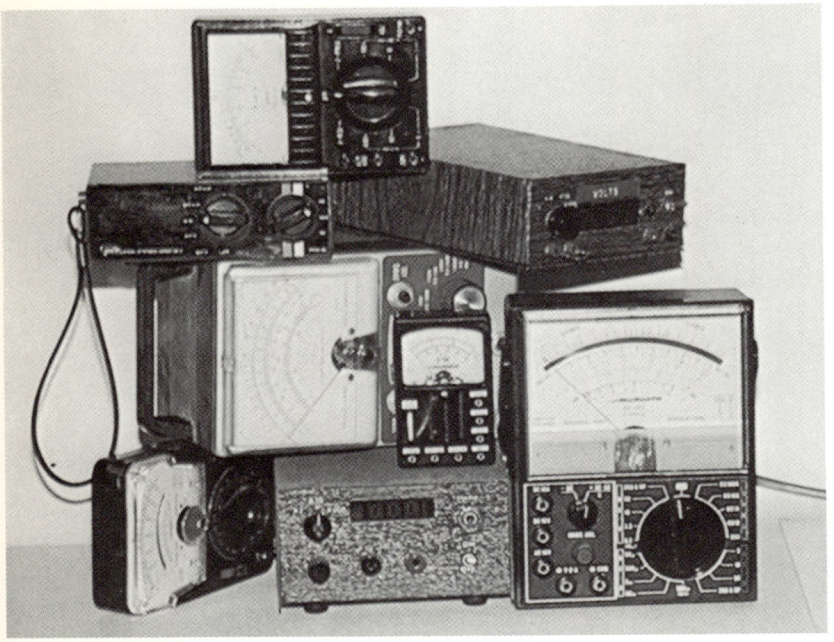

Photo 2: Eight meters (some are multimeters, others are voltmeters) which could be replaced (at least for DC voltage measurements) by the computerized 8 channel voltmeter described here.

Data Format

As I stated earlier, the data from the DVM to the computer is both serial and parallel. There are four digit select lines and four BCD data lines (see table 1).

With respect to what the computer sees through the 74LS04 buffers, the digit select output is low when the respective digit is selected. The most significant digit (½ digit DS1) goes low immediately after an EOC pulse, followed by the remaining digits sequencing from most significant to least significant digit (MSD to LSD). An interdigit blanking time of two clock periods is included to ensure that the BCD data has settled. The multiplex clock rate is equal to the system clock frequency divided by 80.

During the ½ digit (DS1), the polarity and certain status bits are available. It would be confusing to list the status bits, since they are not being used in this application for autoranging. The polarity will be Q_2 and a "1" will indicate negative. The ½ digit value will appear on Q_3 and a "1" will indicate high.

The interface is summarized by port allocations in table 1. (Note: I have assigned particular port numbers to each byte. These designations will run directly with the software driver provided. If the reader wishes to assign different port numbers, that is fine, but remember to modify the driver software to reflect the changes.)

Photo 3: Prototype board for the 8 channel 3½ digit voltmeter.

Designing an Analog to Digital Converter Software Driver

For a hardware personality like me, software is a tedious task. I don't like writing any more than I have to and if it is possible to write a universal piece of code which is compatible with any operating system, all the better. Units such as the digital to analog converter I presented in "Control the World" (page 47) do not need software drivers because the hardware is explicitly designed to be independent of computer timing. *Timing* is the key word. A "software driver" is the same as its hardware counterpart. Both serve to couple the computer to external devices and synchronize the timing. The most obvious driver already existing in a computer system like my Digital Group system is the asynchronous data link to the tape cassette, video display and printer. The computer is instructed through this program to perform explicitly timed operations which result in the correct serial input and output.

The 3½ digit DVM interface is not unlike a communications driver. To effectively obtain data from the interface, the computer must synchronize itself to the integrated circuit and perform a set instruction repertoire to demultiplex the input data stream. There is a certain trade-off between hardware and software. Another ten or 15 chips could be added to the interface board so that it requires no more software

Photo 4: *An illustration of the accuracy of the computerized voltmeter. A Data Precision 4½ digit digital multimeter and the author's system simultaneously measure a C cell battery. The computer value is 1.540 V compared with the Data Precision reading of 1.5402 V.*

Table 1: *IO port data formats.*

```
Command Output Byte (Port 003 OUT)    (Enable = 1  Disable = 0)
   B7 = EOC/Interrupt Enable/disable
   B6 ⎫
   B5 ⎬  Future Expansion
   B4 ⎭
   B3 ⎫
   B2 ⎪
   B1 ⎬  Channel Select, 0-7
   B0 ⎭
Status Input Byte (Port 002 IN)
   B7 ⎫
   B6 ⎪
   B5 ⎪
   B4 ⎬  Not Used
   B3 ⎪
   B2 ⎭
   B1 = Out of Range (−1.999 < Vin > 1.999)
   B0 = End of Conversion
Data Input Byte (Port 003 IN)                          IC1
                                         Symbol    Pin Number
   B7 = 1st digit (MSD):  When true = B7→0   DS1       19
   B6 = 2nd digit                  B6        DS2       18
   B5 = 3rd digit                  B5 ⎫ N/A  DS3       17
   B4 = 4th digit                  B4 ⎭      DS4       16
   B3 ⎫                     B3 = ½ digit value   Q3    23
   B2 ⎬ BCD Digit Value     B2 = Polarity        Q2    22
   B1 ⎪                     B1 = N/A             Q1    21
   B0 ⎭                     B0 = Status Bit      Q0    20
```

Listing 1: An assembly program for driving the 8 channel 3½ digit voltmeter in figure 3. It is designed to run on the Z-80 and is assembled to occupy memory page octal 140.

```
ASSM 140000 140000

140000                    0100 *
140000                    0110 *** MC14433 3 1/2 DIGIT A/D CONVERTER DRIVER
140000                    0120 *
140000                    0125 * REV 1.6
140000                    0130 *
140000                    0140 DIP    EQU   3      DATA INPUT PORT NUMBER
140000                    0150 SIP    EQU   2      STATUS INPUT PORT NUMBER
140000                    0160 COP    EQU   3      COMMAND OUTPUT PORT NUMBER
140000                    0170 EEOC   EQU   200    ENABLE EOC INPUT
140000                    0180 DEOC   EQU   000    DISABLE EOC INPUT
140000                    0190 *
140000                    0200 *
140000                    0210 * CONVERTED CHANNEL DATA BUFFERS
140000                    0220 *
140000 000 000            0230 CHAN0  DW    000000
140002 000 000            0240        DW    000000
140004 000 000            0250 CHAN1  DW    000000
140006 000 000            0260        DW    000000
140010 000 000            0270 CHAN2  DW    000000
140012 000 000            0280        DW    000000
140014 000 000            0290 CHAN3  DW    000000
140016 000 000            0300        DW    000000
140020 000 000            0310 CHAN4  DW    000000
140022 000 000            0320        DW    000000
140024 000 000            0330 CHAN5  DW    000000
140026 000 000            0340        DW    000000
140030 000 000            0350 CHAN6  DW    000000
140032 000 000            0360        DW    000000
140034 000 000            0370 CHAN7  DW    000000
140036 000 000            0380        DW    000000
140040                    0390 *
140040                    0400 * INTERMEDIATE DATA BUFFERS
140040                    0410 *
140040 000                0420 POLVAL DB    000    LAST POLARITY VALUE (0=POSITIVE)
140041 000                0430 CHAN   DB    000    CURRENT CHANNEL NUMBER
140042 000 000            0440 CCP    DW    000000 COMMAND CHANNEL PARAMETER
140044 000 000            0450 STATUS DW    000000 RETURN STATUS PARAMETER
140046                    0460 *
140046                    0470 *
140046                    0480 *** START A/D CONVERTER
140046                    0490 *
140046                    0500 *     INPUT PARAMETER=DE REGISTER WITH CHANNEL SELECT BITS
140046                    0510 *                    SET FOR DESIRED CHANNEL (BIT 0=1
140046                    0520 *                    FOR CHANNEL 0, ETC.)
140046                    0530 *     OUTPUT PARAMETER=HL REGISTER(BIT 0 FOR CHANNEL 0
140046                    0540 *                    WHERE 0=GOOD VALUE;1=OUT OF RANGE)
140046                    0550 *
140046 353                0560 START  EX    DE,HL  SAVE INPUT PARAMETER
140047 042 042 140        0570        LD    (CCP),HL
140052 257                0580        XOR   A      INITIALIZE CHANNEL NUMBER
140053 375 041 040 140    0590        LD    IY,POLVAL INITIALIZE INTERMEDIATE DATA POINTER
140057 375 167 001        0600        LD    (IY+1),A ZERO CHANNEL NUMBER
140062                    0610 *
140062                    0620 * START A/D CONVERTER AND ESTABLISH POLARITY
140062                    0630 *
140062 006 002            0640        LD    B,2    CYCLE TWO TIMES
140064 076 007            0650        LD    A,7    SELECT CHANNEL 8
140066 323 003            0660 AGAIN  OUT   COP    SELECT CHANNEL
140070 366 200            0670        OR    EEOC
140072 323 003            0680        OUT   COP    ENABLE EOC INPUT
140074 333 002            0690 WAIT   IN    SIP    READ STATUS
140076 313 107            0700        BIT   0,A    TEST FOR EOC
140100 050 372            0710        JR    Z,WAIT JUMP IF NOT TRUE
140102 020 362            0720        DJNZ  AGAIN  JUMP IF NOT DONE
140104 006 200            0730        LD    B,200  SELECT DIGIT 1
140106 315 361 140        0740        CALL  RDIG   READ DIGIT
140111 016 000            0750        LD    C,0    POLARITY=POSITIVE
140113 313 122            0760        BIT   2,D    TEST POLARITY BIT
140115 040 001            0770        JR    NZ,POS JUMP IF POSITIVE
140117 014                0780        INC   C      POLARITY=NEGATIVE
140120 375 161 000        0790 POS    LD    (IY+0),C SAVE CURRENT POLARITY
140123                    0800 *
140123                    0810 * SELECT NEXT CHANNEL FOR CONVERSION
140123                    0820 *
140123 072 042 140        0830 SELNXT LD    A,(CCP) LOAD CHANNEL COMMAND PARAMETER
140126 313 077            0840        SRL   A      TEST NEXT CHANNEL BIT
140130 062 042 140        0850        LD    (CCP),A RESTORE
140133 070 010            0860        JR    C,SEL001 JUMP IF CHANNEL SELECTED
140135 312 355 140        0870        JP    Z,RAPUP
140140 375 064 001        0880 INCCN  INC   (IY+1) INCREMENT CHANNEL NUMBER
140143 030 356            0890        JR    SELNXT
140145 335 041 000 140    0900 SEL001 LD    IX,CHAN0 LOAD DATA BUFFER BASE ADDRESS
140151 026 000            0910        LD    D,0
140153 375 136 001        0920        LD    E,(IY+1) LOAD CURRENT CHANNEL NUMBER
140156 313 043            0930        SLA   E      CALCULATE BUFFER OFFSET
140160 313 043            0940        SLA   E
140162 335 031            0950        ADD   IX,DE
140164                    0960 *
140164                    0970 * SELECT CHANNEL AND START CONVERSION
140164                    0980 *
140164 072 041 140        0990 SCSC   LD    A,(CHAN) LOAD CHANNEL NUMBER
140167 323 003            1000        OUT   COP    SELECT CHANNEL
140171 366 200            1010        OR    EEOC   ENABLE EOC OUTPUT
140173 323 003            1020        OUT   COP    COMMAND A/D CONVERTER
140175                    1030 *
140175                    1040 * WAIT FOR EOC
140175                    1050 *
140175 333 002            1060 WEOC   IN    SIP    READ CONVERTER STATUS
140177 313 107            1070        BIT   0,A    TEST FOR EOC
140201 050 372            1080        JR    Z,WEOC JUMP IF NOT READY
140203 313 117            1090        BIT   1,A    TEST FOR OVERAGE
140205 040 124            1100        JR    NZ,OVER JUMP IF TRUE
140207                    1110 *
140207                    1120 * CONVERSION DONE;PROCESS FIRST (MSD) DIGIT
140207                    1130 *
140207 006 200            1140 MSD0   LD    B,200  SELECT DIGIT 1
140211 315 361 140        1150        CALL  RDIG   WAIT AND READ DIGIT 1
140214 057                1160        CPL
140215 017                1170        RRCA         RIGHT JUSTIFY DIGIT VALUE
140216 017                1180        RRCA
140217 017                1190        RRCA
140220 346 001            1200        AND   1      ISOLATE
140222 036 000            1210        LD    E,0    INITIALIZE STATUS BYTE
140224 113                1220        LD    C,E
140225                    1230 *
```

than the digital to analog converter board, but the cost justification is not there.

Driver programs can be triggered by either a poll from another program or an interrupt which initiates execution. While both can be equally effective in certain applications, using interrupt initiated drivers which give the appearance of simultaneous computer operation can be hazardous. By now, most experimenters have mastered BASIC and are trying to find more challenging applications. But consider for a moment the BASIC interpreters most systems are provided with. They may execute divinely, but they have no source listing and therefore cannot be modified very easily. If a program utilizes information provided through interrupt driven peripherals, but has no way of knowing when the information will arrive, it is of no use. Attempting to add interrupt analog data acquisition to unsourced sequentially interpreted BASIC is more than I intend to explain in this article.

Adding this DVM interface to BASIC requires a polled driver. A machine language program is written which can be inserted anywhere in the computer's memory (assuming it's assembled to execute there, of course) and called as a subroutine when the peripheral is to be exercised. The Digital Group Maxi BASIC, like many others, has instructions which allow memory and IO port manipulation as well as calling machine language subroutines. It is this latter call instruction which initiates the analog to digital conversion cycles and communicates with the interface driver program. When it executes this call instruction, it passes a channel convert code in the DE register pair. The driver program returns control to the BASIC interpreter at the conclusion

---

Constructing the Interface

1. Use IC sockets and solder in all passive components.
2. Turn on the power and ensure that the correct supply voltages are presented to ICs 1, 2 and 6. Turn off power.
3. Insert IC2 and apply power. The output at pin 2 should be 2.5 V and should not drift. Adjust the pot so that there is exactly 2.000 V on IC1 pin 2. Turn off power.
4. Insert the rest of the ICs including the MC14433. Be careful when inserting the 4051 and MC14433. You are now ready to wire the board to some convenient input and output ports and see if it flies.
5. Turn on power. A driver program obviously is necessary to see if the circuit actually works and I have included one. If you are really anxious, you can try a couple of quickies: an oscilloscope attached to digit select or data lines will tell you immediately if the circuit is running. You should see square waves of various duty cycles. Another method is to write a short program which scans the end of conversion bit (remember to reset it first) and halt. If it halts, there must be an EOC.

of the analog to digital conversion. This provides a convenient method of synchronization. BASIC waits for the driver to finish storing the converted input data before trying to use it. Perhaps the next level is to write an interrupt driver which continually updates a value in the interpreter's tables of variables; but this would require a source listing and further documentation of the interpreter in order to accomplish the goal.

The Driver Is a Relocatable Subroutine

The actual program which interfaces to and stores the values to the DVM chip is written in the form of a single callable subroutine. To maintain the relocatability of the subroutine to any page in memory, all information necessary for the proper execution of the driver is provided at the time of the call. The additional information about which channels are to be converted is loaded into the DE registers at the time of the call. One bit of the E register is allocated for each analog to digital channel. Channel 1 is the least significant bit and channel 8 is the most significant. Setting a "1" value for the channel bit will tell the driver to convert that channel and a "0" means to ignore it. Loading E with binary 10 110 011 will indicate to the driver that channels 1, 2, 5, 6 and 8 are to be converted. Setting all bits to "1" will cause all channels to be read and converted. Indicating to the driver which, if any, channels are to be read rather than scanning all of them is a method of saving time. By computer standards, this analog to digital interface is slow; it is better not to waste any more time than is necessary.

The driver starts the conversion process by selecting a channel address to convert. This is accomplished by looking at the least significant bit of the E register. If it is a "1" it will convert on that channel. If it is a "0" it shifts and inspects the next bit, and so on until it finds one that is set. When a bit set condition is found, the channel address of that particular channel is sent out via port 003 to the analog input multiplexer IC6 and the end of conversion flip flop IC5 is reset. The DVM then starts the process of converting the analog input signal.

Demultiplexing the output of the DVM is fairly straightforward. The processor hangs in a loop waiting for an end of conversion signal. When this happens, the program knows that the next four digits of data are what is wanted. The DVM integrated circuit sets each of the digit select lines successively, and the program records the values of the four data lines each time. It strips the status and polarity bits from the most significant

Listing 1, continued:

```
140225                  1240 * TEST POLARITY OF CHANNEL
140225                  1250 *
140225 313 122          1260 MSD1     BIT   2,D         TEST POLARITY
140227 040 017          1270          JR    NZ,MSD2     JUMP IF POSITIVE
140231                  1280 *
140231                  1290 * NEGATIVE POLARITY
140231                  1300 *
140231 014              1310          INC   C
140232 036 200          1320          LD    E,200       LOAD NEGATIVE SIGN
140234 375 313 000 106  1330          BIT   0,(IY+0)    TEST PREVIOUS POLARITY
140240 040 022          1340          JR    NZ,MSD3     JUMP IF ALSO NEGATIVE
140242 375 313 000 306  1350          SET   0,(IY+0)    MAKE PREVIOUS VALUE NEGATIVE
140246 030 314          1360          JR    SCSC        CONVERT AGAIN
140250                  1370 *
140250                  1380 * POSITIVE POLARITY
140250                  1390 *
140250 375 313 000 106  1400 MSD2     BIT   0,(IY+0)    TEST PREVIOUS POLARITY
140254 050 006          1410          JR    Z,MSD3      JUMP IF ALSO POSITIVE
140256 375 313 000 206  1420          RES   0,(IY+0)    MAKE PREVIOUS VALUE POSITIVE
140262 030 300          1430          JR    SCSC        CONVERT AGAIN
140264                  1440 *
140264                  1450 * SAVE MSD AND CURRENT POLARITY
140264                  1460 *
140264 263              1470 MSD3     OR    E           ADD POLARITY SIGN TO MSD
140265 335 167 000      1480          LD    (IX+0),A    SAVE IN DATA BUFFER
140270 375 161 000      1490          LD    (IY+0),C    SAVE CURRENT POLARITY
140273                  1500 *
140273                  1510 * PROCESS 2ND DIGIT
140273                  1520 *
140273 313 010          1530          RRC   B           SELECT DIGIT 2
140275 315 361 140      1540          CALL  RDIG        WAIT AND READ DIGIT
140300 346 017          1550          AND   017         ISOLATE
140302 335 167 001      1560          LD    (IX+1),A    STORE SECOND DIGIT
140305                  1570 *
140305                  1580 * PROCESS 3RD DIGIT
140305                  1590 *
140305 313 010          1600          RRC   B           SELECT 3RD DIGIT
140307 315 361 140      1610          CALL  RDIG        WAIT AND READ DIGIT
140312 346 017          1620          AND   017         ISOLATE
140314 335 167 002      1630          LD    (IX+2),A    STORE
140317                  1640 *
140317                  1650 * PROCESS 4TH DIGIT
140317                  1660 *
140317 313 010          1670          RRC   B           SELECT 4TH DIGIT
140321 315 361 140      1680          CALL  RDIG        WAIT AND READ DIGIT
140324 346 017          1690          AND   017         ISOLATE
140326 335 167 003      1700          LD    (IX+3),A    STORE
140331 030 205          1710          JR    INCCN
140333                  1720 *
140333                  1730 * LOAD 2.000 OVERRANGE VALUE INTO DATA BUFFER
140333                  1740 *
140333 076 002          1750 OVER     LD    A,2         LOAD MSD VALUE
140335 335 167 000      1760          LD    (IX+0),A
140340 257              1770          XOR   A
140341 335 167 001      1780          LD    (IX+1),A    LOAD LSD VALUES
140344 335 167 002      1790          LD    (IX+2),A
140347 335 167 003      1800          LD    (IX+3),A
140352 303 140 140      1810          JP    INCCN
140355                  1820 *
140355                  1830 * END OF CHANNEL CONVERSIONS
140355                  1840 *
140355 052 044 140      1850 RAPUP    LD    HL,(STATUS)
140360 311              1860          RET               RETURN TO CALLER
140361                  1870 *
140361                  1880 *
140361                  1890 * READ DIGIT ROUTINE
140361                  1900 *
140361 333 003          1910 RDIG     IN    DIP         READ DATA BYTE
140363 057              1920          CPL               CONVERT TO HIGH TRUE LOGIC
140364 127              1930          LD    D,A         SAVE COPY
140365 240              1940          AND   B           TEST FOR GIVEN DIGIT READY
140366 050 371          1950          JR    Z,RDIG      JUMP IF NOT
140370 172              1960          LD    A,D         RESTORE A REGISTER
140371 311              1970          RET               RETURN TO CALLER
```

digit (the 3½ digit) and reformats the value into four bytes of memory. The three whole digits will be stored in BCD notation and occupy three of the bytes. The ½ digit, polarity and out of range will be located in the remaining data byte. Polarity is indicated by setting the most significant bit. A positive reading is a zero condition and negative is a one in that bit. The ½ digit value can only be a one or zero and occupies the least significant bit of the quantity. Out of range is accomplished with a little program manipulation. If the driver detects that the incoming reading is not within range, it sets the equivalent of +2 in the ½ digit byte. Obviously, this is an illegal condition for a DVM capable of only counting to 1999, but it is easy for BASIC to check the authenticity of the data by checking that all incoming values are between −1999 and +1999. The driver program continues to do

Table 2: Power wiring table for figure 3.

IC Number	Type	+5V Pin	−5V Pin	GND Pin
IC1	MC14433	24	12	1&13
IC2	MC1403	1		3
IC3,4	74LS04	14		7
IC5	7474	14		7
IC6	CD4051	16	7	8

Note: All resistors ¼ W 5% unless otherwise noted.
All capacitors are 100 V ceramics unless otherwise noted.

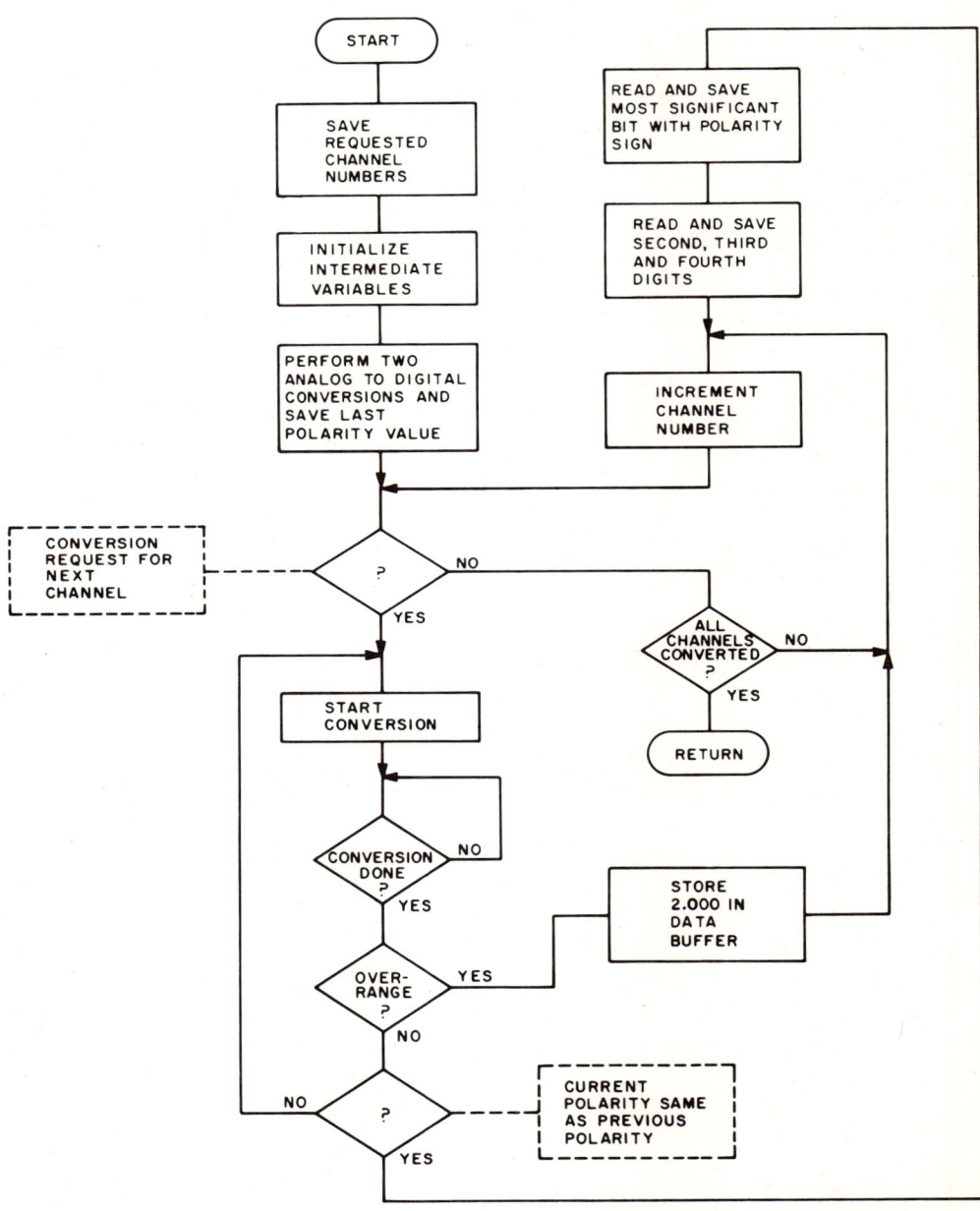

Figure 3: Flowchart of the digital voltmeter driver program of listing 1.

this same sequence until all designated channels have been converted.

There is a slight peculiarity with DVM chips: they don't like changes in polarity. The first conversion after a change in polarity will be 0.000 and will have to be discarded. In a single channel DVM this wouldn't present a problem, but when reading eight channels, some will be negative inputs and others will be positive.

The initial conversion also has the same problem to contend with, since the conversion history when the driver is not active is unknown. The solution is to write a smarter driver. Following a call, the driver program initializes the interface and determines the polarity. After that, any time the polarity changes between successive readings on designated channels, another conversion is initiated and stored. Figure 3 is a simplified flow diagram showing the logical design of the driver.

The end product of the driver is a 32 byte memory resident table which contains the eight 4 byte values corresponding to the eight channels. The values are sequentially arranged in the table. A simple formula locates a particular channel location at L + (4(N-1)) where L is the starting address of the table and N is the channel number. A complete assembly listing of the DVM driver is outlined in listing 1. It is made to run on a Z-80 and is assembled to occupy page 140 (octal).

The driver can be assembled for practically any portion of memory, but take care not to overlap into operating system or source files. If you own Digital Group software, there are some alternatives depending on what version you have. For people with straight (non-universal) 32 character Z-80 Maxi BASIC Version 1.0, page 012 is empty and has been left for future expansion. If you have the 64 character Maxi BASIC Version 1.1, it's better not to try to bury the driver within the interpreter unless you're an experienced programmer. Owners of 8080 systems have only to reassemble the code using 8080 instructions and locate it in a similar manner. The logic behind the driver is not so involved that it necessitates using the Z-80. Any microprocessor should be able to work with the interface.

Using the Interface with BASIC

This DVM interface is specifically designed to run with a BASIC interpreter such as Maxi BASIC or the equivalent. Listing 2 illustrates a BASIC program which does data acquisition and computes results from this input data. Often, the best method of explanation is to illustrate the actual use

Listing 2: A BASIC program (written in Maxi BASIC) which performs data acquisition and computes results from the output of the 8 channel digital voltmeter.

```
LIST
100 REM
110 REM
120 REM 8 CHANNEL 3 1/2 DIGIT SCANNING PROGRAM -S.CIARCIA
130 REM REV 1.5
140 REM SPECIAL ANALYSIS SECTION ---
150 REM TTL TO MOS VOLTAGE LEVEL CONVERTER
160 REM
170 REM
180 REM
190 LET M1=24576
192 REM PAGE 140(OCTAL)
200 REM M1 IS SET TO BE THE DECIMAL STARTING LOCATION OF
210 REM THE VALUE TABLE
220 LET M2=24614
230 REM M2 IS THE MACHINE LANGUAGE CALL ADDRESS LOCATION FOR THE A/D
240 LET M3=10
250 REM M3 IS THE GAIN. IN THIS APPLICATION, THE RANGE OF THE CONVERTER
260 REM IS +19.99 TO -19.99 VOLTS
270 REM TO USE THE CONVERTER FOR -1.999 TO +1.999, LET M3=1
280 GOTO 300
290 PRINT"TO REPEAT THE SAME SELECTION, TYPE AN X"
291 PRINT"TO SELECT A NEW OPTION,TYPE AN O" :INPUT B$
292 IF B$="X" THEN GOTO 420
294 PRINT : PRINT : PRINT
300 PRINT"                    OPTION LIST"
310 REM WE START THE PROGRAM WITH AN OPTION LIST
320 PRINT"-----------------------------------------------"
330 PRINT"0 ----SELECT CHANNELS"
340 PRINT"1 ----SCAN AND DISPLAY ALL CHANNELS"
350 PRINT"2 ----SCAN AND DISPLAY SELECTED CHANNELS ONCE"
360 PRINT"3 ----SCAN AND DISPLAY SELECTED CHANNELS CONTINUOUSLY"
370 PRINT"4 ----SCAN CHANNEL 1 CONTINUOUSLY 100 TIMES"
380 PRINT"5 ----GO TO SPECIAL ANALYSIS SUBROUTINES"
390 REM THESE ROUTINES ARE DEPENDENT UPON THE PARTICULAR A/D APPLICATION
400 PRINT"6 ----EXIT"
410 PRINT"WHICH OPTION ":INPUT S
420 IF S=0 THEN 520
430 IF S=1 THEN 930
440 IF S=2 THEN 1060
450 IF S=3 THEN 1280
460 IF S=4 THEN 1380
470 IF S=5 THEN 1470
480 IF S=6 THEN PRINT"THANKYOU" :END
490 GOTO 410
500 REM
510 REM FIRST WE DETERMINE WHICH ANALOG CHANNELS TO READ
520 PRINT "INDICATE YOUR CHOICES WITH A Y OR N AFTER THE CHANNEL NUMBER
530 FOR C=1 TO 8
540 PRINT"CHANNEL ";C,
550 INPUT A$
560 REM ACCEPT ONLY TRUE INPUTS
570 IF A$="Y" THEN LET A(C)=1 :GOTO 610
580 IF A$="N" THEN LET A(C)=0 :GOTO 610
590 PRINT"INPUT A Y FOR YES OR A N FOR NO"
600 GOTO 540
610 NEXT C
620 GOTO 290
630 REM
640 REM
650 REM
660 REM SET D EQUAL TO THE DECIMAL MEMORY ADDRESS OF THE
670 REM BEGINNING OF VALUE TABLE
680 REM THIS SUBROUTINE DETERMINES THE 3 1/2 DIGIT VALUE
690 REM FROM THE TABLE IN MEMORY
700 LET Q1=EXAM(D)
710 LET Q=Q1
720 IF Q1>128 THEN LET Q=Q1-128
730 D=D+1
740 LET W=EXAM(D)
750 D=D+1
760 LET E=EXAM(D)
770 D=D+1
780 LET R=EXAM(D)
790 LET D=D+1
800 LET Y=Q+(.1*W)+(.01*E)+(.001*R)
810 LET Y1=M3*Y
820 RETURN
830 REM
840 REM THIS SUBROUTINE PRINTS OUT THE VOLTAGE VALUES
850 PRINT"CHANNEL ";X;" IS ";
860 IF Q1<128 THEN PRINT" "; :GOTO 880
870 IF Q1>=128 THEN PRINT "-";
880 IF M3=10 THEN PRINT %5F2;Y1;" VOLTS" :GOTO 900
890 PRINT %6F3;Y1;" VOLTS"
900 RETURN
910 REM
920 REM
930 LET R=CALL(M2,255)
940 REM THE CALL INSTRUCTION TELLS THE A/D INTERFACE TO START CONVERTING
950 REM 255 IS ALL BITS SET
960 REM THIS WILL CAUSE THE A/D TO CONVERT AND STORE ALL EIGHT CHANNELS
970 LET D=M1
980 REM D IS THE START ADDRESS OF THE VALUE TABLE
990 FOR X=1 TO 8
1000 GOSUB 700
1010 REM GET 3 1/2 DIGIT VALUE FROM MEMORY
1020 IF Y>=2 THEN PRINT"CHANNEL ";X;" IS OUT OF RANGE" :GOTO 1040
1030 GOSUB 850
1040 NEXT X
1050 GOTO 290
1060 LET D=M1
1070 GOSUB 1130
1080 GOTO 290
1090 REM
1100 REM
1110 REM
```

Listing 2, continued:

```
1120 REM THIS SUBROUTINE PRINTS ONLY THE SELECTED CHANNELS
1130 LET L=A(1)*1+A(2)*2+A(3)*4+A(4)*8+A(5)*16+A(6)*32+A(7)*64+A(8)*128
1140 REM THIS EQUATION SETS THE BIT PATTERN FOR THE CALL TO THE A/D
1150 LET H=CALL(M2,L)
1160 REM H WILL RETURN FROM THE CALL WITH THE HL REG. VALUE BUT
1170 REM IS NOT BEING USED PRESENTLY IN THIS PROGRAM
1180 FOR X=1 TO 8
1190 GOSUB 700
1200 LET Z=A(1)+A(2)+A(3)+A(4)+A(5)+A(6)+A(7)+A(8)
1210 IF Z=0 THEN PRINT"NO CHANNELS HAVE BEEN SELECTED" :EXIT 290
1220 IF A(X)=0 THEN 1250
1230 IF Y>=2 THEN PRINT"CHANNEL ";X;" IS OUT OF RANGE" : GOTO 1250
1240 GOSUB 850
1250 NEXT X
1260 RETURN
1270 GOSUB 1130
1280 LET D=M1
1290 REM THIS SUBROUTINE IS A CONTINUOUS LOOP --- EXIT WITH RESET SWITCH
1300 FOR J=1 TO 1000
1310 LET D=M1
1320 GOSUB 1130
1330 PRINT : PRINT : PRINT
1340 NEXT J
1350 GOTO 290
1360 REM
1370 REM THIS SUBROUTINE CONTINUOUSLY SCANS AND PRINTS CHANNEL 1
1380 FOR R=1 TO 100
1390 LET H=CALL(M2,1)
1400 REM GO AND CONVERT CHANNEL 1 ONLY
1410 LET D=M1
1420 GOSUB 700
1430 LET X=1
1440 GOSUB 850
1450 NEXT R
1460 GOTO 290
1470 LET B=CALL(M2,255)
1480 REM SCAN AND STORE ALL CHANNELS
1490 LET D=M1
1500 FOR X=1 TO 8
1510 GOSUB 700
1520 LET V(X)=Y1
1530 REM SET VALUES INTO AN 8 VALUE ARRAY
1540 NEXT X
1550 REM CHECK CALIBRATION
1560 IF V(8)>=2.006 THEN PRINT"OUT OF CALIBRATION" :GOTO 290
1570 IF V(8)<=1.994 THEN PRINT"OUT OF CALIBRATION" :GOTO 290
1580 PRINT"TTL TO MOS LEVEL CONVERTER ---TTL LOW INPUT STATE":PRINT:PRINT
1590 PRINT"DIODE D1"
1600 PRINT"VOLTAGE DROP =",V(2)-V(1);" VOLTS"
1610 PRINT :PRINT"R1"
1620 LET T1=(V(2)-V(3))/2200
1630 PRINT"CURRENT = ";T1;" AMPS"
1640 PRINT"POWER = ";T1*T1*2200
1650 PRINT :PRINT"Q1"
1660 PRINT"VCE Q1 = ";V(4)-V(3);" VOLTS"
1670 PRINT"VBE Q1 = ";V(3);" VOLTS"
1680 PRINT"VCB Q1 = ";V(4);" VOLTS"
1690 PRINT :PRINT"R2"
1700 LET T2=(V(5)-V(4))/4700
1710 PRINT"R2 DROP = ";V(5)-V(4);" VOLTS"
1720 PRINT"CURRENT = ";T2;" AMPS"
1730 PRINT"POWER = ";T2*T2*4700;" WATTS"
1740 PRINT :PRINT"R3"
1750 LET T3=(V(6)-V(7))/4700
1760 PRINT"R3 DROP = ";V(6)-V(7);" VOLTS"
1770 PRINT"CURRENT = ";T3;" AMPS"
1780 PRINT"POWER = ";T3*T3*4700;" WATTS"
1790 PRINT:PRINT"Q2"
1800 PRINT"VBE Q2 = ";V(5)-V(4);" VOLTS"
1810 PRINT"VCE Q2 = ";V(7)-V(5);" VOLTS"
1820 PRINT"VCB Q2 = ";V(7)-V(4);" VOLTS"
1830 PRINT"IC OF Q2 = ";T3;" AMPS"
1840 PRINT"POWER DISSIPATION = ";(V(7)-V(5))*T3;" WATTS"
1850 PRINT:PRINT"SUPPLY VOLTAGES"
1860 PRINT V(6)
1870 PRINT"-";V(5)
1880 GOTO 290
READY

RUN
                    OPTION LIST
----------------------------------------------
0 ----SELECT CHANNELS
1 ----SCAN AND DISPLAY ALL CHANNELS
2 ----SCAN AND DISPLAY SELECTED CHANNELS ONCE
3 ----SCAN AND DISPLAY SELECTED CHANNELS CONTINUOUSLY
4 ----SCAN CHANNEL 1 CONTINUOUSLY 100 TIMES
5 ----GO TO SPECIAL ANALYSIS SUBROUTINES
6 ----EXIT
WHICH OPTION
?1
CHANNEL  1 IS    3.54 VOLTS
CHANNEL  2 IS    2.93 VOLTS
CHANNEL  3 IS     .63 VOLTS
CHANNEL  4 IS  -10.75 VOLTS
CHANNEL  5 IS  -11.02 VOLTS
CHANNEL  6 IS    5.04 VOLTS
CHANNEL  7 IS  -11.45 VOLTS
CHANNEL  8 IS    2.00 VOLTS
TO REPEAT THE SAME SELECTION, TYPE AN X
TO SELECT A NEW OPTION, TYPE AN O
?0
                    OPTION LIST
----------------------------------------------
0 ----SELECT CHANNELS
1 ----SCAN AND DISPLAY ALL CHANNELS
2 ----SCAN AND DISPLAY SELECTED CHANNELS ONCE
3 ----SCAN AND DISPLAY SELECTED CHANNELS CONTINUOUSLY
4 ----SCAN CHANNEL 1 CONTINUOUSLY 100 TIMES
5 ----GO TO SPECIAL ANALYSIS SUBROUTINES
6 ----EXIT
WHICH OPTION
?0
INDICATE YOUR CHOICES WITH A Y OR N AFTER THE CHANNEL NUMBER
CHANNEL  1       ?Y
CHANNEL  2       ?N
CHANNEL  3       ?N
CHANNEL  4       ?Y
CHANNEL  5       ?Y
CHANNEL  6       ?N
CHANNEL  7       ?N
CHANNEL  8       ?N
TO REPEAT THE SAME SELECTION, TYPE AN X
TO SELECT A NEW OPTION, TYPE AN O
?0
                    OPTION LIST
----------------------------------------------
0 ----SELECT CHANNELS
1 ----SCAN AND DISPLAY ALL CHANNELS
2 ----SCAN AND DISPLAY SELECTED CHANNELS ONCE
3 ----SCAN AND DISPLAY SELECTED CHANNELS CONTINUOUSLY
4 ----SCAN CHANNEL 1 CONTINUOUSLY 100 TIMES
5 ----GO TO SPECIAL ANALYSIS SUBROUTINES
6 ----EXIT
WHICH OPTION
?2
CHANNEL  1 IS    3.54 VOLTS
CHANNEL  4 IS  -10.75 VOLTS
CHANNEL  5 IS  -11.02 VOLTS
TO REPEAT THE SAME SELECTION, TYPE AN X
TO SELECT A NEW OPTION, TYPE AN O
?0
                    OPTION LIST
----------------------------------------------
0 ----SELECT CHANNELS
1 ----SCAN AND DISPLAY ALL CHANNELS
2 ----SCAN AND DISPLAY SELECTED CHANNELS ONCE
3 ----SCAN AND DISPLAY SELECTED CHANNELS CONTINUOUSLY
4 ----SCAN CHANNEL 1 CONTINUOUSLY 100 TIMES
5 ----GO TO SPECIAL ANALYSIS SUBROUTINES
6 ----EXIT
WHICH OPTION
?5
TTL TO MOS LEVEL CONVERTER ---TTL LOW INPUT STATE

DIODE D1
VOLTAGE DROP =       -.61 VOLTS
R1
CURRENT =  1.0454545E-03 AMPS
POWER  =  2.4045452E-03
Q1
VCE Q1 =  10.12 VOLTS
VBE Q1 =   .63 VOLTS
VCB Q1 =  10.75 VOLTS
R2
R2 DROP =  .27 VOLTS
CURRENT =  5.7446809E-05 AMPS
POWER  =  1.5510639E-05 WATTS
R3
R3 DROP = -6.41 VOLTS
CURRENT = -1.3638298E-03 AMPS
POWER  =  8.742149E-03 WATTS
Q2
VBE Q2 =  .27 VOLTS
VCE Q2 =  .43 VOLTS
VCB Q2 =  .7 VOLTS
IC OF Q2 = -1.3638298E-03 AMPS
POWER DISSIPATION = -5.8644681E-04 WATTS
SUPPLY VOLTAGES
 5.04
- 11.02
TO REPEAT THE SAME SELECTION, TYPE AN X
TO SELECT A NEW OPTION, TYPE AN O
?0
                    OPTION LIST
----------------------------------------------
0 ----SELECT CHANNELS
1 ----SCAN AND DISPLAY ALL CHANNELS
2 ----SCAN AND DISPLAY SELECTED CHANNELS ONCE
3 ----SCAN AND DISPLAY SELECTED CHANNELS CONTINUOUSLY
4 ----SCAN CHANNEL 1 CONTINUOUSLY 100 TIMES
5 ----GO TO SPECIAL ANALYSIS SUBROUTINES
6 ----EXIT
WHICH OPTION
?6
THANKYOU
READY
```

of a device. This program, while being general in nature, provides specific reference to the value of mating BASIC and analog acquisition.

Figure 4 is a circuit of a TTL to MOS voltage level converter. Its use is to convert 0 and 5 V TTL levels to +5 V and −12 V MOS logic levels. It is a relatively simple circuit, but it shows how BASIC can work for you.

Up to this point I have said that the input

range of the DVM is ±1.999 V. By putting resistor voltage dividers in series with the multiplexer channel inputs, other ranges can be accommodated. A 900 K-100 K resistor divider network will change the input range to ±19.999 V. Some channels can be set for 20 V ranges. With the present CD4051, though, separate resistor dividers are needed on the inputs because the maximum voltage handling capability of the 4051 is the range of its power supply. Relays, which could pass the high voltages, could be configured to allow use of only one selectable divider network, but for now we are limited. If you put resistor dividers on the inputs, the only necessity is to instruct the program to multiply the particular channel reading by an appropriate ranging factor. In this particular case, all input channels have been set for ±19.99 V ranges, and the multiplier is ten.

The program presents an option list. It allows general application as an acquisition and data logging tool. With it, one can select to read and print all eight channels, particular channels, or log a single channel continuously. Option 5 is what it's all about. It automatically records the input voltages and computes the circuit parameters such as power dissipation and voltage drops. A very complicated circuit example would probably have been more impressive, but that is merely a case of applying programming talents to the same set of input data.

One further note of explanation: the call instruction in Maxi BASIC has been misinterpreted by some people. It is not a directly executable instruction, but is rather used in a statement like LET X = CALL (2560,9). The BASIC interpreter will go to memory location decimal 2560 and start executing a machine language subroutine. The number in parentheses after the comma is the value which is put in the D and E registers at the same time. This is a 16 bit value with a range of 0 to 65,535. When the machine language subroutine is finished, it returns to the interpreter. X will then have a value equal to whatever was in the H and L registers when the subroutine ended.

Conclusion

Having eight channels is better than having one, especially if it doesn't cost any more. I've attempted to present a low cost solution to a usually expensive data acquisition problem. As is always the case with computers, the maximum utilization of the device is dependent upon the programmer, and as my college textbooks used to say, this is an exercise left to the reader.■

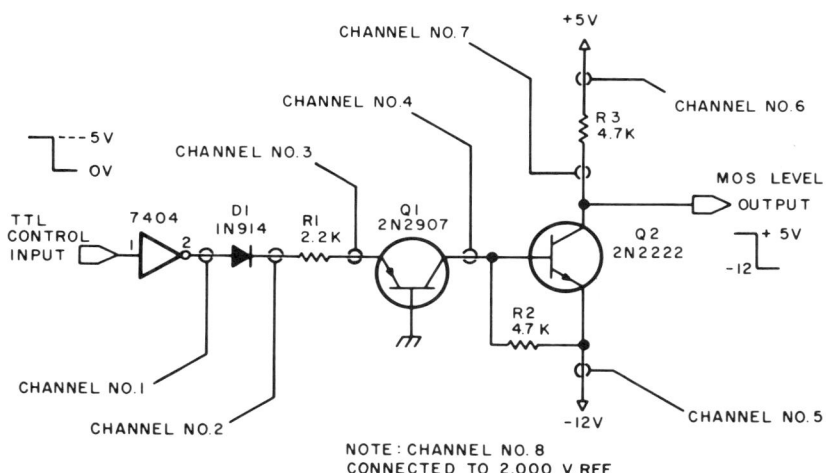

Figure 4: A sample circuit illustrating the use of the 8 channel 3½ digit voltmeter. The circuit is a TTL to MOS voltage level converter.

The author would like to extend special thanks to Dave Hardenbrook for his help in writing the DVM driver program.

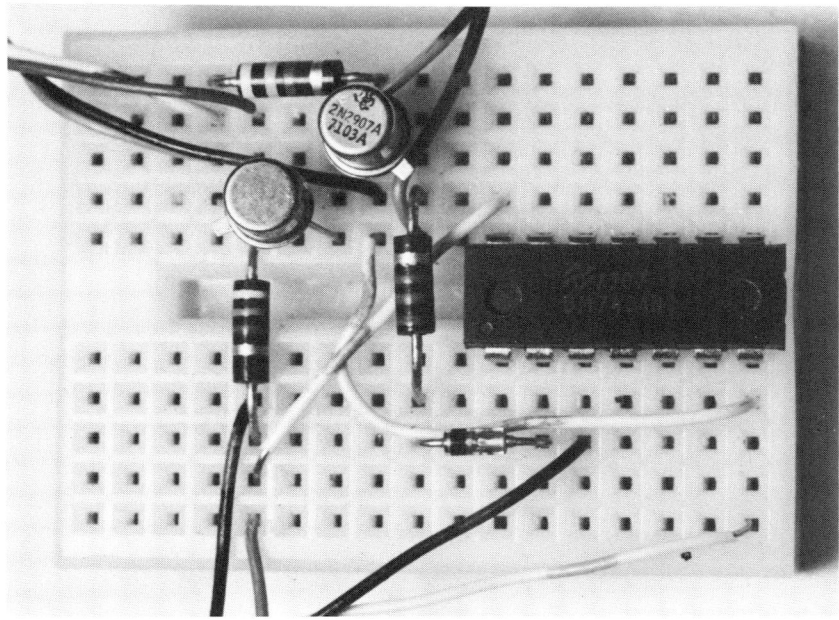

Photo 5: The breadboard circuit of the schematic in figure 4 used to test the 8 channel voltmeter.

Photo 1: The prototype board for the expanded digital voltmeter.

Add More Zing to the Cocktail

"Try an 8 Channel DVM Cocktail" brought you a design for an 8 channel 3 1/2 digit 0 to 2 V digital voltmeter (DVM) interface. The article introduced multiplexed analog data acquisition by means of a construction project.

I'm sure that the majority of the readers who have built the DVM will be satisfied with the results. There is of course that small group of problem makers who don't believe the whole world exists in the range from 0 to 2 VDC: a point well taken.

Actually, I planned to expand the capabilities of the basic DVM all along. I'll elaborate in detail; the end result will be a DVM interface with these additional specifications:

Super Cocktail DVM
- 8 programmable input channels
- AC or DC capability
- programmable gain of 1, 10, or 100
- ranges of 0 to 200 mV, 0 to 2 V, 0 to 20 V, or 0 to 200 V
- input overvoltage protection

I had hoped that by presenting the basic 0 to 2 V interface first, more readers would attempt to build it due to its low cost. The extra capabilities presented in this article can be added directly to the previously described hardware interface.

A Quick Review of the Interface Hardware

This DVM is designed around the Motorola MC14433 3 1/2 digit low power complimentary MOS analog to digital converter. The MC14433 is a modified dual ramp integrating analog to digital converter with multiplexed binary coded decimal (BCD) output. With the resistor values chosen it will perform approximately 25 conversions per second.

The full scale voltage value (ie: the value represented by the 3-1/2 digits after any input voltage division) is set by an MC1403 voltage reference integrated circuit. With 2.000 V applied to the V_{Ref} input of the MC14433, full scale is ±1.999 V. If 0.200 V is applied, full scale would be ±0.1999 V or ±199.9 mV.

The MC14433 can directly drive one LS TTL load. Since not all parallel input ports are LS TTL compatible, 74LS04s act as buffers and drivers on all digital voltmeter integrated circuit output pins. Data output is of course inverted and must be complemented before use.

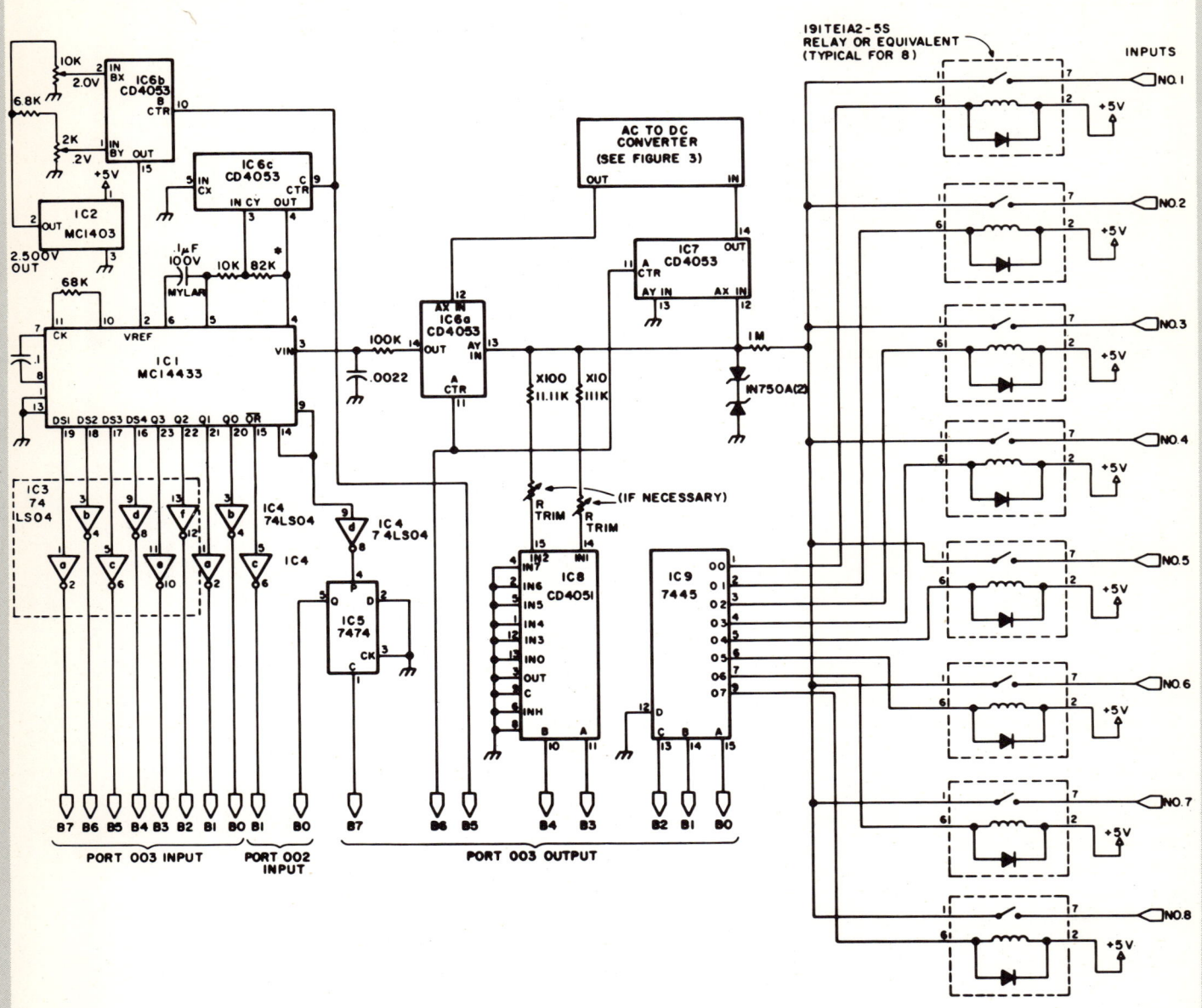

Figure 1a: The modified digital voltmeter, an expansion of the basic design presented in "Try an 8 Channel DVM Cocktail!" (page 13). Changes include the addition of an input multiplexer, made up of eight dual in line package relays, and IC9, a 1 of 10 decoder. The modification allows the voltmeter to handle a wider variety of input voltages, both AC and DC. All resistors are 5% 1/4 W, and all capacitors are 100 V ceramic, unless otherwise indicated.

Table 1: Power wiring table for figure 1.

Number	Type	+5 V	GND	−5 V
IC1	MC14433	24	13	12
IC2	1403	1	3	
IC3	74LS04	14	7	
IC4	74LS04	14	7	
IC5	7474	14	7	
IC6	CD4053	16	8	7
IC7	CD4053	16	8	7
IC8	CD4051	16	8	7
IC9	7445	16	8	

The data from the digital voltmeter to the computer is serial and parallel. There are four digit select lines and four binary coded decimal (BCD) data lines:

    pin 23 Q3   (Most significant bit)
    pin 22 Q2
    pin 21 Q1   BCD, digit value outputs
    pin 20 Q0
    pin 19 DS1 (Most significant digit)
    pin 18 DS2
    pin 17 DS3 Digit select outputs
    pin 16 DS4

With respect to what the computer sees through the 74LS04 buffers, the digit select output is low when the respective digit is selected. The most significant digit (1/2 digit DS1) goes low immediately after an end of conversion pulse followed by the remaining digits sequencing from the most significant to the least significant digit. An interdigit blanking time of two clock periods is included internally to ensure that the BCD data has settled.

During the 1/2 digit (DS1), the polarity and certain status bits are available. Polarity is on Q_2 and a 1 will indicate negative. The 1/2 digit will appear on Q_3 and a 1 will indicate high.

Enhancements to the Basic DVM Interface

Photo 1 and figure 1 illustrate the fully modified DVM interface. It retains the basic interface structure outlined in the original article, but with some additional goodies. The interface is designed for attachment to decoded 8 bit parallel input and output ports and can be polled by a machine language subroutine. More on this later.

The following is a summary of the interface by port allocations. (Note: I have assigned particular octal port numbers to each byte. These designations will run directly with the software driver provided. If the reader wishes to assign some other port numbers, this is fine, but remember to modify the driver software to reflect the changes.)

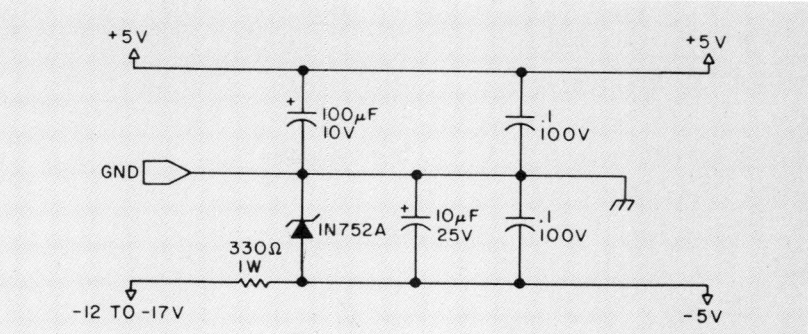

Figure 1b: A circuit enabling the experimenter to derive −5 VDC from an existing power supply having any output from −12 to −17 VDC. −5 VDC is needed to power the various CMOS switches used in this design (see figure 1c).

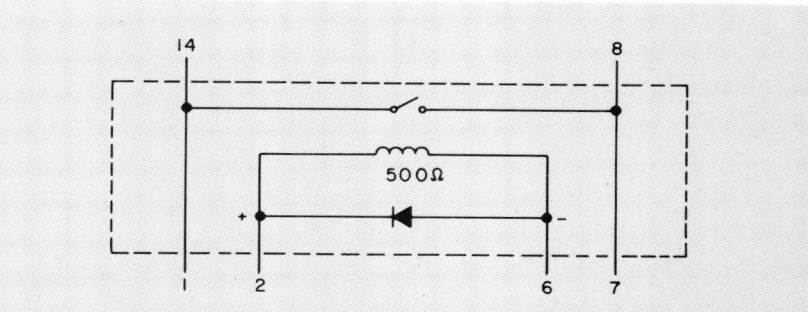

Figure 1c: Pin diagram of a Sigma relay, type 191TE1A2-5S 14 pin dual in line package. For further details and prices, contact SIGMA Instruments, Braintree MA 02184.

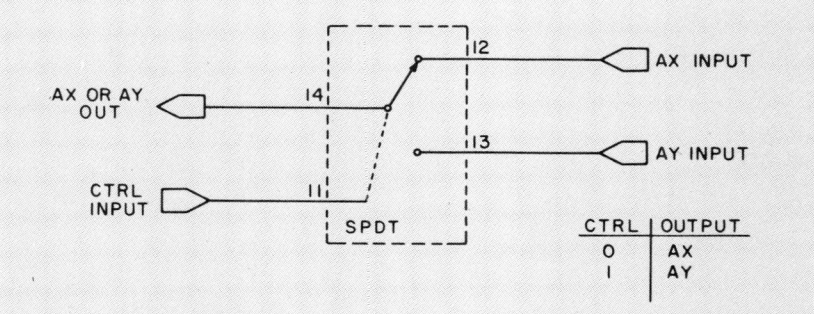

Figure 1d: Functional description of one switching section of a CD 4053 CMOS switch. The device acts like a remote controlled single pole double throw switch.

Command Output Byte (Port 003 Out)

```
B7 = EOC enable or disable    (Disable = 0  Enable = 1)
B6 = AC or DC select          (AC = 0; DC = 1)
B5 = 2.0 V or 0.2 V V_Ref select  (2.0 V = 0; 0.2 V = 1)
B4 ⎫
B3 ⎬ = Gain Code              B4 B3 | Gain
                              0  0  | ×1
                              0  1  | ×10
B2 ⎫                          0  0  | ×100
B1 ⎬ = Channel select, 0 to 7  1  1  | N/A (will result in ×1)
B0 ⎭
```

Status Input Byte (Port 002 In)

```
B7 ⎫
B6 ⎪
B5 ⎪
B4 ⎬ Not used
B3 ⎪
B2 ⎭
B1 = Out of range       ⎰ −1.999 V  > V_IN > 1.999 V  ⎱
B0 = End of conversion  ⎱ −199.9 mV > V_IN > 199.9 mV ⎰
```

Data Input Byte (Port 003 In)

```
B7 = 1st digit      Most significant digit: when low true = B7 = 0
B6 = 2nd digit                                              B6 ⎫
B5 = 3rd digit                                              B5 ⎬ N/A
B4 = 4th digit                                              B4 ⎭
B3 ⎫                                                        B3 = 1/2 digit value
B2 ⎬ BCD digit value                                        B2 = Polarity
B1 ⎪                                                        B1 = N/A
B0 ⎭                                                        B0 = Ranging status bit
```

The most obvious change to the newly modified DVM board is the input multiplexer. Up to this point all the inputs were multiplexed through a CMOS CD4051 integrated circuit. This device performs quite satisfactorily for inputs in the range of 0 to 2 V. The maximum input voltage range it can handle is limited by its supply voltage (in this case ±5 V). Even if the supplies were increased to ±9 V (18 V absolute, which is the maximum supply for a CD4051B) a separate voltage divider would still be required at each input channel to keep the applied voltages within safe limits. To have a 0 to 200 V range selectable unit incorporating a CD4051 input maximum would require having eight separate programmable dividers and an overvoltage protection circuit on each channel in case the wrong divider values are chosen.

The preferred approach is to have only one divider network and one overvoltage circuit, but such an alternative requires that the input multiplexer be capable of handling all input voltage levels from 0 to 200 V! The answer is to use relays. Not the big 10 A clunkers you see in surplus catalogs, but the new generation of (dual in line package) reed relays such as the Series 191 by SIGMA (see photo 2). These particular relays can be driven directly by TTL logic, exhibit maximum 1 ms bounce, and have a rated life of 100 million operations.

The new input multiplexer section consists of dual in line package relays RL1 thru RL8 and a 1 of 10 decoder, IC9. When a latched output port 3 bit channel address is impressed on the input lines of IC9, it puts a 0 voltage level on the output pin corresponding to that address and pulls in the proper channel select relay. The outputs of all eight relays are wired together and are next directed to the overvoltage and gain divider circuitry.

The input impedance of the DVM chip is very high (on the order of 1000 MΩ). Placing a 1 MΩ resistor in series with the relay outputs facilitates the addition of protection circuitry without compromising the interface's capabilities. This current limiting 1 MΩ resistor and two back-to-back zener diodes limit the absolute voltage seen by the MC14433 to about ± V. (The MC14433's absolute limit is its power supply range, even though its usable input range is ±2 V.) If the correct gains are chosen and programmed to the interface, this protection should never be required. But, no one is perfect.
perfect.

In addition to this function, the 1 MΩ resistor is one leg of a programmable divider network. Figure 2 shows the input subsystem in simplified terms. An AC to DC converter is also included and will be explained later. SW1 and SW2, parts of IC8, represent the gain selection section. The switches are illustrated in a unit gain DC input mode. When an input relay is closed, its applied voltage is sent directly to the DVM integrated circuit input through the 1 MΩ resistor. The AC to DC converter is switched out of the system and with both SW1 and SW2 open, no dividers are in the circuit. If 1.400 V is applied through a closed relay, the DVM will read 1.400 V for that channel. If, on the other hand, 150 V is suddenly switched in on another relay with this SW1 and SW2 setting, the chips would be fried were it not for Z1 and Z2. At

Photo 2: The Sigma dual in line package relay, type 191TE1C2-5S, similiar to that used in the design of the expanded digital voltmeter's input multiplexer.

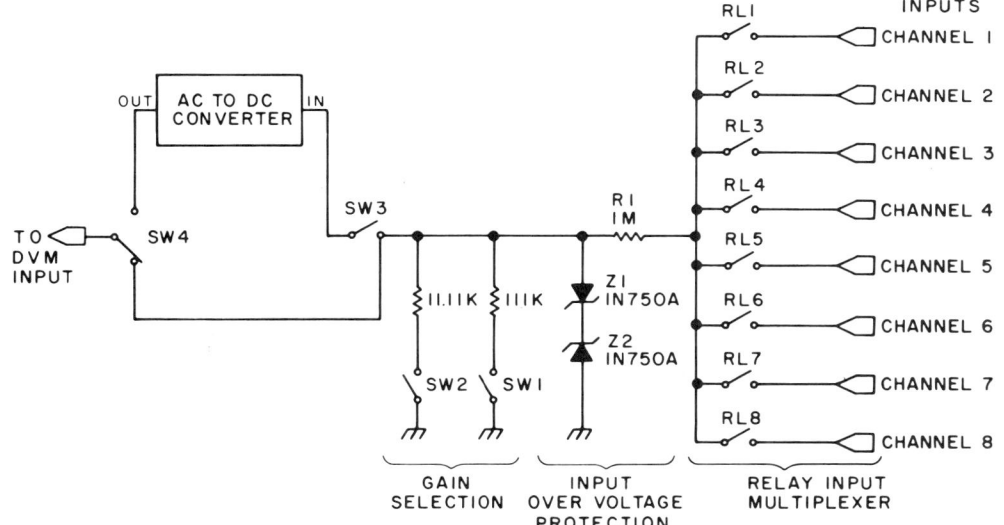

Figure 2: A simplified representation of the input section of the expanded digital voltmeter. The amount of gain and the AC to DC conversion option are selectable by means of CMOS switches.

voltages of less than 4 absolute (±4 V) the diodes do nothing. When inputs exceed this absolute value, Z1 and Z2 clamp them to 4 V. The data acquired by the computer will indicate an out of range condition, since it is over 2 V, but at least it will not have evaporated.

How Do We Read 0 to 200 V Inputs?

Closing switch 2 forms a 10:1 divider network. If 8 V is applied and switch 1 is closed, the result is:

$$VA = \left(\frac{8}{R_1 + R_2}\right) \times R_2$$

$$= \left(\frac{8}{1.111 \, M\Omega}\right) \times 111 \, K$$

$$= 0.799 \, V$$

$$\approx 0.800 \, V$$

As you can see, the result of closing SW1 and applying the 111 K resistor is to divide the 8 V by 10 to get 0.799 V. Proper trimming of this 111 K resistor will give an output of 0.800 V. This value is compatible with the DVM integrated circuit input range, and when read by the computer, will be equal to 0.800 V. The programmer should keep in mind that a divider is used on this channel and should multiply the result by 10 to obtain 8.00 V.

Closing switch 2 forms a 100:1 divider. The mathematics is the same except that the divider resistor is 11.11 K instead of 111 K. An 8 V input appears at the DVM input as 0.080 V, while 150 V becomes 1.500 V.

AC to DC Converter

An additional bonus of this interface is AC to DC conversion on any input channel. Figure 3 shows the schematic of the AC to DC converter section of the interface. Bit 6 of output port 003 controls the application of this function. When it is high, SW3 and SW4 are in the positions shown in figure 2. In this state the AC to DC converter is switched out of the circuit and the DVM gets its input directly from the divider section. When bit 6 is programmed to be a low level, switches 3 and 4 switch to their alternate positions and route the input signal from the divider network through the AC to DC converter. The resulting signal is equal to the average RMS value of the applied input signal. This is basically the same type of circuit as the kind included in many single channel digital meters.

The AC to DC converter consists of three sections of an LM324, IC10. IC10A is a high impedance input buffer with variable offset adjustment. When the converter is switched into play, it must have a high input impedance to avoid loading down the divider network. IC10B is the actual AC to DC conversion section. Its output is a current proportional to the AC input voltage. IC10C converts this current to a voltage and provides ripple filtering. One consideration to keep in mind is that, since this is a multiplexing analog to digital converter, the usual DC blocking capacitor at the input of the AC to DC converter has been removed. Given the particular circuit impedances and desired frequency range the converter should cover, the input capacitor had to be removed because it couldn't respond quickly enough. The result is an AC to DC converter that will pass both AC and DC

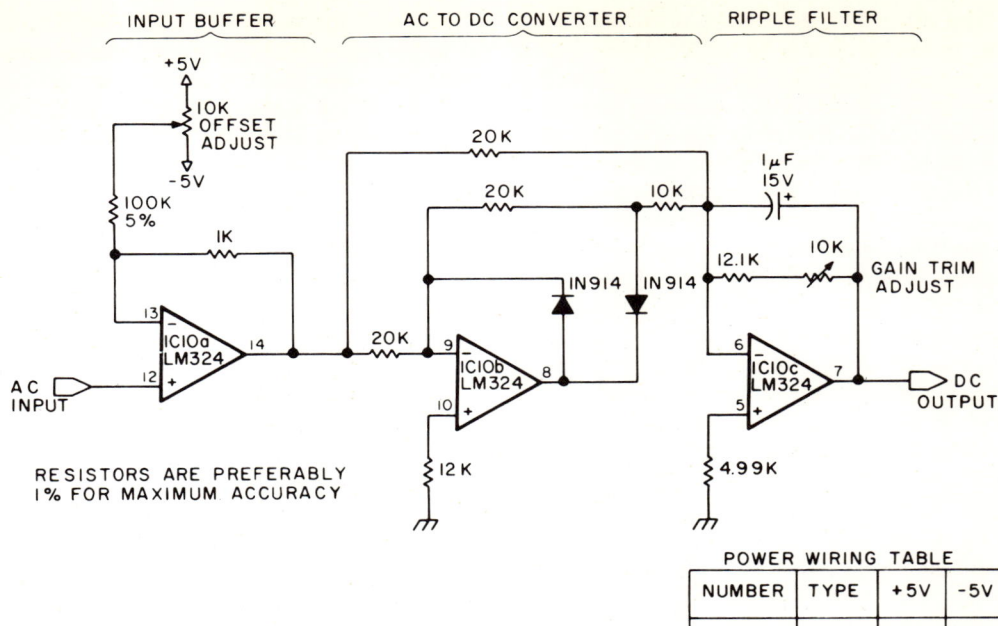

Figure 3: Circuitry of the AC to DC converter used by the digital voltmeter. All resistors are 1% except where shown.

signals; only the AC converted signals should be used, however.

When a 1.0 V peak AC signal (60 Hz) is applied to the converter, the output should be +0.707 VDC. If by accident the AC converter is switched into a DC signal, the output of the converter will be 1.414 times the true DC input. Keep a close watch on your program command byte to the interface.

Adding a 199.9 mV Range

Up to this point we have discussed additions to the basic circuit that allow range selections of 0 to 2 V, 0 to 20 V, and 0 to 200 V. Circuit changes can be incorporated to extend the DVM range in the opposite direction. Figure 4 illustrates the voltage reference and range selection setup of this interface. The MC14433 can also be configured to cover a range of 0 to ±199.9 mV. When bit 5 of port 003 is low, switches 5 and 6 are in the positions shown. A ratiometric converter has a range determined by the applied V_{Ref}, which would be 2.000 V in this instance. With SW5 open, the integrating time constant is set by using a 82 K resistor (this can be formed by a series combination of resistors). With bit 5 set to a 1, the converter changes its V_{Ref} level to 0.200 V and its integration resistor to 10 K. These changes are the only ones necessary for 0 to 0.2 V range selection.

A Less Complicated Driver

The driver was explained in "Try an 8 Channel DVM Cocktail" in detail. It was designed to be as fast as possible. The relay multiplexer added this month unfortunately cannot operate at that speed without modification. I have included a new driver subroutine written especially for this application (see listing 1).

The interface driver is a relocatable subroutine which is polled by a call instruction. The driver is written for page 140 (octal) but is easily relocatable. It occupies less than one 256 byte page of memory and is written for the Z-80 processor. It is especially designed to run with an Extended BASIC which has instructions to access memory and IO ports, and can call a machine language program.

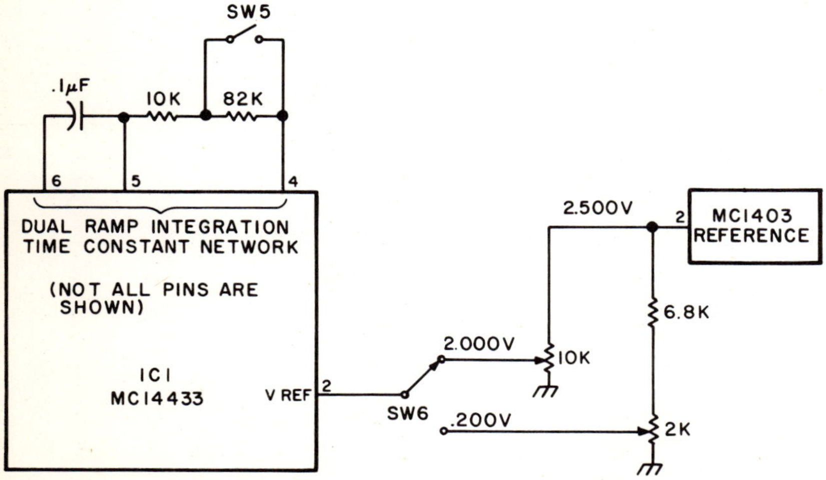

Figure 4: A simplified detail of figure 1, showing the V_{ref} and integration time constant circuitry.

The driver is exercised by a call instruction. In Digital Group Maxi BASIC, the call instruction looks like this: LET X=CALL (24611,64). The BASIC interpreter goes to decimal location 24611 to execute the call and decimal 64 is put in the DE register pair. To the driver, this call is a signal to perform an analog to digital conversion. The contents of the DE register tell it which channel to convert, whether it should be AC or DC, and which V_{Ref} and gain to use. One channel is converted every time the driver is called. The information sent in the DE register at the time of the call is the command output byte (port 003), and each bit has the designations previously listed. The only difference is that bit 7 (the enable disable bit to the analog to digital converter) is sent out as a 0 when doing a call. The driver will set it to an enable condition after it has pulled in the proper relay and allowed a 1.3 ms bounce delay.

When the driver concludes its operation, it has acquired a 3 1/2 digit voltage reading from the DVM which is represented by four bytes. These four bytes are placed in a table in memory. The eight channels of data constitute a 32 byte table. The location of a particular channel's data can be found by a simple expression:

4 byte data location
starts at $L + [4(N-1)]$

where L = starting address of table
N = channel number (1 to 8)

To use the converter with BASIC, the program merely calls for a particular channel conversion and then extracts the appropriate data from the table. Listing 2 is a BASIC program which details the entire procedure.

Conclusion

I often see construction projects which are beyond the means of some experimenters. With these two articles I've attempted to reverse the trend by giving the complete design of a low cost DVM interface. By adding more components, such as relays, this interface can become a full fledged data acquisition system. ■

CAUTION:
One caution should be kept in mind when using this interface to measure AC signals: the ground on the interface board is the same ground as the computer. If you use the interface board to read 115 VAC line voltage, a potential short circuit exists unless either the computer or the measured voltage is isolated. Since isolating the computer equipment would constitute a violation of many electrical codes, only isolated AC signals should be read. A common measurement case which meets this criterion is the AC secondary section of a low voltage power supply such as the unit which runs your computer.

Listing 1: An assembly language program for driving the MC14433 3 1/2 digit analog to digital converter, written for the Z-80.

```
140000                      0140 DIP    EQU   3        DATA INPUT PORT NUMBER
140000                      0150 SIP    EQU   2        STATUS INPUT PORT NUMBER
140000                      0160 COP    EQU   3        COMMAND OUTPUT PORT NUMBER
140000                      0170 EEOC   EQU   200      ENABLE EOC INPUT
140000                      0180 DEOC   EQU   000      DISABLE EOC INPUT
140000                      0190 *
140000                      0200 *
140000                      0210 * CONVERTED CHANNEL DATA BUFFERS
140000                      0220 *
140000 000 000              0230 CHAN0  DW    000000
140002 000 000              0240        DW    000000
140004 000 000              0250 CHAN1  DW    000000
140006 000 000              0260        DW    000000
140010 000 000              0270 CHAN2  DW    000000
140012 000 000              0280        DW    000000
140014 000 000              0290 CHAN3  DW    000000
140016 000 000              0300        DW    000000
140020 000 000              0310 CHAN4  DW    000000
140022 000 000              0320        DW    000000
140024 000 000              0330 CHAN5  DW    000000
140026 000 000              0340        DW    000000
140030 000 000              0350 CHAN6  DW    000000
140032 000 000              0360        DW    000000
140034 000 000              0370 CHAN7  DW    000000
140036 000 000              0380        DW    000000
140040                      0390 *
140040                      0400 * INTERMEDIATE DATA BUFFERS
140040                      0410 *
140040 000                  0430 CHAN   DB    000      CURRENT CHANNEL NUMBER
140041 000 000              0440 CCP    DW    000000   COMMAND CHANNEL PARAMETER
140043                      0460 *
140043                      0470 *
140043                      0480 *** START A/D CONVERTER
140043                      0490 *
140043                      0550 *
140043 173                  0560 START  LD    A,E
```

The following interface is available postpaid in the continental US from:

General Digital Corporation
700 Burnside Av
East Hartford CT 06108

ICs 1, 2, 3, 4, 5 and 8 to build the 0 to 2 V 8 channel unit described in the first part of this 2 part article.

Listing 1, continued:

```
140044 062 041 140        0570            LD      (CCP),A
140047 346 007            0580            AND     007
140051 062 040 140        0590            LD      (CHAN),A
140054 335 041 000 140    0600            LD      IX,CHAN0
140060 026 000            0910            LD      D,0
140062 137                0920            LD      E,A
140063 313 043            0930            SLA     E       CALCULATE BUFFER OFFSET
140065 313 043            0940            SLA     E
140067 335 031            0950            ADD     IX,DE
140071                    0960    *
140071                    0970    * SELECT CHANNEL AND START CONVERSION
140071                    0980    *
140071 006 003            0985            LD      B,3     SET CYCLE COUNT
140073 072 041 140        0990    SCSC    LD      A,(CCP)
140076 323 003            1000            OUT     COP     SELECT CHANNEL
140100 315 243 140        1005            CALL    DELAY
140103 366 200            1010            OR      EEOC    ENABLE EOC OUTPUT
140105 323 003            1020            OUT     COP     COMMAND A/D CONVERTER
140107                    1030    *
140107                    1040    * WAIT FOR EOC
140107                    1050    *
140107 333 002            1060    WEOC    IN      SIP     READ CONVERTER STATUS
140111 313 107            1070            BIT     0,A     TEST FOR EOC
140113 050 372            1080            JR      Z,WEOC  JUMP IF NOT READY
140115 020 354            1085            DJNZ    SCSC
140117 313 117            1090            BIT     1,A     TEST FOR OVERANGE
140121 040 066            1100            JR      NZ,OVER JUMP IF TRUE
140123                    1110    *
140123                    1120    * CONVERSION DONE;PROCESS FIRST (MSD) DIGIT
140123                    1130    *
140123 006 200            1140    MSD0    LD      B,200   SELECT DIGIT 1
140125 315 232 140        1150            CALL    RDIG    WAIT AND READ DIGIT 1
140130 057                1160            CPL
140131 017                1170            RRCA            RIGHT JUSTIFY DIGIT VALUE
140132 017                1180            RRCA
140133 017                1190            RRCA
140134 346 001            1200            AND     1       ISOLATE
140136 036 000            1210            LD      E,0     INITIALIZE STATUS BYTE
140140 313 122            1220            BIT     2,D     TEST POLARITY
140142 040 002            1230            JR      NZ,MSD3 JUMP IF POSITIVE
140144 036 200            1240            LD      E,200   LOAD POLARITY SIGN
140146                    1440    *
140146                    1450    * SAVE MSD AND CURRENT POLARITY
140146                    1460    *
140146 263                1470    MSD3    OR      E       ADD POLARITY SIGN TO MSD
140147 335 167 000        1480            LD      (IX+0),A SAVE IN DATA BUFFER
140152                    1500    *
140152                    1510    * PROCESS 2ND DIGIT
140152                    1520    *
140152 313 010            1530            RRC     B       SELECT DIGIT 2
140154 315 232 140        1540            CALL    RDIG    WAIT AND READ DIGIT
140157 346 017            1550            AND     017     ISOLATE
140161 335 167 001        1560            LD      (IX+1),A STORE SECOND DIGIT
140164                    1570    *
140164                    1580    * PROCESS 3RD DIGIT
140164                    1590    *
140164 313 010            1600            RRC     B       SELECT 3RD DIGIT
140166 315 232 140        1610            CALL    RDIG    WAIT AND READ DIGIT
140171 346 017            1620            AND     017     ISOLATE
140173 335 167 002        1630            LD      (IX+2),A STORE
140176                    1640    *
140176                    1650    * PROCESS 4TH DIGIT
140176                    1660    *
140176 313 010            1670            RRC     B       SELECT 4TH DIGIT
140200 315 232 140        1680            CALL    RDIG    WAIT AND READ DIGIT
140203 346 017            1690            AND     017     ISOLATE
140205 335 167 003        1700            LD      (IX+3),A STORE
140210 311                1710    RAPUP   RET
140211                    1720    *
140211                    1730    * LOAD 2.000 OVERRANGE VALUE INTO DATA BUFFER
140211                    1740    *
140211 076 002            1750    OVER    LD      A,2     LOAD MSD VALUE
140213 335 167 000        1760            LD      (IX+0),A
140216 257                1770            XOR     A
140217 335 167 001        1780            LD      (IX+1),A LOAD LSD VALUES
140222 335 167 002        1790            LD      (IX+2),A
140225 335 167 003        1800            LD      (IX+3),A
140230 030 356            1810            JR      RAPUP
140232                    1870    *
140232                    1880    *
140232                    1890    * READ DIGIT ROUTINE
140232                    1900    *
140232 333 003            1910    RDIG    IN      DIP     READ DATA BYTE
140234 057                1920            CPL             CONVERT TO HIGH TRUE LOGIC
140235 127                1930            LD      D,A     SAVE COPY
140236 240                1940            AND     B       TEST FOR GIVEN DIGIT READY
140237 050 371            1950            JR      Z,RDIG  JUMP IF NOT
140241 172                1960            LD      A,D     RESTORE A REGISTER
140242 311                1970            RET             RETURN TO CALLER
140243 016 377            1980    DELAY   LD      C,377
140245 015                1990    DEL1    DEC     C
140246 310                2000            RET     Z
140247 030 374            2010            JR      DEL1
```

Listing 2: A supervisory program for controlling the expanded digital voltmeter written in extended BASIC.

```
120 REM 8 CHANNEL 3 1/2 DIGIT AC/DC PROGRAMABLE RANGE DVM -S.CIARCIA
130 REM REV. 1.9
140 REM BOARD CHECK OUT PROGRAM
150 REM
160 REM
170 LET M1=24576
180 REM THIS IS PAGE 140(OCTAL)
190 LET M2=24611
200 REM THIS IS THE CALL ADDRESS
210 REM
220 PRINT
230 PRINT
240 PRINT"DO YOU WANT TO SCAN PREVIOUSLY CHOSEN CHANNELS OR"
250 PRINT"SELECT NEW ONES ?   SCAN OR SELECT OR STOP"
260 INPUT S$
265 IF S$="STOP" THEN GOTO 2000
270 IF S$="SCAN" THEN GOTO 830
280 PRINT"SELECT ALL VALUES OR CHANGE ONE CHANNEL"
290 PRINT"ALL OR ONE"; :INPUT S$
300 IF S$<>"ONE" THEN GOTO 420
310 PRINT
320 PRINT"WHICH CHANNEL DO YOU WISH TO CHANGE "; :INPUT C
330 PRINT"PRESENTLY CHOSEN VALUES ARE "
340 IF D(C)=1 THEN R1=.2 ELSE R1=2.0
350 PRINT"VREF.=";R1;" VOLTS   DIVIDER GAIN IS X";F(C);"    CONDITIONING IS FOR ";
360 IF C(C)=1 THEN PRINT"DC" ELSE PRINT"AC"
370 LET A(C)= 1 :GOSUB 590
380 GOSUB 750
390 PRINT"ANOTHER CHANNEL TO CHANGE ?   Y OR N"; :INPUT R$
400 IF R$<>"N" THEN GOTO 320
410 GOTO 830
420 PRINT
425 PRINT"INPUT CHANNEL PARAMETERS"
430 PRINT"GAIN MULTIPLIER IS  1,10 OR,100"
440 PRINT"ENTER CHANNEL PARAMETERS AS REQUIRED"
450 PRINT :PRINT: PRINT
460 FOR C=1 TO 8
470 PRINT"DO YOU WANT TO READ CHANNEL ";C;"            Y OR N OR EXIT";
480 INPUT A$
490 IF A$="EXIT" THEN GOTO 240
500 LET A(C)=0
510 IF A$="N" THEN GOTO 710
520 IF A$="Y" THEN LET A(C)=1
530 IF A$<>"Y" THEN GOTO 470
540 GOSUB 590
550 GOTO 700
560 REM
570 REM
580 REM THIS IS THE PARAMETER SETTING SUBROUTINE
590 PRINT"GAIN ",
600 INPUT B(C)
610 LET F(C)=B(C)
620 LET E(C)=0
630 IF B(C)=10 THEN LET E(C)=8 :GOTO 650
640 IF B(C)=100 THEN LET E(C)=16 :GOTO 650
650 PRINT"ENTER 1 FOR DC OR 0 FOR AC",
660 INPUT C(C)
670 PRINT"ENTER 1 FOR .2 VOLT, OR 0 FOR 2.0 VOLT'DVM VREF.";
680 INPUT D(C)
690 RETURN
700 PRINT
710 NEXT C
720 REM X1 TO X8 ARE THE CALL SETPOINTS
730 GOSUB 750
740 GOTO 810
750 FOR J=1 TO 8
760 LET X(J)=64*C(J)+32*D(J)+E(J)+J-1
770 REM X(J) IS LOADED WITH THE BIT PATTERN WHICH IS
780 REM PUT IN THE DE REG. PAIR DURING THE CALL INSTRUCTION
790 NEXT J
800 RETURN
810 PRINT
820 PRINT
830 REM THIS ROUTINE DETERMINES WHICH CHANNELS ARE TO BE CONVERTED"
840 FOR C=1 TO 8
850 IF A(C)=0 THEN GOTO 870
860 LET H=CALL(M2,X(C))
870 NEXT C
880 REM THIS ROUTINE PRINTS THE VALUES IN THE MEMORY TABLE
890 LET Z=A(1)+A(2)+A(3)+A(4)+A(5)+A(6)+A(7)+A(8)
900 IF Z=0 THEN PRINT"NO CHANNEL PARAMETERS HAVE BEEN CHOSEN" :GOTO 450
910 LET D=M1
920 FOR L=1 TO 8
930 GOSUB 1030
940 IF A(L)=0 THEN 990
950 IF D(L)=0 THEN GOTO 970
960 IF Y1>=.2 THEN PRINT"CHANNEL ";L;" IS OUT OF RANGE" : GOTO 990
970 IF Y1>=2 THEN PRINT"CHANNEL ";L;" IS OUT OF RANGE" :GOTO 990
980 GOSUB 1230
990 NEXT L
1000 GOTO 170
1010 REM
```

Listing 2, continued:

```
1020 REM
1030 REM THIS ROUTINE EXAMINES THE MEMORY TABLE
1040 REM AND CONVERTS THE 4 BYTES TO A 3 1/2 DIGIT VOLTAGE
1050 LET Q1=EXAM(D)
1060 LET Q=Q1
1070 IF Q1>=128 THEN LET Q=Q1-128
1080 D=D+1
1090 LET W=EXAM(D)
1100 D=D+1
1110 LET E=EXAM(D)
1120 D=D+1
1130 LET R=EXAM(D)
1140 LET D=D+1
1150 LET Y=Q+(.1*W)+(.01*E)+(.001*R)
1160 LET Y1=Y
1170 LET Y=B(L)*Y
1180 IF D(L)=1 THEN LET Y1=Y/10
1190 RETURN
1200 REM
1210 REM
1220 REM
1230 REM THIS SUBROUTINE PRINTS OUT THE VOLTAGE VALUES
1240 PRINT"CHANNEL ";L;" IS ";
1250 IF Q1<128 THEN PRINT" "; : GOTO 1270
1260 IF Q1>=128 THEN PRINT"-";
1270 IF D(L)=1 THEN PRINT %7F4;Y1;" VOLTS "; :GOTO 1310
1280 IF B(L)=100 THEN PRINT %5F1;Y;" VOLTS ";
1290 IF B(L)=10 THEN PRINT %5F2;Y;" VOLTS ";
1300 IF B(L)=1 THEN PRINT %6F3;Y;" VOLTS ";
1310 IF C(L)=0 THEN PRINT"AC";
1320 PRINT
1330 RETURN
2000 END
READY
```

Listing 3: A sample of the program in listing 2 being used to read five different inputs.

```
DO YOU WANT TO SCAN PREVIOUSLY CHOSEN CHANNELS OR
SELECT NEW ONES ?   SCAN OR SELECT OR STOP
?SELECT
SELECT ALL VALUES OR CHANGE ONE CHANNEL
ALL OR ONE?ALL

INPUT CHANNEL PARAMETERS
GAIN MULTIPLIER IS  1,10 OR,100
ENTER CHANNEL PARAMETERS AS REQUIRED

DO YOU WANT TO READ CHANNEL  1      Y OR N OR EXIT?Y
GAIN      ?1
ENTER 1 FOR DC OR 0 FOR AC      ?1
ENTER 1 FOR .2 VOLT, OR 0 FOR 2.0 VOLT DVM VREF.?0

DO YOU WANT TO READ CHANNEL  2      Y OR N OR EXIT?Y
GAIN      ?1
ENTER 1 FOR DC OR 0 FOR AC      ?1
ENTER 1 FOR .2 VOLT, OR 0 FOR 2.0 VOLT DVM VREF.?0

DO YOU WANT TO READ CHANNEL  3      Y OR N OR EXIT?N
DO YOU WANT TO READ CHANNEL  4      Y OR N OR EXIT?N
DO YOU WANT TO READ CHANNEL  5      Y OR N OR EXIT?N
DO YOU WANT TO READ CHANNEL  6      Y OR N OR EXIT?Y
GAIN      ?10
ENTER 1 FOR DC OR 0 FOR AC      ?1
ENTER 1 FOR .2 VOLT, OR 0 FOR 2.0 VOLT DVM VREF.?0

DO YOU WANT TO READ CHANNEL  7      Y OR N OR EXIT?Y
GAIN      ?10
ENTER 1 FOR DC OR 0 FOR AC      ?0
ENTER 1 FOR .2 VOLT, OR 0 FOR 2.0 VOLT DVM VREF.?0

DO YOU WANT TO READ CHANNEL  8      Y OR N OR EXIT?Y
GAIN      ?100
ENTER 1 FOR DC OR 0 FOR AC      ?1
ENTER 1 FOR .2 VOLT, OR 0 FOR 2.0 VOLT DVM VREF.?0


CHANNEL  1 IS    1.515 VOLTS
CHANNEL  2 IS     .114 VOLTS
CHANNEL  6 IS -  9.48 VOLTS
CHANNEL  7 IS    9.40 VOLTS AC
CHANNEL  8 IS  118.2 VOLTS
```

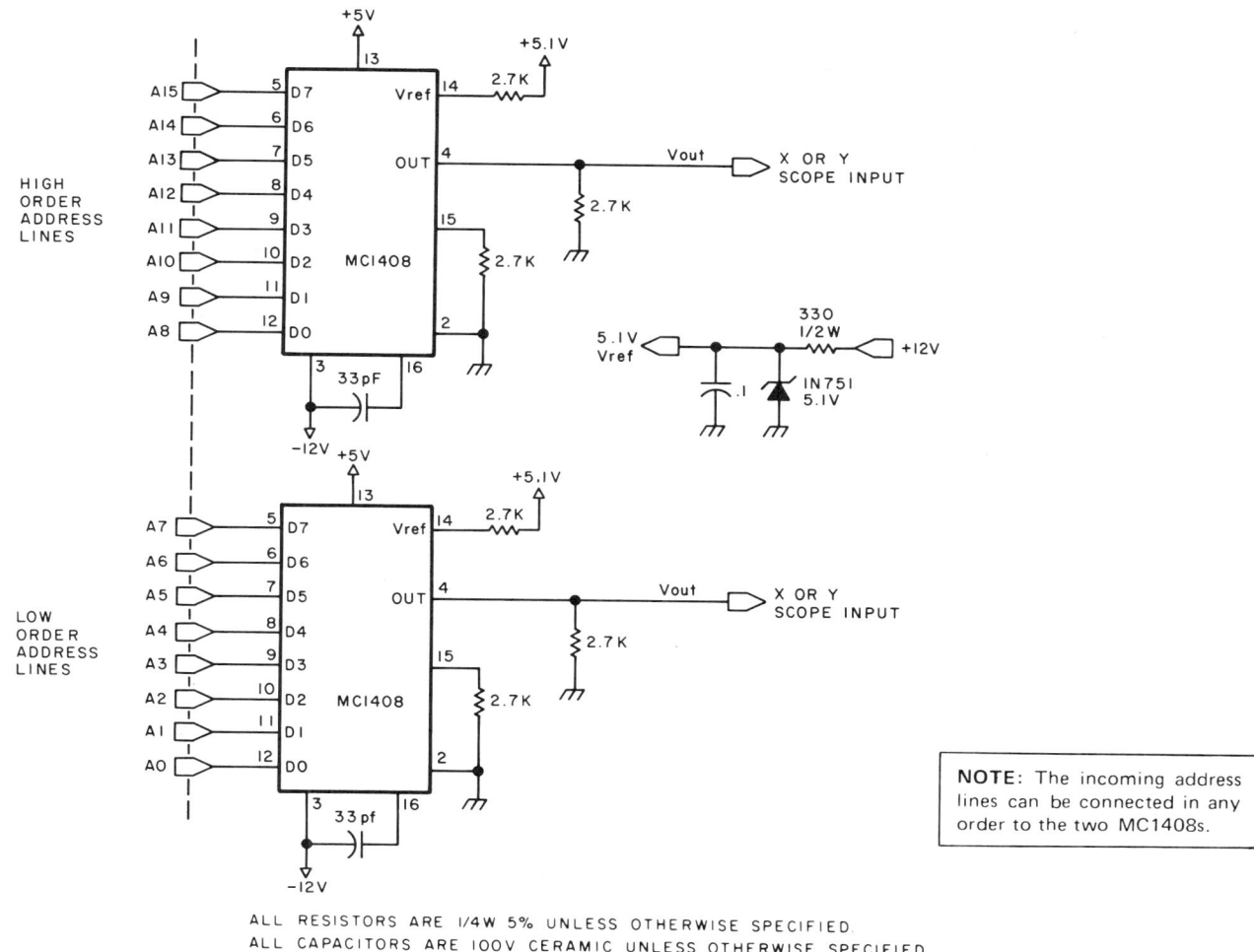

Figure 1: A 256 by 256 point address state analyzer that displays dynamic fluctuations of a computer's 16 bit memory address bus. Two 8 bit digital to analog converters drive the horizontal and vertical inputs of an oscilloscope with the analog equivalent of the eight high order and eight low order address lines. The display gives a visual "signature" of the computer in action. Accessing of unexpected memory locations which distort this "signature" becomes instantly visible for troubleshooting purposes.

A Penny Pinching Address State Analyzer

Some years ago I got my first home microcomputer, a Scelbi 8H. This was before the advent of widespread interest in personal computers and it was naturally based upon the Intel 8008 processor. Back then I was satisfied with the tedious task of hand toggling a program into the computer and watching the front panel memory address and data buffer lights twinkle, signifying that the program was executing something. After that I bought more memory which consisted of 2102s. That gave me enough space to write only the simplest of monitor programs, again using the front panel as the display medium. At the end of its evolution, my 8008 did have a rudimentary video display and 300 bps cassette interface; but, if there was one major physical characteristic of the first generation home computers, it was the predominance of the front panel display and data entry switches. The concept of the integrated home computer "system" was yet to be seen. A computer required display and data entry switches if it was to be powered up and exercised. Additional IO devices such as video displays and keyboards were luxuries.

Well, it was inevitable. The prices of components have dropped drastically in

Photo 1: *The author's computer system, showing the address state analyzer in operation with a BASIC program (see oscilloscope in center of picture). The program is printing an integer sequence of ASCII characters on the display to the right using the function CHR$(X). On the left is a 50 K byte Digital Group Z-80 system.*

the past few years and the experimenter now thinks in terms of a home computer system incorporating a processor, cassette interface, read only memory systems software, keyboard and video display. Fewer and fewer microcomputers have front panels that display memory lines or data buffers. The memory address in addition to the contents of all other pertinent processor registers is now usually available through a monitor program command. The cost effectiveness of the front panel lights and toggle switches has diminished to the vanishing point.

I would never advocate a return to front panels, by any means. But recall how many times you have checked the rhythmic pulsations of particular lights to assure yourself that your program was executing correctly. Or, how many times have you recognized that the program had obviously vectored off into the unknown by the graphical representation of the 16 address bus lights? Adding 16 lamps on the memory address lines can be done on any microcomputer, and this would give us some indication of what the program is doing. But the LEDs are truly readable only when the processor is in a hold state, halted, or otherwise not changing the memory address. The chances of obtaining a recognizable visual pattern on the LEDs are small when running programs written in languages like BASIC that jump around in memory as they interpret each statement. And with LEDs there are only 16 graphical elements; this gives poor resolution.

A $15 Video Analyzer

There is another way to watch the internal program sequence that far exceeds a 16 bit lamp display: a 256 by 256 point analyzer that displays the dynamic fluctuations of the 16 bit memory address bus. This gadget can be added using only two integrated circuits and any X-Y oscilloscope with sufficient bandwidth. The result is a graphical presentation of the computer in action. It is not graphics in the classic sense: no pictures can be drawn, and alphanumeric capability is nonexistent. It is instead a point plot of the memory address states, dynamically changing during the execution of a program.

The 6800, 8080, Z-80, 6502 and other processors all have 16 bit address buses. They directly address 64 K bytes of memory (ie: there are 65,536 possible address combinations). The address bus can be divided into eight bits of high order address and eight bits of low order address.

If either of these address portions is attached to the eight input lines of a pair of digital to analog converters, two unique analog voltage values are produced for each address location. The two voltage outputs, *one for high address and one for low address,* can then be attached to the vertical and horizontal inputs of an oscilloscope. The result is a fascinating animated display of a computer in action.

Constructing the State Analyzer

It isn't often that I can outline a design in which layout, physical components, absolute voltages, input and output polarities, or input attachments are so flexible. This 2

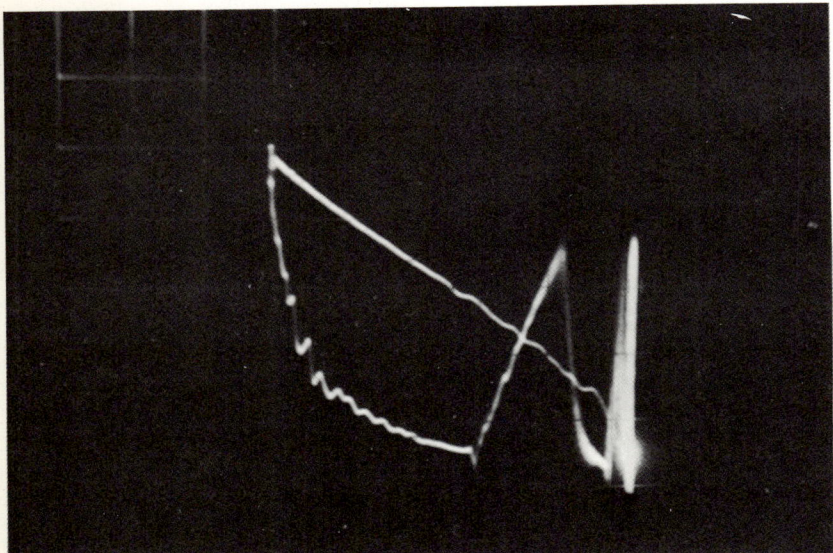

Photo 2: *A close-up of the penny pinching address state analyzer display showing the result of a power on reset in the computer. Execution begins in the 256 byte EROM bootstrap program; the program continually vectors to the cassette input port 001 (thin excursion line to the upper left in the photo) to see if data is present.*

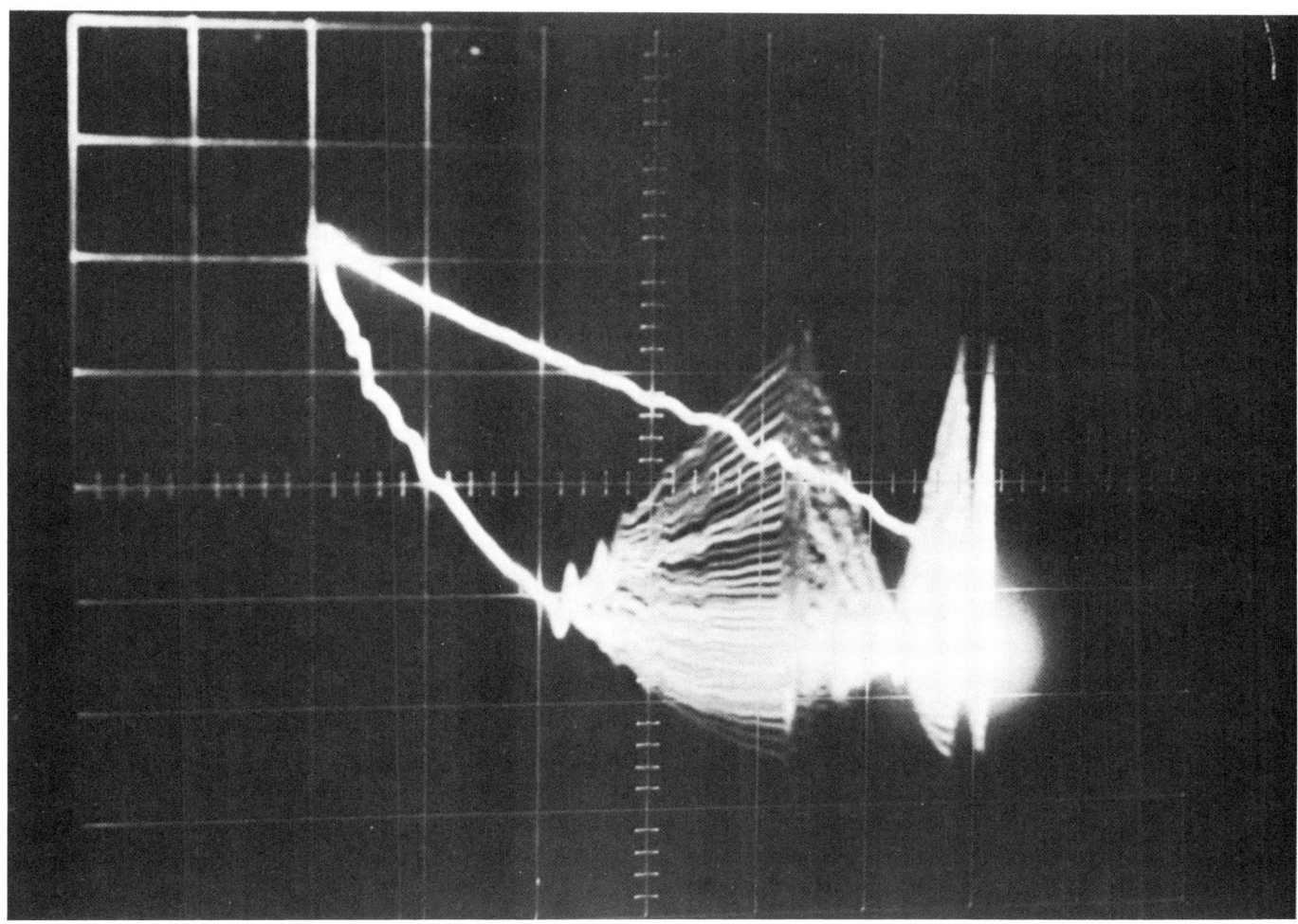

chip circuit can be hooked up any way you want it. You can mix the address bits between the two digital to analog converters. If you separate the address bytes as I have and attach one byte to each converter, the display tends to dwell in a narrow region along a vertical line.

The 8 bit digital to analog converter I have chosen is the Motorola MC1408. The L6, L7 or L8 version can be used since absolute accuracy is not important. What is being produced is a system signature unique to your system and your programming. Figure 1 illustrates the schematic of the circuit as I attached it to my computer address lines. For a more complete description of how the MC1408 works, see "Control the World" (page 47).

Evaluating the Results

The oscilloscope traces in photos 1, 2, 3 and 4 are particular to my system and software only; but similar, though not exact versions, should be produced on other systems. As diagrammed in the schematic, I have used the high order address lines to drive the X axis and the low order address lines to drive the Y axis. Another peculiarity of my system is a logically inverted address bus. The result is that the display moves in the opposite direction from what one might expect. The higher the address, the lower the output voltage. Again, as I stated earlier, human pattern recognition, not methodology, is important.

After attaching this video drive to an oscilloscope, turn on the power. In my case the pattern displayed (as in photo 2) illustrates that the computer is operating in the region of memory occupied by the monitor software; it regularly vectors to another address, that of the cassette input (the 8 bit low order memory address lines of the Z-80 or 8080 are also used to address input and output ports) at port 001. Later, when running BASIC, repeated addressing of keyboard input port 000 can be recognized as in photo 3 taken after TDL 12 K BASIC was loaded.

One of the programs which best illustrates this new visual dimension of the computer is a basic memory test program as it scans through memory. Dynamically

Photo 3: Effect of a carriage return while executing TDL 12 K BASIC. The long streamer shows the program's reference to the input port of the keyboard.

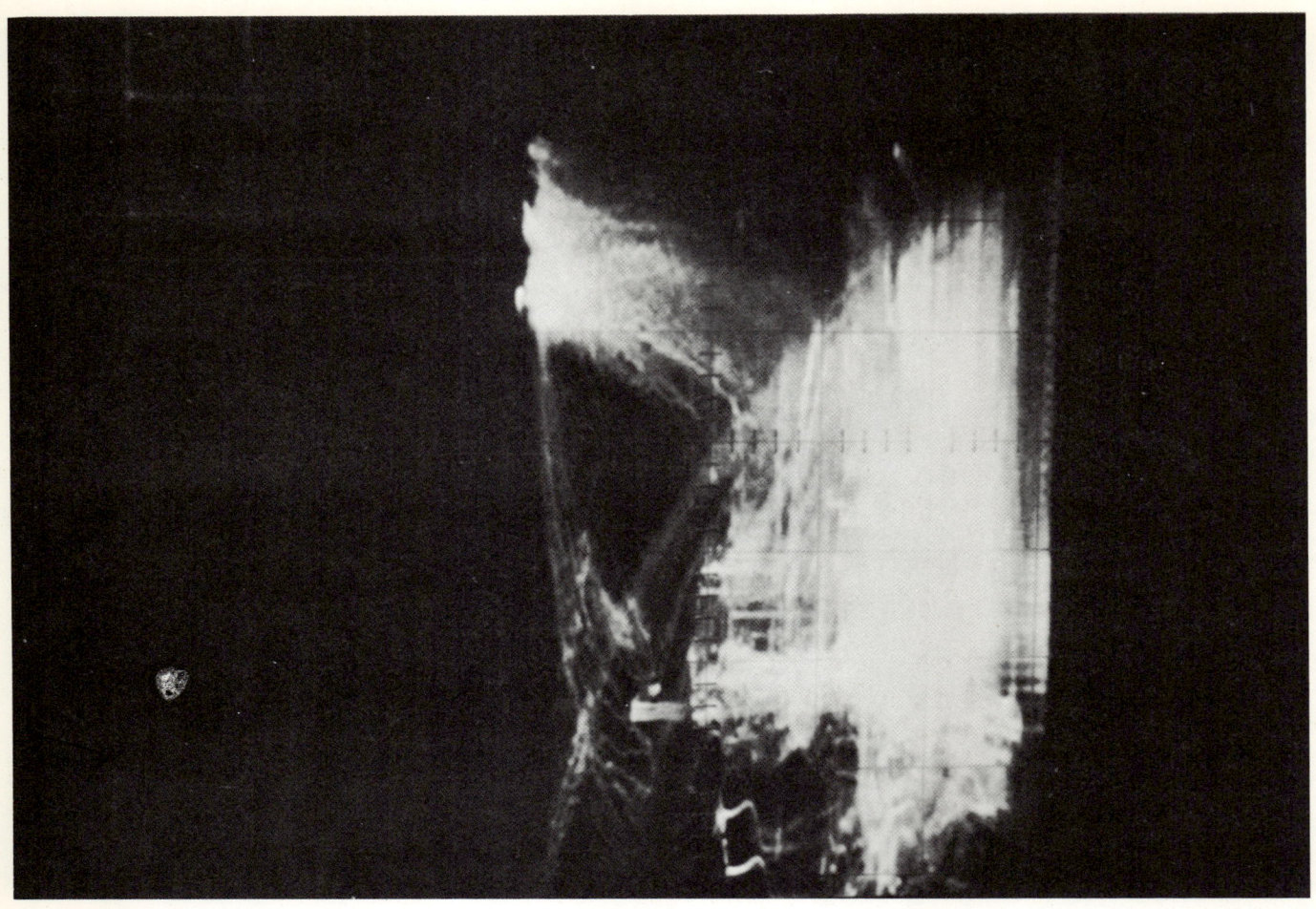

Photo 4: A complex bus addressing pattern during the execution of a BASIC program.

varying displays such as these are very difficult to photograph and would appear as blurs. The photos I have included are those of programs with addressing sufficiently repetitive so that the pattern appears stable (see photo 4).

There is one particular instance that proved the worth of the address state analyzer on my system. I had received and was in the process of checking out the TDL 12 K Super BASIC software package distributed by Micro COM for the Digital Group Z-80 system, and was having trouble getting the software to execute in 26 K of memory. Rather than call the company and complain of a possible bad tape, I turned on the address state analyzer and loaded the tape. I could see the computer cycling through the cassette input section of the monitor and depositing it in increasingly higher portions of memory. At its conclusion, the words "Highest Memory" appeared on the screen. I promptly typed in 26000 and hit a carriage return. The computer took off and started doing a scan across memory in a pattern similar to that of a memory test program. Following this, the computer went into visible convulsions (or the electronic equivalent) on the ocilloscope and never returned to the display. I loaded the program once again and this time answered the question with 20000. The result was an introductory blurb indicating that BASIC was fully operational. A quick scan of the 2 K bytes of memory on the processor board verified that they were wired for something other than 24 K to 26 K. The address state analyzer (in which I now had considerably more faith) told the complete story. After replying to the "Highest Memory," the program apparently scanned memory and tried to verify that the typed input was indeed plausible. In a false case it got hung up. Resetting the memory bank decoding circuit for 24 K to 26 K, of course, solved the problem. ∎

Program Your Next EROM in BASIC

"Steve, you just gotta help me!" was my not so usual frantic midafternoon introduction to Jerry. He burst into my office with a manner reminiscent of a storm trooper. The vacuum he created as he rushed toward me around the obstacles in his path caused disturbed paper work to flutter slowly to the floor in his wake. He stopped abruptly at my desk and held the contents of his hand under my nose, hoping to exact an immediate response from me. Being abruptly summoned and having objects stuffed in my face is not generally how I like to be approached.

"I hope I'm not disturbing you, Steve, but I need some help." He extended his hand again but knew enough not to stick it in my face. "I accidently blew one of the EROM chips that contains the data acquisition software you gave me. We have a computer club meeting tomorrow night and I'm supposed to demonstrate my computer. I'm just going to look dumb to all those guys if I don't have a good demonstration..."

I could understand his plight. If Jerry were to sit down and discuss his problem with his children, I'm sure his 9 year old son would describe it as a classic case of peer pressure. Designing control systems for factories on paper is different from a direct demonstration of one's capabilities in front of a knowledgeable group of fellow computerists. Jerry was terrified that he would be a flop.

"Hold it Jerry... what's the problem? You have a computer... I thought you bought an EROM programmer?", I asked, still trying to ascertain the true depth of his difficulty. "You have a listing of the EROM contents."

"I've been meaning to get a programmer one of these days, but it costs a fortune. I wouldn't use it enough to justify the expense. I called Bob and he let me look at the assembly listing of an EROM programmer. I brought it along so we could cut another on your system. I've never been very good at assembly language programming. The listing of his programmer looks quite involved. I'm sure I wouldn't be able to incorporate it into my operating system by tomorrow night. You just gotta help me, Steve... please?"

His pleading was a bit sickening but I could understand what he was going through. "Jerry, why don't you write your own quick programmer?", I asked. "What do you think it entails?" The reason for this line of questioning wasn't to antagonize or delay him, but rather to get a handle on what may be a problem for more people than Jerry.

"What do you mean? How to do it? You write an assembly language program that gets the address and data to the EROM and you hold it there until it's burned in, and step to the next address. But it's all those program loops to keep track of the address, data and timing. I really bought this computer to use on BASIC, remember?"

"You've done some extensive BASIC programming, haven't you? You have a computer with plenty of parallel input and output ports, don't you? Write the EROM programmer in the language you understand best. True, it can be written in assembly language, but it can just as well be written in BASIC."

"Huh?", he grunted, still not quite believing me. "What do you mean?"

I felt I had his interest now. I was telling him that solving his dilemma need not entail using any more than the canned software supplied with his system, and that he didn't have to get involved with the "black magic" of assembly language.

Photo 1: A closeup of a 2708 erasable read only memory. Visible through the transparent quartz window are the two banks of FAMOS (Floating gate Avalanche injection Metal Oxide Semiconductor) storage devices. The contents of this memory storage circuit are erased by exposing the window to ultraviolet light.

"You already said that programming an EROM entailed getting the address and data to the EROM and stepping the address sequentially. Right?", I said.

"Yes, but BASIC?", he responded.

"Sure, why not BASIC?", I said. "By using INP and OUT commands, address and data can be set, and PEEK and POKE commands allow the interface data to be read into or from memory." It was important to convince him of the true value of high level languages. "You have a monitor program resident in your system that could allow you to just key the EROM data list into memory somewhere, don't you?"

"Yes, but . . . ."

"No buts! Just write a BASIC program that transfers this memory table one byte at a time to the read only memory." I felt I was really on the move now; I was going to "learn" him something if it killed him.

"Yes, but my BASIC is an interpreter. It runs pretty slowly. It's no match for an assembly language program. Assembly language loaders can program an EROM in 100 seconds; BASIC would be an order of magnitude. . . ." It was necessary to interrupt him at this point. Jerry was caught up in the old argument of potential versus accomplishment.

"Jerry, except for the time taken for data entry and printing, how long do your average BASIC programs run?"

"Oh, 5 or 10 minutes I suppose; why?" Jerry was not so curious that he had forgotten his problem, but his responses had become less acidic.

"And what do you do in between program runs or when you go upstairs for supper?" As oblique as my question may have seemed, I was driving to a point.

"I leave the computer on, of course, so I don't have to reload the BASIC. Everybody does that. Don't you?" His response was reminiscent of a child not sure whether he would be reprimanded for raiding the cookie jar or not telling that he raided the cookie jar.

"Jerry, what you just said is that if no operator interaction is required with the computer, execution time is irrelevant. Furthermore, if you started a program like an EROM loader on off peak use periods, you couldn't care less if it took a minute or an hour to run."

"Yes. . .but. . . well, I guess you're right." He had apparently never thought to use BASIC.

"In conclusion, Jerry, what language are you best able to program?" I had to be careful I didn't come across too strongly, but it was never too late to learn.

"BASIC, of course. I know how to program in assembly language, but. . .," he continued, still believing that there was something wrong about taking a different approach to the accepted norm.

"Then program the bloody EROM in BASIC! In fact, I had the same problem a few weeks ago and built the interface board already. If you drop over to my house this evening, I'll show you how it works and give you an EROM." The look on Jerry's face was one of relief, but I was sure he'd eventually realize I could have answered his question when he first walked in. It was important that he understand what he was trying to accomplish as well as obtain satisfactory results.

This seems like an overamplified introduction to a simple construction article, but I find it easier to present such topics if I explain how I got involved with them. There's no reason that read only memory programmers should remain as black magic to the personal computer enthusiast. There are a number of 2708 EROM programmers on the market in the $100 to $150 range. But most of the readers who correspond with me say they only want to program one or two for bootstraps and the like. It is for this reason I'd like to present a $9 EROM loader which, when tied to parallel ports such as those described in "Memory Mapped IO" (page 7), can provide this function. Rather than be completely confusing, maybe I ought to start at the beginning.

What Is an EROM?

If you presently own a personal computer, even in its minimum configuration, it contains programmable memory. Most likely the memory you own is made of semiconductor memory chips configured as boards with 4 K, 8 K, 16 K or more bytes. Programmable memory means that any element can be addressed and read from or written to (that is to say, programmed) individually. Addressing is random and is determined by program necessity rather than configuration. Any number of electronic elements can function as programmable memories. TTL 7474 flip flops, bistable relays, core memory, etc, can all function in this manner, but are not necessarily cost effective for personal computer applications. Since the majority of programmable memory storage in personal computers is of the semiconductor type, one major problem is created. Semiconductor programmable memory is volatile. When the power is removed, the data is destroyed.

One solution to the volatility of semiconductor programmable memory is to configure a certain quantity of the storage as nonvolatile read only memory (ROM). ROMs exhibit the same random addressing capabilities as volatile programmable memory, but the data stored in them is permanent. The required bit patterns are programmed into them during manufacture, or during a special postmanufacturing procedure, and any time power is applied, these bit patterns will be the same. Most computer systems containing read only memory use this vehicle to store bootstrap loaders or monitor routines that allow ease of system startup.

A further extension of the read only memory is the programmable read only memory, or PROM. When a programmable read only memory comes from a manufacturer, no program data is stored in the device. To use this type of read only memory, a special programmer is required to alter the internal structure of the chip and impress specific bit patterns permanently into the addressable memory locations.

It is often desirable to have the nonvolatility of ROMs and the read and write capabilities of semiconductor programmable memories. An effective compromise is the EROM or erasable read only memory. It is used as a read only memory for extended periods of time, erased occasionally and reprogrammed as necessary. Erasure is accomplished by removing the EROM integrated circuit from the system and exposing the chip (covered by a transparent quartz window) to ultraviolet light. I'll describe erasure and programming later.

The erasable read only memory technology used by Intel and most other manufacturers is a stored charge type called a FAMOS transistor, for *floating gate avalanche injection metal oxide semiconductor*. It is similar to what is known as a P-channel silicon gate field effect transistor with the lower, or "floating," gate totally surrounded by an insulator of silicon dioxide. The 1 or 0 storage value of the FAMOS cell is a function of the charge on the floating gate. A charged cell will have the opposite storage output of an uncharged cell. By applying a 25 V charging voltage to selectively addressed cells, particular bit patterns making up the program can be written into the memory. This charge, because it is surrounded by insulating material, can last for years. When this silicon dioxide insulator is exposed to intense ultraviolet light, it becomes somewhat conductive. The result is erasure of all programmed information as the charge leaks away.

There are many erasable read only memories on the market: 1702s, 2708s and 2716s are the major ones. For the most part, experimenters have moved away from the very difficult-to-program 1702s toward the more desirable and more easily programmed 2708s. An added benefit is the fourfold increase in storage capacity of the 2708. The 2716 is the newest version of this erasable technology on the market, and at the time of this writing is considerably more expensive than the 2708. It is for this reason that the methods outlined in this article are used for programming 2708s.

Programming a 2708

The 2708 is an ultraviolet erasable read only memory. It is configured as 1024 single byte memory locations (eight bits per byte). Figure 1 illustrates a simple interface that allows the user to both read and program a 2708.

When reading the contents of the memory, a 10 bit address is presented to address lines A0 thru A9, and the eight bits of data stored in that location will appear as outputs of the memory on D0 thru D7. The interface is attached to three 8 bit output ports and one 8 bit input port. 10 bit addressing is accomplished by using two bits of port 18 in addition to the eight bits of port 17. When B7 and B6 of port 18 are at a zero level, the 8 bit stored data is read by input port 16. The port numbers chosen are peculiar to my system. Any four user defined available parallel IO ports that accomplish the same functions can be chosen instead, substituting for the ports I used.

Programming is straightforward. B6 of the output port 18 is raised to a 1 level to set the interface to the write mode. This signal raises the voltage level on the 2708 chip select pin 20 from a zero volt read enable to +12 V program mode enable. The

IC	Type	+5 V Pin	−5 V Pin	+12 V Pin	Gnd Pin
1	74125	14			7
2	74125	14			7
3	74121	14			7
4	7406	14			7
5	2708	24	21	19	12

Notes:

1. All resistors are 1/4 W 5% unless otherwise noted.
2. Transistor Q1 is rated for VCE = 40 V. Suggested type: 2N2222A.
3. Note that IC4 is a 7406 A 7416 should not be substituted.
4. Programming pulse voltage should be between 25 to 27 VDC.

Output Port 18

B6	B7	
0	X	Read.
1	0	Program mode enabled.
1	⎍	Low to high transition. Initiates input byte storage into EROM.

("X" indicates a "don't care" condition.)

eight data output lines now become eight data input lines to the memory. The program mode signal also gates output port 16 through a pair of 74125s to these data input lines and presents the "data to be stored" to the 2708.

According to the manufacturer's specifications for the 2708, it takes 100 seconds to fully program or "burn in" the EROM. A little simple division would lead one to believe that each address byte should be programmed for 100 ms. Yes and no! Each byte has a cumulative programming time of 100 ms, but it is done in 1 ms pulses. All addresses must be cycled through the program sequence before repeating the pulse on a particular location. In plain English, as each byte is addressed it is given a 1 ms program pulse. To accumulate 100 ms per byte, the program must be repeated 100 times. More on this later.

IC3 and two sections of IC4 provide the +25 V program pulse to the 2708. IC3 is set for a duration of 1 ms and is triggered by a logic 0 to 1 transition at its input. The 2708 both sources and sinks current through programming pin 18, so a combination of devices is necessary rather than a simple

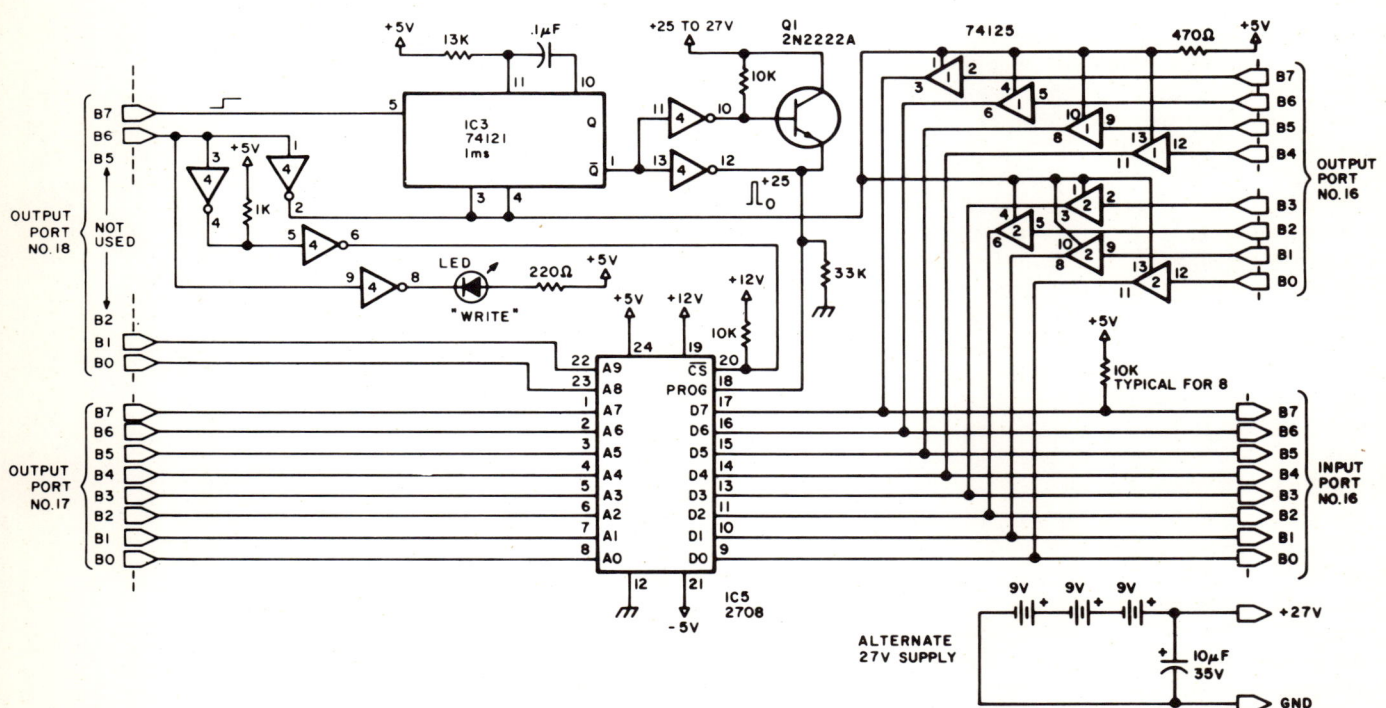

Figure 1: A 2708 erasable read only memory reader and programmer. During reading, the 2708 (IC5) receives a 10 bit address on address lines A0 thru A9. The eight bits of data stored at that location will then appear as outputs on lines D0 thru D7. The circuit is shown attached to three 8 bit output ports and one 8 bit input port of a microcomputer. (The port numbers chosen are peculiar to the author's system and are necessary to fully describe the software interaction.) During programming, bit B6 of output port 18 is set high, which causes the interface to enter the write mode. This signal raises the voltage level on the 2708 select pin 20 from a 0 V read enable to a +12 V program mode enable. The eight data output lines now become data input lines. The program mode signal also gates output port 16 through ICs 1 and 2 to these data input lines and presents the data to be stored to the 2708. Each 8 bit data byte is then burned in for 100 ms in 1 ms pulses using ICs 3 and 4.

Photo 2: A 2708 programmer built from the circuit in figure 1. This board uses parallel IO ports to set data and address.

open collector driver. In the write mode, when $\overline{CS}$/WE pin 20 is at +12 V and between programming pulses, pin 18 has to be pulled down by an active device because it sources a small amount of current. The 1 ms programming pulse itself is about 30 mA and cannot be easily accommodated without emitter follower configured Q1. This pulse should be between 25 and 27 V at pin 18. Three 9 V transistor radio batteries will suffice for this application or a commercial 24 V, 50 mA power supply can be used. Most supplies can be resistor trimmed to produce the desired 25 to 27 V.

Using the Interface with BASIC

The logic behind this interface is simple: set an address and read data, or set an address and write data. Every EROM programmer I have seen uses an assembly language routine to sequence the operation. This interface is no exception. It will run faster if controlled in that manner, especially if wired to the memory bus for read operations rather than through IO ports. It does not have to be controlled through BASIC.

BASIC is the predominent high level language in personal computer use today. It is only natural for an experimenter proficient in BASIC to consider using this method. It is important to remember that most BASIC systems use interpreters and will perform operations very slowly compared with assembly (machine) language programs; but, if fast operation is not a particular requirement, BASIC can perform the same functions.

Reading the contents of a 2708 is a simple procedure, as shown in listing 1. Obviously, it takes a long time to print the 1024 bytes in the memory chip even though formatting would speed it up. Another operation which is useful is to read the 2708 and load it into memory, such as in the case of a utility program or interface driver. The concept is the same, but the print statement is deleted. The new program, which reads the EROM and loads it into memory, is shown in listing 2.

Programming the 2708 is no more complicated than reading it. There are two sources for the data to be placed in the 2708. It can come from a 1 K byte listing presently resident in memory (such as that produced by an assembler), or via keyboard entry. Keyboard entry, while possible, is very time-consuming and requires that an array be produced with 1024 variables. If keyboard entry is desirable, it would be far

```
100 REM FIRST WE CLEAR THE OUTPUT AND SET IT
110 REM TO THE READ MODE
130 OUT 18,0
140 FOR N=0 TO 3
150 FOR M=0 TO 255
155 OUT 17,M : OUT 18,N
160 PRINT "ADDRESS"; (N*256)+M;"=";INP(16)
170 NEXT M
180 NEXT N
200 END
```

Listing 1: A BASIC program used to read the contents of an erasable read only memory. This program and the programs in listings 2 and 3 were written in 8 K Zapple BASIC marketed by Micro Com.

```
100 OUT 18,0 :REM SET TO READ MODE
110 LET X=26000 :REM
114 REM SET X=DECIMAL ADDRESS OF THE
115 REM START OF THE MEMORY TABLE
120 FOR N=0 TO 3
130 FOR M=0 TO 255
135 OUT 17,M:OUT 18,N
140 POKE X, INP(16)
150 LET X=X+1
160 NEXT M
170 NEXT N
180 PRINT "TABLE LOADED"
200 END
```

Listing 2: A BASIC program used to read the contents of a 2708 erasable read only memory and store the data in memory.

```
90  FOR T=1 TO 100
100 LET A=64 :OUT 18,A :REM 64 IS BIT 6 SET
110 REM THIS SETS THE INTERFACE TO THE PROGRAM MODE
120 LET X=26000
130 REM X IS THE START OF THE MEMORY TABLE
140 FOR N=0 TO 3
150 FOR M=0 TO 255
155 LET D=PEEK(X)
160 OUT 17,M : OUT 18,N+A :OUT 16,D
165 REM LINE 160 SETS THE ADDRESS + DATA BYTES
170 OUT 18,N+A+128 :REM 128 IS THE PROGRAM PULSE BIT
180 OUT 18,N+A :REM RESET B7
190 LET X=X+1
200 NEXT M
210 NEXT N
220 LET M=0 :LET N=0
230 NEXT T
240 PRINT "DONE"
250 END
```

Listing 3: A BASIC program used to program a 2708.

better to use an existing resident monitor program to load memory directly from the keyboard and produce a memory-resident table which is then transferred to the 2708.

The program write pulse timing takes advantage of the fact that BASIC is slower than assembly language. To load a memory with data, output port 18 bit B6 is set to a logic 1 level. This enables the program pulse generator, IC3, and data input source through the 74125s. After the address and data words are sent to the outputs, port 18 bit B7 is raised to a logic 1, causing the oneshot to fire. The duration of the pulse is 1 ms. If this were an assembly language program, a timing routine would have to be used to time out 1 ms before stepping into the next address and data combination. BASIC takes approximately 5 ms to interpret and execute each of the commands used in this program. With such interpretation delays, the program can't possibly overdrive the programming sequence, and therefore needs no timing loops. As stated earlier, to meet manufacturers' specifications, 100 1 ms sequences must be performed. *[If you reprogram the algorithm for another language, or use a BASIC interpreter, make sure the timing is comparable...CH]* Such a program is shown in listing 3.

How About a 2 Minute 2708 Write Cycle?

This program is not very fast, and in fact, takes 30 to 40 minutes to run for the full 100 loops. This is fine if you aren't in a hurry, but a better way is to write an intelligent programming routine. Yes, the manufacturer states that to be absolutely sure the 2708 is programmed, 100 loops should be executed. But, it has been my experience with the many 2708s I've programmed using this interface, that it takes only one loop. This is not to say that all devices will perform similarly, but it does lead to some interesting programming compromises. Eliminate the FOR and NEXT loop at lines 90 and 230 in listing 3. Next, at line 230, insert a program that will read the data. After each complete loop, read the 2708 byte by byte and compare it to the source table in memory. If it is equal, then stop. Programming is done. If any one or more bytes do not correspond, return and sequence through another complete program cycle. In my experience with premium 2708s, I have yet to require a second loop. This will allow fast temporary writing for program checkout. When the software is finalized, reprogram the 2708, when time allows, with the full 100 loops to ensure longevity of the stored data. While conceptually it may seem more feasible to rewrite only errant data bytes, in practice this is not advised.

Erasing an EROM

When 2708s are bought directly from a manufacturer they come completely erased (every byte is hexadecimal FF). If you plan to write a 2708 program once and you either don't want to modify it or you don't make mistakes, forget about erasing. The majority of experimenters will undoubtedly want to reprogram 2708s and similar erasable read only memories. It then becomes necessary to know how to erase them. We all know that the 2708 is ultraviolet erasable. However, duration, distance from the light source, and intensity determine the quality of the erasure.

People concerned about maintaining manufacturer's specifications during the programming sequence should also be advised of the proper erasing methods. Unlike the test-read-after-write loop method for programming, 2708s are usually removed from the circuit during erasing. It is therefore advisable to perform the procedure correctly or it will have to be repeated.

The typical 2708 can be erased by exposure to high intensity shortwave ultraviolet light with a wavelength of 2537 Å. The recommended integrated dose (ultraviolet intensity × exposure time) is 12.5 Watt-seconds per square centimeter (Ws/cm^2). The time required to produce this exposure is a function of the ultraviolet light intensity.

Choice of a particular ultraviolet eraser should be equally divided between cost and safety. A commercial unit not only specifies its intensity (which allows computation of exposure time), but also includes some very important interlocks. It is conceivable that some homebrew erasers might have improper shielding that can allow the ultraviolet light to escape or be accidently turned on while being viewed. Such possibilities can lead to permanent eye damage.

One of the most cost effective erasers on the market is the UVS-11E by Ultra Violet products in San Gabriel CA. This $59.50 unit is made especially with the home computer market in mind and includes some very important safety features. The lamp will not operate unless properly seated in its holding tray and, if lifted from the tray, will automatically shut off. At the standard exposure distance of 1 inch (2.54 cm), the UVS-11E produces an intensity of 5000 μW per square centimeter (μW/cm^2). Exposure time for the 2708 is easily calculated. Exposure time (T_E):

$T_E = J/I$

where:

J = required erasure density of device,
I = incident power density of eraser.

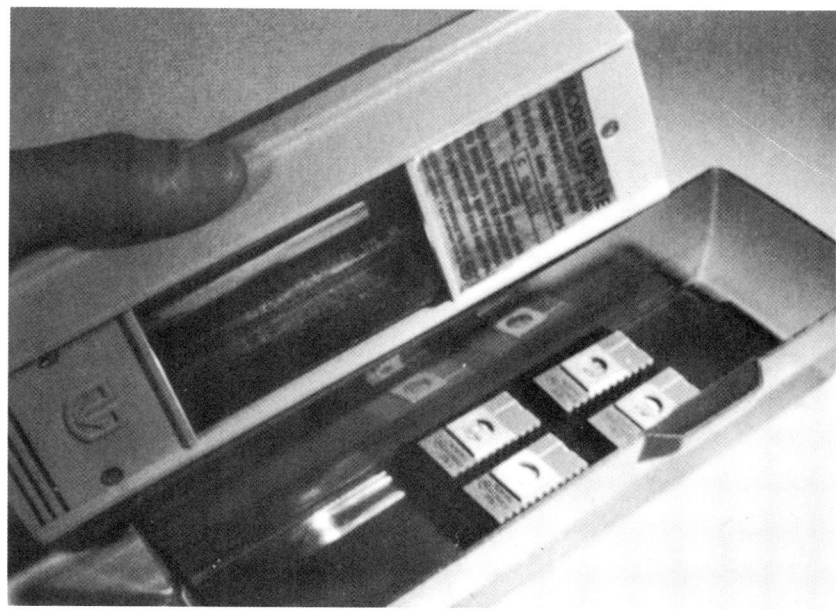

Photo 3: An Ultra Violet Products UVS-IIE ultraviolet eraser for 2708s and similar erasable read only memories. This unit can hold four circuits at a time on conductive foam inside the tray.

For a 2708 which requires 12.5 Ws/cm^2:

I = 5000 μW/cm^2,
J = 12.5 Ws/cm^2,

$$T_E = \frac{12.5}{5000 \times 10^{-6}} = 2500 \text{ seconds};$$

or:

T_E = 41.6 minutes for complete erasure.

"Well, Jerry, it wasn't all that bad, was it? We got your 2708 programmed with plenty of time to spare and now you know how easy it is to do it yourself." I sensed he felt relieved that he didn't have to cancel his grand computer expo for the computer club that evening.

"Thanks, Steve. I knew that anyone with as much computer junk in his cellar as you have had to have the solution to my problems. It's so much easier when you're working with someone experienced in these matters."

The temporary glow produced by his first statement quickly subsided. I got this strangely familiar tinge of pain as I started to recognize the now familiar line. Other coworkers had involved me in computer gambling and stock market schemes that turned into real fiascos. Rather than argue in my defense, I just shrugged off the desire to take the 2708 back from Jerry, throw it on the floor, and jump on it. How do I get myself into these things? Sanity prevailed and I just said softly, "We'll see."■

Photo 1: The author's prototype for the 4 channel self-refreshing digital to analog converter shown in figure 9. Also contained on the board is a prototype 4 channel analog to digital converter circuit.

Control the World!

(Or at Least a Few Analog Points)

"Ka-chunk! OK, get the reading quick! Ka-chunk! Pop! Pop! Bang!! The darn thing crapped out again! We'll never get one of these detectors to pass a life test."

The burly mechanic puffed his fat cigar and with a disgusted sigh continued, "The dime store engineers who design these kludges should be the ones who have to test them! That's if you could ever get them out of that puzzle factory upstairs!"

That was my cue. I was indeed an engineer descended from the puzzle factory and my mission was to discover why we were having so much trouble life test qualifying one of the pressure detectors we intended for future manufacture. Hearing the preceding commentary as I approached the testing lab, I decided that an authoritative professional type would not be very popular at the moment, so I went into my innocent nonmanagerial mode and entered the lab.

This lab was not unlike any other small production qualification and testing lab. It had the usual machinery and instrumentation and many artifacts of former test programs lying about. The most prominent artifact was the leader of the instrumentation group, Ned. Ned's large frame amply filled the white lab coat though it was barely discernable in the dense cloud of cigar smoke. The combined scent of hydraulic oil, burned resistors, and cigar smoke convinced me that today was not going to be my day.

"Hi, Ned. What's the problem with the new detector?", I asked.

"It's about time one of you guys came down and asked. This has got to be the most fragile pressure detector I have ever tested. So far, we have wiped out four engineering prototypes and haven't gotten to 20,000 pressure cycles, let alone the 50,000 life test," he bellowed.

My eyes rolled slightly as he mentioned the failed units. These pressure detectors were not in the least bit fragile; they were ruggedized units with a prospective sale price of $4700 each. The four engineering prototypes were handmade and far more costly. Before it became too apparent that I was coming to a slow burn, I asked the obvious question. "Ned, are you following the engineering test specification?"

"You guys are really something! I've been in this business for 30 years. I was testing..."

"OK, OK, Ned! Just tell me what your test procedure is. Pretend I'm a novice and tell me by the numbers." I was sure that he felt that was the way he had to work with any engineer, so I humored him and just listened.

"All right. The pressure detector is rated at 7500 PSIG and we are life testing it," he said with a cigar chomping smile. "The pressure is cycled between 0 pounds per square inch gauge (PSIG) and 10,000 PSIG every ten seconds and remains at 5,000 PSIG between cycles. [PSIG, or gauge pressure, is a differential pressure measurement using the ambient pressure as a reference. Usually, standard sea level pressure (14.7 pounds per square inch) is used as the reference...CM] At the conclusion of each cycle, the detector reading is compared to an out-of-tolerance spec. Oven temp and other control parameters are constantly monitored. Every 10,000 cycles, a calibration run is taken and compared to the accuracy specification quoted. We just haven't been able to get one of the bloody things to hang together long enough to finish the test. The pressure diaphragm keeps breaking."

So far, what he was relaying was exactly the procedure I had outlined. Nothing sounded wrong, so the next obvious question was a description of the test apparatus.

"I decided to automate the testing procedure," he gleamed like a kid describing a new toy. "I made a sequencing circuit with relays to cycle the pressure automatically. All the operator does is record the data and run the calibrations. Here, let me draw you a diagram."

It was unbelievable! True, Ned was following the spec, but what a way to do it! Pressure transducers are expected to withstand a certain amount of overpressuring, which was the reason for the test. But overpressure in combination with a 10,000 PSIG impulse was like a jackhammer. The engineering group upstairs would be amazed that the test made it though 20,000 cycles. I

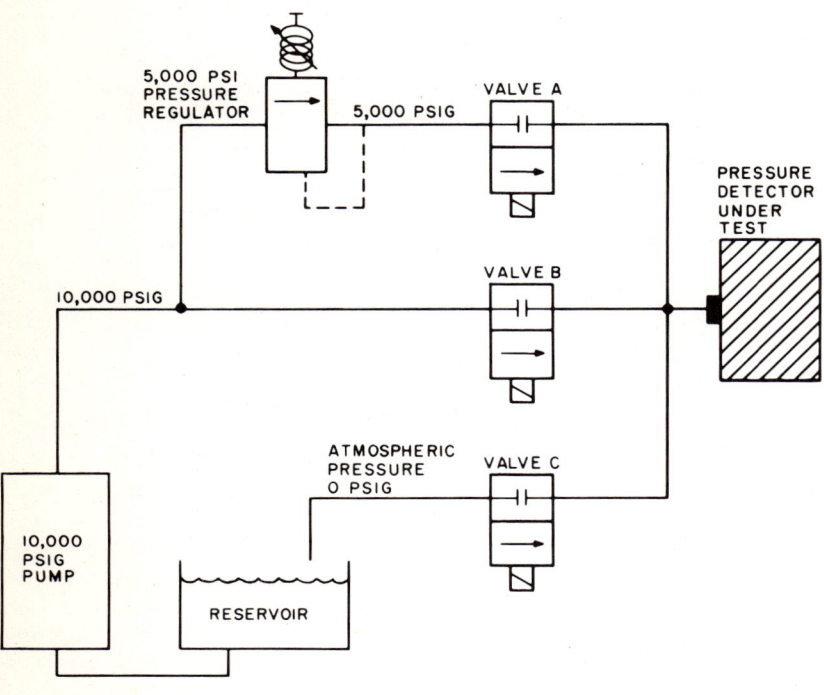

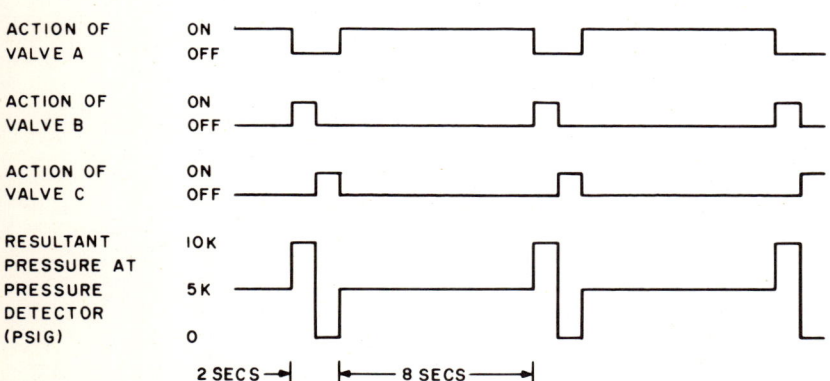

Figure 1: Configuration of a conventional impulse pressure calibration test setup. Note that the pressure detector under test receives what amounts to a square wave input. This type of violent pressure change can shorten the life of the detector and give a false indication of its long term life expectancy. PSIG, or "gauge pressure," is explained in the text.

wiped my brow, leaned against the concrete wall and asked with a pathetic whimper, "I suppose the failed detectors make good boat anchors."

"What?", he asked, not having heard what I had said.

"Ned, while I think your intention is fine, your method may be a little too rough on the unit. Why don't we change the square wave pressure being applied to the detector to a sinusoidal waveform." This was the method I had assumed he was going to use initially.

"I can't have a guy sitting there cranking a pressure controller knob ten hours a day. It's going to take two weeks to run this test as it is. That's why I automated it!" He seemed to get mad as I challenged his inventiveness.

"You don't have to compromise anything. Get a DC proportional control valve from the stock room and modulate the pressure sinusoidally. In fact, you can use the minicomputer which you ordinarily use for mathematical calculations over there in the corner to drive it directly, collect the data, and run the calibration automatically."

"You guys upstairs must be suffering from thin air. I know about computers; ones and zeros and all that stuff. We're talking about a DC voltage controlled valve. That isn't consistent with computer binary voltage levels. You would have exactly the same on and off situation as my relay controller," he stated.

It was going to be an uphill fight, but I knew I was going to have to introduce Ned to the world of analog to digital and digital to analog conversion. I first mapped out the life test circuit and diagrammed the waveforms.

Ned was no neophyte. He felt that he knew a lot about computers and in fact was quite familiar with the uses of BASIC and FORTRAN on the lab minicomputer. But Ned had never considered that this number crunching machine has the same logical abilities to control analog devices if properly interfaced.

General Considerations

While this may have been a lengthy introduction to computer analog interfacing, it often takes a real life situation to make one realize the added potential of the computer when it is combined with analog capabilities.

Since natural parameters such as displacement, temperature, volume and magnetic field strength are analog, and most practical methods of data acquisition, manipulation and visual presentation are digital, conversion between analog and digital qualities is a fundamental operation in computing and control systems. The basic building blocks are the digital to analog converter (DAC), and the analog to digital converter (ADC).

Because these converters are essentially interface devices, the basic conversion circuitry must be adapted to properly mate the application to the computer. Such variables include the possible necessity for buffers, registers, clock circuitry and reference voltages, all of which are external supports for the actual conversion device. The exact design requirements can be lengthy and are handled separately by necessity. Digital to analog conversion is the first topic to be discussed.

Digital to Analog Conversion

The digital to analog converter can be thought of as a digitally controlled programmable potentiometer which produces an analog output. This output value (V_o) is the product of a digital signal (D) and an analog reference (V_{ref}) and is related by the following equation:

$$V_o = (D)(V_{ref})$$

To a large extent, no digital to analog or analog to digital converter can be of much

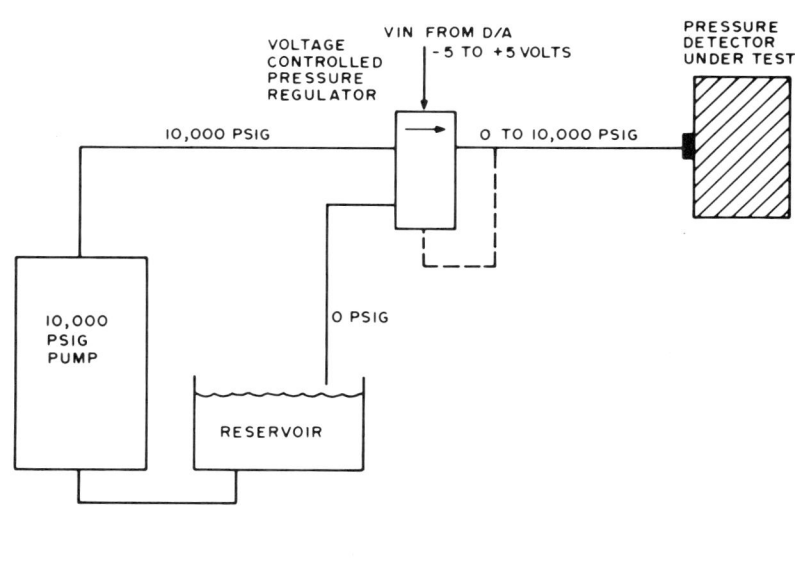

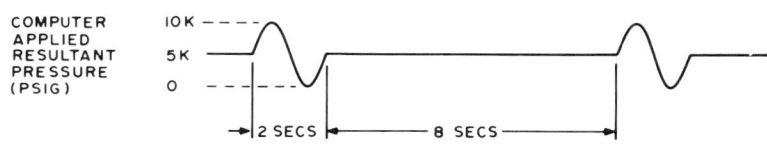

Figure 2: The same pressure detector as in figure 1 being tested here with a computer controlled system which applies the test pressure sinusoidally. This approach gives a much better indication of the unit's true life expectancy, and incidentally shows one practical application of digital to analog conversion.

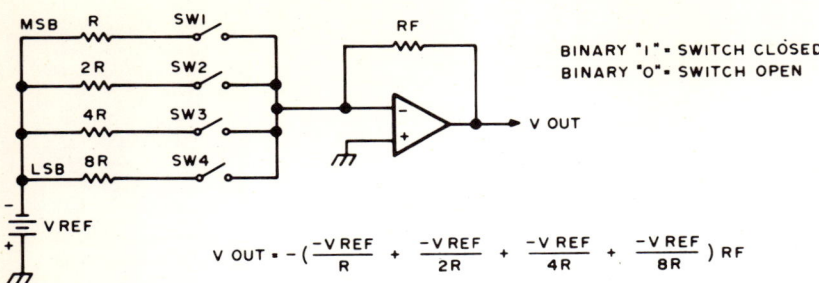

Figure 3: A 4 bit weighted resistor digital to analog converter. A 4 bit word is used to control four single-pole single-throw switches. Each of these switches is in series with a resistor. The resistor values are related as powers of 2, as shown. The other sides of the switches are connected together at the summing point of an operational amplifier. Currents with magnitudes inversely proportional to the resistors are generated when the switches are closed. They are summed by the op amp and converted to a corresponding voltage.

practical use to anyone without specifying the type of code utilized to represent digital magnitude.

Converters work with either unipolar or bipolar digital codes. Unipolar includes straight binary and binary coded decimal (BCD). Even floating point converters have been used on occasion: witness the auto ranging digital voltmeter. Offset binary, one's and two's complement and Gray code are usually reserved for bipolar operation. Since the obvious sphere of this article is home computer applications, straight and offset binary will be the only digital methods addressed.

It is important to remember that the binary quantity presented by the computer is a representation of a fractional value to be multiplied by a reference voltage. In binary fractions, the most significant bit has a value of $1/2$ or 2^{-1}, the next most significant bit is $1/4$ or 2^{-2}, and the least significant bit is $1/2^N$ or 2^{-N}. It can be seen that adding up all the bits approaches a value of 1. (The more bits, the closer the value is to 1). The discrepancy between the binary value approaching 1 and the actual value 1 is the quantization error of the digital system. I'll discuss this later.

Offset binary is nothing more than straight binary except that the binary number zero is set to represent the maximum negative analog quantity. In the easiest terms, the most significant bit is a zero for negative analog values, and a one for positive analog values.

The conversion of digital values to proportional analog values is done by either of two basic conversion techniques: the weighted resistor digital to analog converter and the R–2R digital to analog converter. The weighted resistor digital to analog converter is by far the simplest and most straightforward. This parallel decoder requires only one resistor per bit. In the weighted resistor digital to analog converter, switches are driven directly from the signals that represent the digital number D. Currents with magnitudes of $1/2$, $1/4$, $1/8$, ... $1/2^N$ are generated by connecting resistors with magnitudes of $R, 2R, 4R, ... 2^NR$ between a reference voltage, $-V_{ref}$, and the summing point of an operational amplifier by means of a set of switches. The various currents are summed and converted to a voltage by the operational amplifier (see figure 3).

While this may appear to be a simple answer to an otherwise complex problem, this method has some potentially hazardous ramifications. The accuracy of this converter is a function of the combined accuracies of the resistors, switches (since all switches have some resistance) and the op amp. In conversion systems of greater than ten bits resolution, the magnitudes of the resistors become exceptionally large and the resultant current flow is reduced to such a low value as to be lost in circuit noise.

A reasonable alternative to the weighted resistor digital to analog converter is the R–2R converter. This is often referred to as a resistor ladder digital to analog converter. The R–2R digital to analog converter is the most widely used type of digital to analog converter, even though it uses more components. This circuit is illustrated in figure 4 and also contains a reference voltage, a set of binary switches and an op amp, but the basis of this converter is a ladder network constructed with two resistor values, R and 2R.

One resistor (2R) is in series with the bit switch, while the other (R) is in the summing line, so that the combination forms

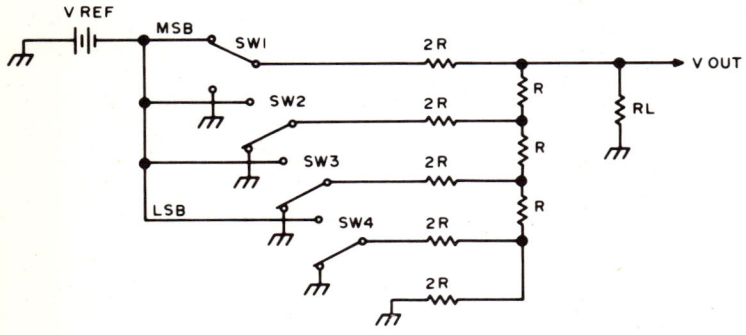

Figure 4: A 4 bit "R – 2R" ladder network digital to analog converter. This type of digital to analog converter makes use of a resistor ladder network constructed with resistors of values R and 2R. The topology of this network is such that current flowing into any branch of a 3 branch node will divide itself equally through the two remaining branches. Because of this, the current will divide itself in half as it passes through each node on its way to the end of the ladder. The four switches are again related as powers of 2. The position of each switch with respect to its distance from the end of the ladder determines its binary significance.

what electrical engineers call a "pi" network. This suggests that the impedances of the three branches of any node are equal, and that a current, I, flowing into a node through one branch flows out as I/2 through the other two branches. In other words, a current produced by closing a bit switch is cut by half as it passes through each node on the way to the end of the ladder. Simply speaking, the position of a switch, with respect to the point where the current is measured, determines the binary significance of the particular switch closure.

This type of converter is easy to manufacture because only two resistor types are needed and can be reduced to one value, R, if three components are used for each bit. Keeping matched resistor values with the same temperature coefficients contributes to a very stable design. Certain tradeoffs are required between ladder resistance values and current flow to balance accuracy and noise.

One form of the R–2R ladder digital to analog converter is the multiplying digital to analog converter. Digital to analog converters are available with either a fixed reference or with an external variable reference. Multiplying digital to analog converters, which utilize external variable analog references, produce outputs which are directly proportional to the product of the digital input multiplied by this variable reference. Functionally, these converters are available as current or voltage output types. The current output devices are necessarily faster because they do not include output amplifiers which limit the bandwidth. Because this output amplifier is not included, current digital to analog converters tend to be a little less expensive than voltage types.

Probably one of the most useful and cost effective multiplying digital to analog converters available on the hobby market today is the Motorola MC1408L-8 8 bit digital to analog converter (see figures 5 and 6).

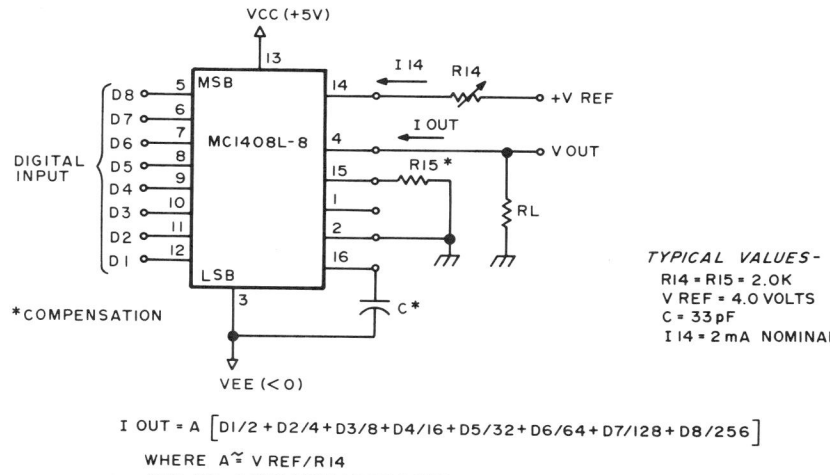

Figure 5: A typical current output monolithic multiplying digital to analog converter. This Motorola integrated circuit contains an R–2R network like the one in figure 4 plus additional current switching logic. The relative accuracy of this 8 bit unit is ±1 least siginificant bit, or 0.19% of full scale.

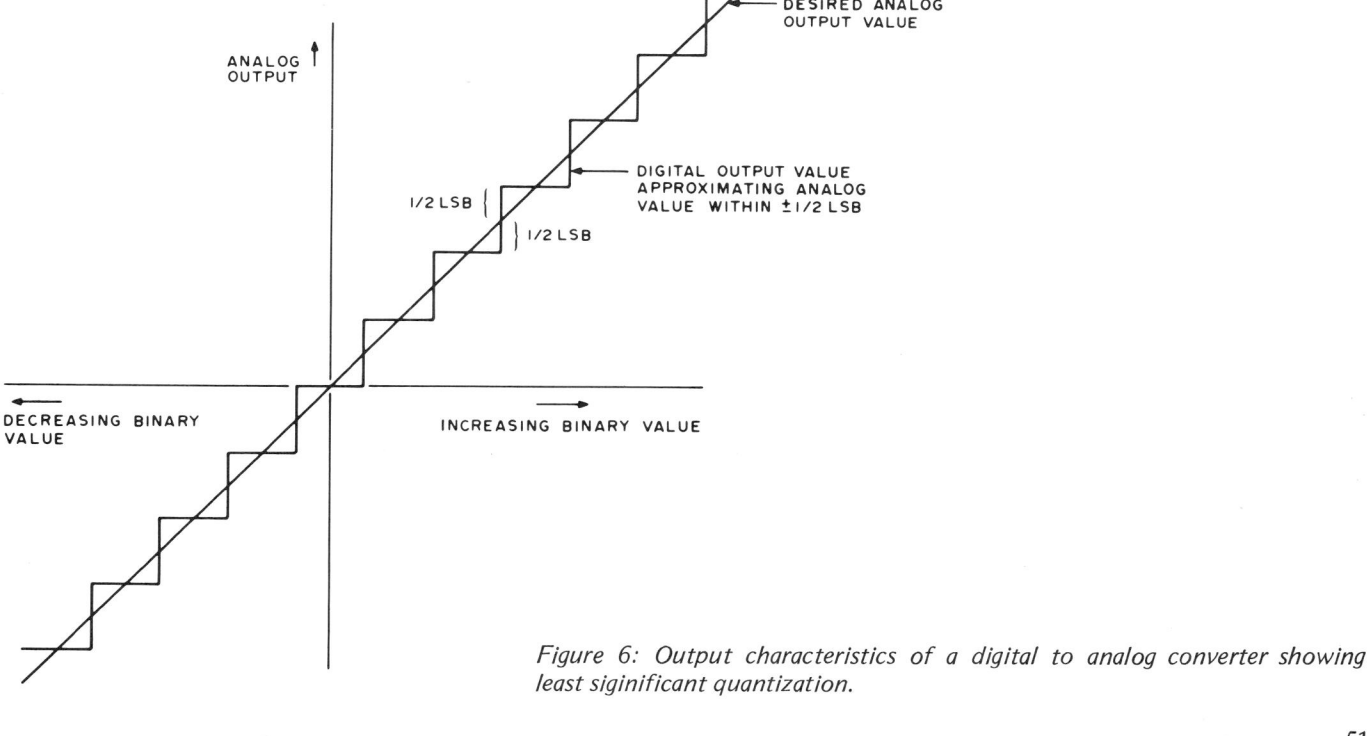

Figure 6: Output characteristics of a digital to analog converter showing least siginificant quantization.

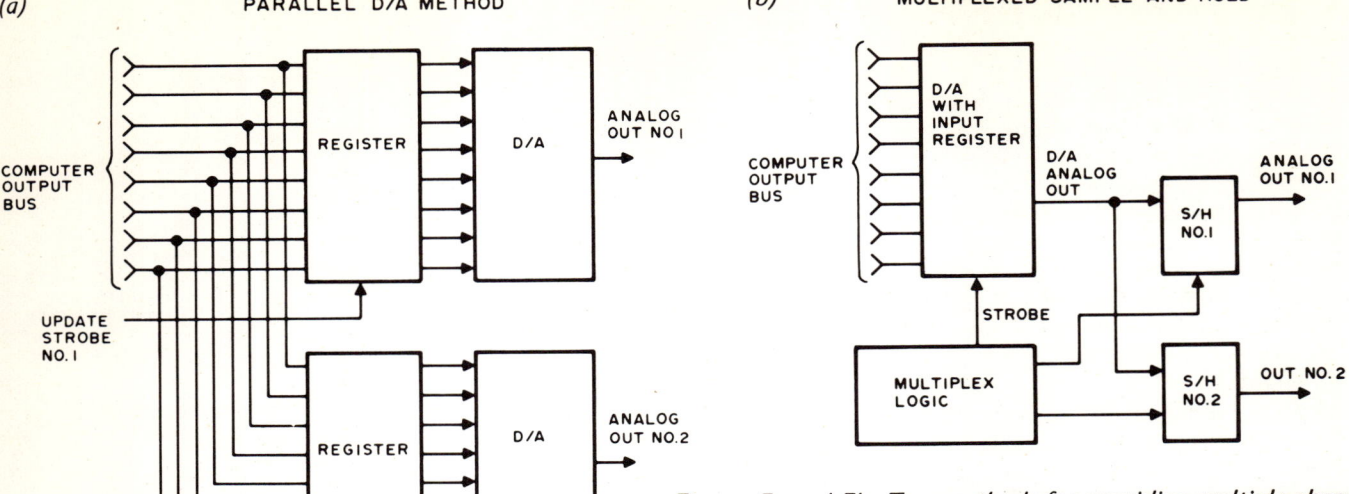

Figures 7a and 7b: Two methods for providing multiple channel output capability. Figure 7a shows a parallel digital to analog converter method in which the computer routes information to two different digital to analog converters. In figure 7b, two sample and hold circuits are fed by the same digital to analog converter. Multiplex logic switches the output of the converter between the two sample and hold circuits. The latter do just what their name implies: when strobed, they store the value of the incoming voltage and stay very close to that value until strobed again, at which time they change to the new value. The sample and hold technique of figure 7b is economically more attractive than the multiple digital to analog converter approach.

As previously mentioned, this monolithic converter contains an R–2R ladder network and current switching logic. Each binary bit controls a switch which regulates the current flowing through the ladder. If an 8 bit digital input of 11000000 (192_{10}) is applied to the control lines of the illustrated converter, the output current would be equal to (192/256) (2 mA) or 1.50 mA. Note that when binary 11 111 111 (or 255 decimal) is applied, there is always a remainder current which is equal to the least significant bit. This current is shunted to ground, and the maximum output current is 255/256 of the reference amplifier current, or 1.992 mA for a 2.0 mA reference current. The relative accuracy for the MC1408-L8 version is ±1/2 least significant bit, or 0.19% of full scale, and is more than adequate for most home computer analog control applications.

A Design with the User in Mind

I could actually stop right now and be satisfied that the reader has at least some idea of what a digital to analog converter is, but no mention has been made as to its uses. BYTE magazine has published articles on digital to analog converters, but few actually using them in detail designs.

When we last left Ned in the testing lab, he was hooking up a voltage controlled pressure regulator and attaching it to the computer through a digital to analog interface. Though only the voltage requirement of the value was mentioned, the pressure detector is situated in an environmental control chamber with the temperature maintained by a setpoint controller.

At various times during the testing phase, the temperature is elevated. To adequately automate this test procedure, therefore, two analog output values are required: one for temperature setpoint and the other for pressure setpoint. It takes one digital to analog converter for the first voltage and we could add another separate digital to analog converter for the second voltage, but this is overly expensive and not necessary. The preferred method is to use multiplexed digital to analog conversion. This technique uses a single converter and switches it back and forth between the two channels doing the respective digital to analog conversion 50% of the time on each channel. To insure that each channel does not go on and off as the converter switches back and forth between them, a circuit called a sample and hold is employed on each channel to maintain the output at a constant level until the next refresh by the digital to analog converter. Figures 7a and 7b illustrate the separator versus multiplexed digital to analog approach, and figure 8 illustrates a basic sample and hold circuit.

A sample and hold circuit is simply a charged capacitor analog storage device. Amplifier A1 is an impedance isolating buffer connected to the digital to analog converter or other voltage supply and connected to the capacitor through a switch. This switch is normally open in the "hold" state. When the output is to be updated, the switch is closed, the circuit enters the "sample" or acquisition mode, causing the capacitor to charge exponentially toward the new value present at the output of A1. When the switch is reopened and again in the "hold" state, the output of A2 will be equal to the capacitor voltage level.

The secret of good sample and hold is to use good high input impedance buffers to minimize the leakage from the capacitor and hold the output for long periods of time. No sample and hold can be designed without some droop during the holding period. The best that the designer can do to minimize this feature is to use precision components (usually more expensive) and refresh the sample and hold frequently enough to overcome decay problems.

Is There a Way to Overcome the Necessity to Refresh Sample and Hold Outputs?

For the home computer experimenter, sample and hold outputs, which require periodic refreshing, can become a bother. This is especially true during step-by-step checkout of system software.

Refreshing a multiplexed digital to analog interface usually requires a separate digital to analog refresh subroutine which must be called at regular intervals while executing the program. Simple, inexpensive sample and holds may require updating tens of times per second, while the better designed circuits available to the hobbyist can do satisfactorily with a once per second update. The fact remains, though, that the refresh is a requirement. This can limit digital to analog interface applications.

Drive the Digital to Analog Converter with BASIC?

Many extended BASIC programs such as the Digital Group MaxiBASIC can directly interface with computer input and output ports. This means that analog devices can be driven with a digital to analog converter, analog data processed through an analog to digital converter, and the acquired data mathematically manipulated using BASIC. The implication is a pseudoreal time analog control scheme utilizing BASIC. This is a realistic capability in slow process control applications where control feedback does

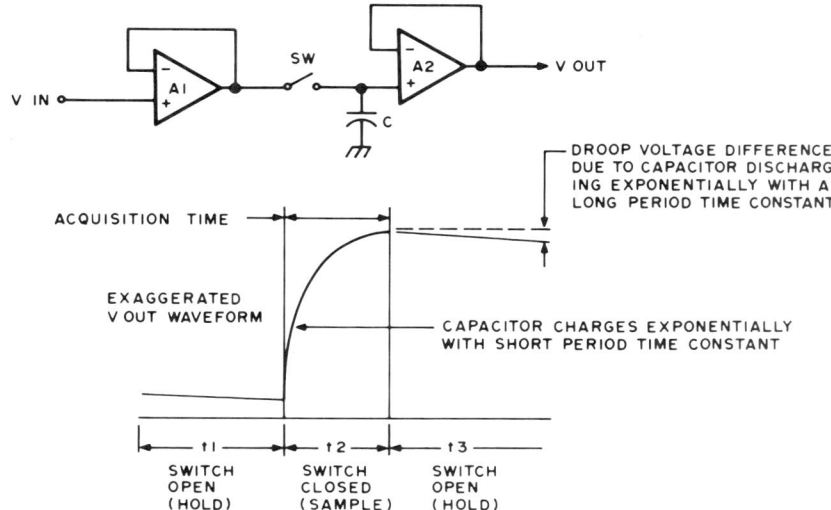

Figure 8: A basic sample and hold circuit. When the switch is closed, the capacitor begins to charge up exponentially to the value of the input voltage. Theoretically, the capacitor will maintain this value indefinitely after the switch is opened, but in reality a certain amount of voltage "droop" (exponential decay) will occur over time as the capacitor slowly discharges.

not have to be activated within microseconds of an initiating event. Solar heating, low duty cycle repetitive machine functions, building environmental control systems, and supervisory control of setpoint controllers are examples of slow processes where slow computer response is of no major consequence.

The Final Configuration

Utilization of BASIC as a real time operating system does imply some constraints. If analog control is involved, the time between updates to an analog output interface can be on the order of tens of seconds, especially if the computer is required to do extensive calculations and record outputs to a printer. Of course, a special interrupt driver could be added to the BASIC and the processor interrupted frequently to service the external devices; but why make life difficult? The idea of using BASIC in the first place was to provide a control capability without adding special machine language drivers, a capability which would enable anyone to try his or her hand at closed loop control programming. This approach, though, tends to eliminate the classical sample and hold multichannel digital to analog method from consideration. It would also seem that the only approach left is the separate storage register and digital to analog converter combination previously illustrated. A more intelligent alternative is a combination of the two methods.

The necessary interface is essentially a

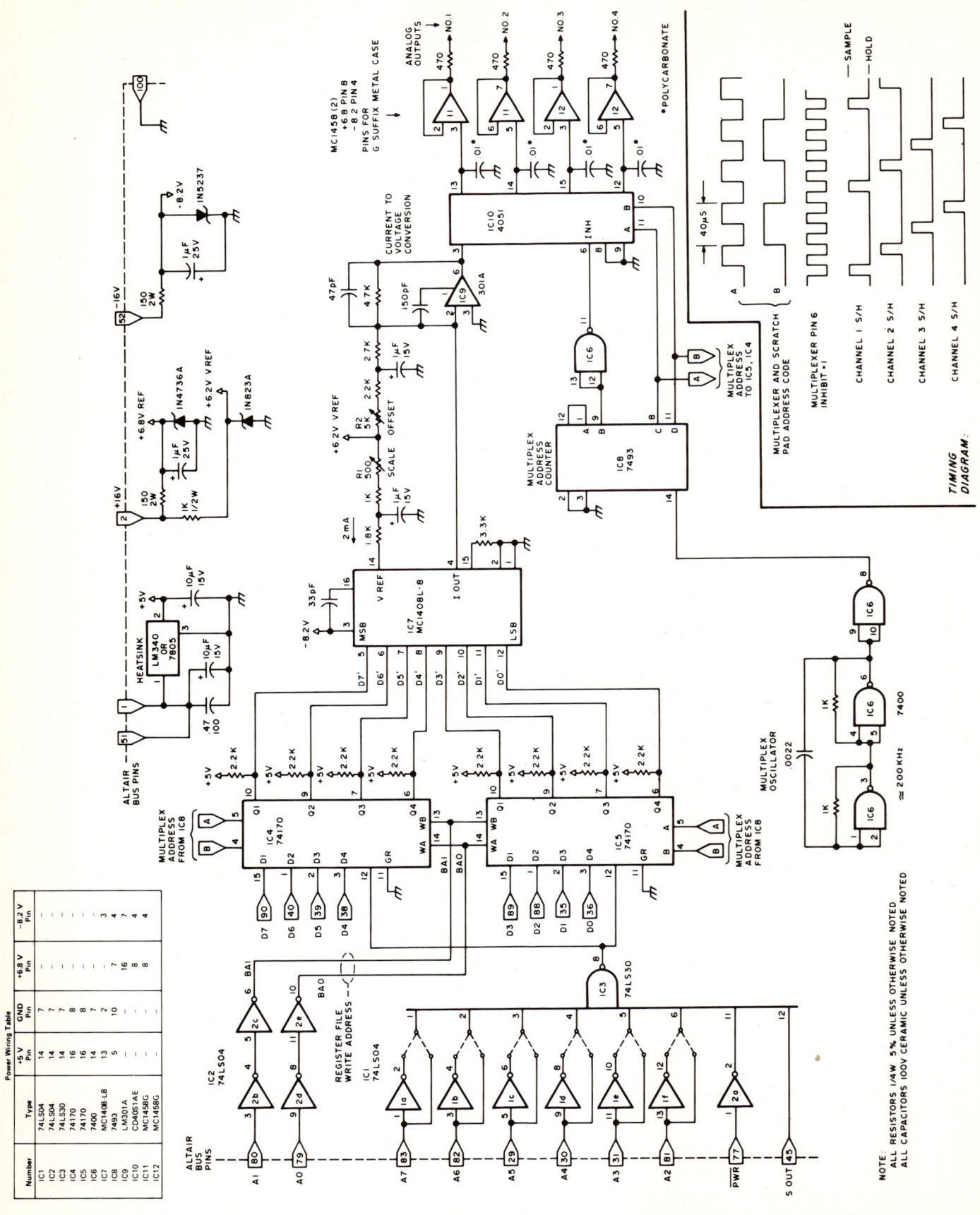

Figure 9: A "smart" 4 channel self-refreshing digital to analog converter. The circuit is self-refreshing and asynchronous in the sense that it maintains its analog outputs independent of computer timing. IC1, IC2 and IC3 form an address decoding network which decodes the 8080 or Z-80 processor's output port address and strobes the computer data bus contents into IC4 and IC5, which form an 8 bit random access scratch pad. IC7 performs the actual analog to digital conversion. The remaining portion of the circuit consists of timing generation and an analog multiplexer with sample and hold circuitry.

smart multiplexed digital to analog converter which maintains its analog setpoints independent of the computer timing. The design of this interface is illustrated in figure 9. It is a hybrid system composed of separate digital storage sample and hold circuits for each of four output channels. Internal timing generators sequentially read the storage registers, initiate the digital to analog conversion, and refresh the sample and holds. Photo 1 shows how this card looks when built using a Vector board with 44 pin edge connector.

The key feature of this unit is the input storage buffer. Two 74170 4 by 4 bit registers are configured to form a 4 word by 8 bit random access scratch pad. An address decoding network composed of IC1, IC2, and IC3 decodes the processor's output port address and strobes the computer data bus contents into the appropriate scratch pad location. These four jumper selectable port addresses can be set to be any four consecutively numbered output ports. The exact selection and jumpering details are outlined in the check out procedure. This particular scratch pad can be written into and read from simultaneously. The interface is completely asynchronous and does not have to be synchronized with the computer in any way.

There are four basic sections to the interface: the scratch pad and port decoding, digital to analog converter, timing generator and analog multiplexer, and sample and holds. A basic timing diagram of the interface is illustrated as part of figure 9.

The timing section consists of a 200 kHz clock generator IC6 and address counter IC8. The 7493 counts down the 200 kHz clock and drives the address lines of the scratch pad and multiplexer at a 50 kHz conversion rate. Each channel is accessed, converted and sampled in a similar manner. When the address lines have settled on a particular channel, the output lines of the scratch pad (IC4 and IC5) present the respective stored digital word to the digital to analog converter IC7. The converter immediately starts moving towards the new value.

Since its settling time is dependent upon the magnitude of change from one channel to the next, the worst case being minus full scale to plus full scale, the 20 µs conversion period incorporates a 10 µs settling time.

For the first 10 µs, the analog multiplexer IC10 is inhibited from conducting the signal to the sample and hold. After this settling time has concluded, the inhibit signal is dropped, and for the next 10 µs the sample and hold for that particular channel is in the sample mode. The circuit automatically sequences itself to the next scratch pad address and repeats the process over and over.

Anyone capable of a little quick math can realize that if the digital to analog conversion is proceeding at 50,000 conversions a second, each sample and hold is being updated at the fantastic rate of 12,500 times a second. This seems to be in direct disagreement with a "tens of times a second" statement made earlier. It is important to remember that this is an asynchronous analog interface. When new data is written into the scratch pad, the new value is not available at the sample and hold output until the next regular sampling period, controlled by the timing generator. The high sampling rate is more to increase the response of the interface than refresh the outputs.

At a 50 kHz conversion frequency, there is a worst case delay of 80 µs between a scratch pad update and an appropriate analog output response. This is of no consequence as far as this article is concerned. However, to maintain the ability to use BASIC as a real time operating system and yet not lose the capability to do high speed applications such as voice synthesis, a few simple modifications can be made. The interface clock rate can be increased from 200 kHz to 400 kHz. This has been successfully accomplished on the prototype and will increase the sampling rate on each channel to 25,000 samples per second. Unfortunately, it is far more demanding of the current to voltage converter IC9. Only one out of three LM301As may work successfully over the full range of 10 V. Another quick method is to remove the 7493 (IC8). This causes the interface to stay addressed on channel 4, doing 50,000 uninhibited conversions per second.

The converter itself is an 8 bit MC1408L-8 multiplying digital to analog converter. As previously outlined, "multiplying" means that it uses an external variable reference voltage. In this case, a 6.8 V zener diode regulated voltage is passed through a resistor that sets the current flow-

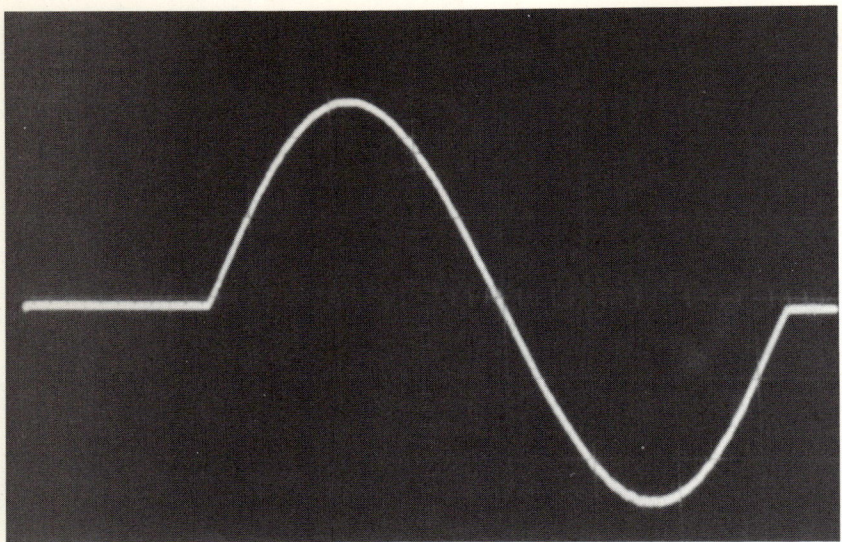

Photo 2: *An oscilloscope display of a sinusoidal waveform synthesized by using the BASIC program in listing 1 in conjunction with the digital to analog converter shown in figure 9.*

ing into pin 14 to approximately 2 mA.

An additional resistor, R_1 (also in this current leg), allows the current to be varied by a small percentage and provides the ability to adjust the full scale range of the digital to analog converter. The output of the converter is a current which is equivalent to the product of this reference current and the binary data on the control lines. The current is converted to a voltage through IC9 and can be zero offset through the use of the offset adjustment pot, R2.

The digital code stored in the scratch pad and presented to the digital to analog converter is in offset binary. A binary value of 00 000 000 produces an output of −5 V from the converter while 11 111 111 is equivalent to +5 V. In offset binary, if the most significant bit is a zero, the output is negative and if the most significant bit is a one, the output is positive. Since the converter has a range of 10 V, and is an 8 bit device, the resolution of the converter is 1/256 of 10 V, or approximately 40 mV. This means that the smallest output increments will be in 40 mV steps. To change this to finer increments requires that the range be shorter, such as +2.56 V to −2.56 V. By adjusting the span and zero pots, any reasonable range may be chosen, but the resolution will always be equal to the least significant bit or 1/256 of the range, and accuracy is estimated to be ±1/2 least significant bit.

Now How Do I Use It?

Once you have conquered the hardware and constructed an interface (see notes in the box) you should be ready to exercise it under program control. There are some interesting applications using the digital to analog interface alone, none the least of which is Ned's problem.

You will remember that my solution to the impulse response problem in Ned's test setup was to vary the pressure sinusoidally using a computer generated voltage to control a pressure regulator. Adding a computer sounds a bit unnecessary, but remember that an analog to digital interface will be attached for data acquisition.

With this particular digital to analog interface, programming an analog control voltage utilizing an extended BASIC such as the Digital Group's MaxiBASIC, is quite easy. To operate a real time sine wave that varies the pressure between 0 and 10,000 PSIG requires a control regulator with a control voltage range of −5 V to +5 V and the following very simple BASIC program:

```
90 REM THIS PROGRAM CALCULATES
   AND OUTPUTS A SINE WAVE.
100 LET A = 3.14/180*360/256
110 FOR B = 0 to 255
120 LET W = INT(127.5+127.5*SIN(A*B))
130 OUT 252,W
140 NEXT B
150 END
```

This program calculates 256 values of a sine wave with an amplitude of −5 to +5 V. When run in real time, the period of the waveform is about two seconds. The period is basically set by the time it takes to compute the expression on line 120 some 256 times. An alternative method is to calculate the points once, load the values in memory and call a subroutine which scans the table when directed to do so by the program.

The first time that the points are computed, it will take two seconds as before. Then they are available in a look up table. A program which constructs such a memory resident table is illustrated in listing 1. Photo 2 shows an oscilloscope trace of the synthesized sine wave created by the digital to analog converter in figure 9 using the table created by listing 1.

A simple program which scans the table and drives the digital to analog converter is assembled into the memory of my particular system at split octal address 012/000 (hexadecimal 0A00) as shown in listing 2. This program can be called at any time with the BASIC command CALL (2560,0), and when driven at faster than 100 ms periods can be easily displayed on an oscilloscope. *[Note that 2560 is decimal for split octal address value 012/000 or hexadecimal 0A00.]* The program in listing 3 incorporates the routine in listing 2 as a called subroutine and can be used to display any waveform defined by the table located at address 100/000 in split octal notation (hexadecimal 4000).

On to Bigger and Better Applications

An obvious application of this programming technique is to mathematically compute and generate complex waveforms which would otherwise require extensive dedicated hardware to duplicate. Music application is an area which is being heavily infiltrated with computer technology. A composer interested in electronic music effects can design discrete waveforms, display and review them before committing them to a performance design.

An alternative approach is to use BASIC to generate all the tables defining envelope or waveform aspects of desired instruments and then let BASIC sit idle while a machine language program selects and calls the tables to produce a musical score.

It's often easier to illustrate one example rather than discuss volumes of theory. One of the least complicated musical envelope waveforms is the ADSR envelope. ADSR stands for Attack, Decay, Sustain and Release. Various combinations of these four variables produce unique sounds similar to such instruments as the piano or trumpet. In an electronic music application the composer would combine the necessary fundamentals and harmonics characteristic of a particular instrument and control the output amplitude with an ADSR waveform feeding a voltage controlled amplifier, or VCA. Both the envelope and harmonic content are separate elements of musical composition. Here they are synthesized separately to illustrate the technique, but mathematically they could be combined into one table. This would impose a far greater limitation on usage than would separate waveforms, but it is not the purpose of this article to investigate electronic music.

The simplest ADSR waveform is composed of four separate linear time dependent functions. Time $T = 0$ to T_1 is the attack, T_1 to T_2 is the decay, T_2 to T_3 is the sustain, and T_3 to T_4 is the release. Each section is defined by a separate equation and is illustrated by the graph in figure 10. Any waveform which is to be synthesized can be graphed in a similar way.

The four lines in the graph are defined by four equations. These equations, and the beginning and end point limits, can be combined into a BASIC program which creates a table of points. The table is stored in page 100 octal and the display routine is the same as was illustrated in listing 3 (see listing 4 and photo 3).

```
80  REM THIS PROGRAM CALCULATES THE VALUES FOR A SINE WAVE AND
82  REM PUTS THEM IN PAGE 100 (OCTAL) OF MEMORY
90  PRINT "SINE WAVE POINT CALCULATOR"
100 LET A=3.14/180*360/256
110 FOR B=0 TO 255
120 LET W=INT(127.5+(127.5*SIN(A*B))
130 FILL 16384+B,W
160 NEXT B
```

Listing 1: An extended BASIC program to compute and load a table in memory with 256 sample points of a sinusoidal waveform. Digital Group MaxiBASIC interpreter.

Split Octal Address	Octal Code	Operation	Commentary
012/000	041 000 100	LXI H&L	Set the program counter to page 100;
012/003	176	MOV A	Move addressed memory to accumulator;
012/004	323 375	OUT	Output accumulator to port 375;
012/006	054	INR L	Increment L register;
012/007	302 003 012	JMP COND.	Jump to 012/003 if L ≠ 0;
012/012	311	RET	Return to BASIC program;

Listing 2: A machine language program which is used to drive the digital to analog converter in figure 9. This program is called by the extended BASIC program in listing 3.

```
300  PRINT "THIS PROGRAM WHICH DRIVES AN 8 BIT D/A PRODUCES "
310  PRINT "ANY WAVEFORM FROM A BINARY TABLE"
400  REM THIS PROGRAM CALLS A SUBROUTINE AT 012/000 (OCTAL)
410  REM WHICH OUTPUTS THE 256     WAVEFORM VALUES TO
420  REM D/A ON OUTPUT PORT 375(OCTAL)
430  REM OCTAL AT 012/000
440  REM 041 000 100 176 323 375 054 302 003 012 311
450  REM MAX SPEED FOR ADSR IS 4 MSEC.
470  REM BINARY TABLE IS ON PAGE 100 (OCTAL)
502  PRINT "GENERATE THE WAVEFORM HOW MANY TIMES ?":INPUT E
505  FOR X=1 TO E
510  LET A=CALL(2560,0)
515  NEXT X
1000 END
```

Listing 3: An extended BASIC program which calculates 256 points of a given waveform which is to be synthesized and then calls the machine language routine in listing 2 to actually drive the digital to analog converter in figure 9. The call to the subroutine in listing 2 occurs at line 510 of this program. Digital Group MaxiBASIC interpreter.

Real satisfaction comes from mathematically recreating complex waveforms. Synthesis is the combining of parts to form a whole. In Fourier analysis it is the recombination of the terms of the trigonometric series, usually the first four or five, to produce the original wave.

Often it is only after synthesizing a wave that the student is convinced that the Fourier series does in fact express the periodic wave for which it was obtained. This technique of mathematically solving the line equations, loading a point table, and either outputting directly to a plotter or calling a subroutine for an oscilloscope display can prove to be an invaluable education tool to a student involved in advanced math or music courses. Using the digital to analog interface as a Fourier waveform syn-

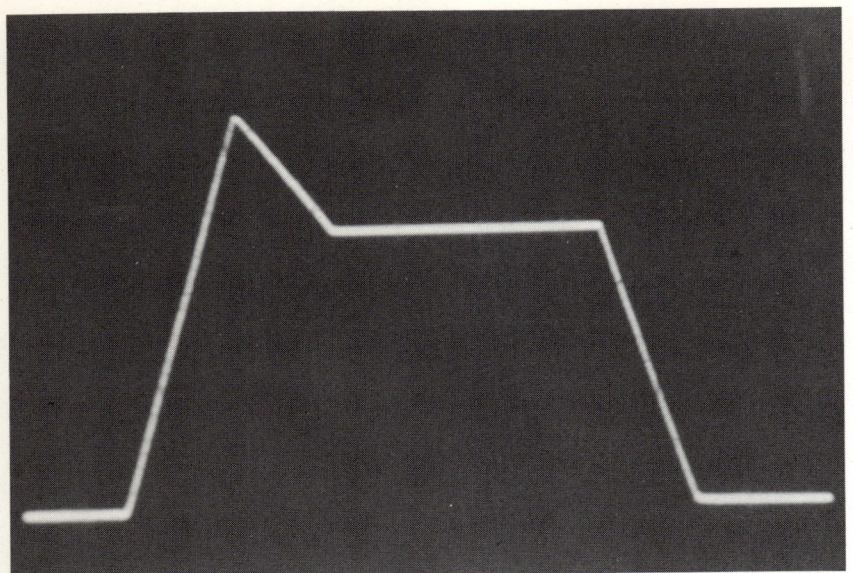

Photo 3: *An oscilloscope display of a musical envelope waveform called an ADSR waveform. "ADSR" stands for Attack, Decay, Sustain and Release, a popular way of characterizing an amplitude envelope which is typical for many musical instrument waveforms. This waveform was synthesized by means of the program in listing 4 which was used to drive the digital to analog converter in figure 9. Also see figure 10.*

thesizer involves the same point plotting methods as previously outlined, with the exception that the equations become more involved.

Consider the trigonometric series for the complex waveform with a peak amplitude of B=127.5 as illustrated in figure 11.

The Fourier series approximating a triangular waveform can be plugged into an extended BASIC program which calculates the points, while the program in listing 3 can be used to display the tabulation. Photo 4 shows the resulting oscilloscope display.

Conclusions

What started out to be just a simple interface for an analog output can be incorporated into control, music and educational applications. The extent and direction of an experimenter's system expansion is of necessity governed by price performance. This is an inexpensive interface which connects an otherwise isolated digital computer to the analog world. When coupled with a high level language such as extended BASIC, its potential is limited only by the program-

```
80   PRINT "ADSR MEMORY LOADER"
90   REM THIS PROGRAM COMPUTES DECIMAL VALUES FOR A PIECE-WISE
91   REM LINEAR ADSR WAVEFORM AND ILLUSTRATES THE METHOD
92   REM THE VALUES ARE THEN LOADED INTO PAGE 100(OCTAL) OF MEMORY
93   REM THEY ARE THEN AVAILABLE FOR MACHINE SUBROUTINES
100  FOR X=0 TO 60
105  REM THIS IS THE "A" SECTION
110  LET Y=INT((255/60)*X)
120  FILL 16384+X,Y
125  NEXT X
130  LET W=61
135  FOR Z=0 TO 39
137  REM THIS IS THE "D" SECTION
140  LET Y=INT((-75/40)*Z+255)
150  FILL 16384+W,Y
152  LET W=W+1
155  NEXT Z
160  FOR X=101 TO 220
170  LET Y=180
172  REM THIS IS THE "S" SECTION
175  FILL 16384+X,Y
180  NEXT X
185  LET N=221
190  FOR X=0 TO 34
192  REM THIS IS THE "R" SECTION
200  LET Y=INT((-180/35)*X+180)
210  FILL 16384+N,Y
212  LET N=N+1
220  NEXT X
1000 END
```

Listing 4: *An extended BASIC program which generates a table of sample points of the ADSR waveform whose graph appears in figure 10. Digital Group MaxiBASIC interpreter.*

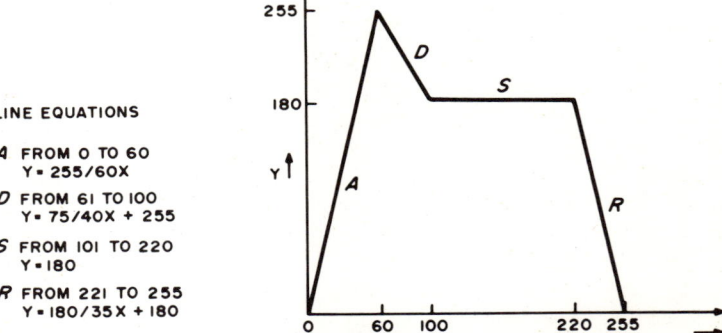

LINE EQUATIONS

A FROM 0 TO 60
  Y = 255/60X

D FROM 61 TO 100
  Y = 75/40X + 255

S FROM 101 TO 220
  Y = 180

R FROM 221 TO 255
  Y = 180/35X + 180

Figure 10: *A simple ASDR (Attack, Sustain, Decay and Release) envelope waveform along with the line equations necessary for digital to analog waveform synthesis (see photo 3 and listing 4).*

mer. To think that the home computer is an expensive toy useful only to bide time between monopoly games is equivalent to thinking that a building is only used to hold the sidewalk down.■

REFERENCES

1. *Digital to Analog Converter Handbook*, Hybrid Systems Corporation, Crosby Dr, Bedford MA.

2. Graeme, Jerald G, *Applications of Operational Amplifiers — Third Generation Techniques*, McGraw Hill Book Company, NY, 1973.

3. Sheingold, Daniel H (ed), *Analog-Digital Conversion Handbook*, Analog Devices Inc, Norwood MA.

4. Stout, David F, and Kaufman, Milton, *Handbook of Operational Amplifier Circuit Design*, McGraw Hill Book Company, NY, 1976.

5. Tobey, et al, *Operational Amplifiers — Designs and Applications*, McGraw Hill Book Company, NY, 1971.

6. Wylie Jr, C R, *Advanced Engineering Mathematics*, McGraw Hill Book Company, NY.

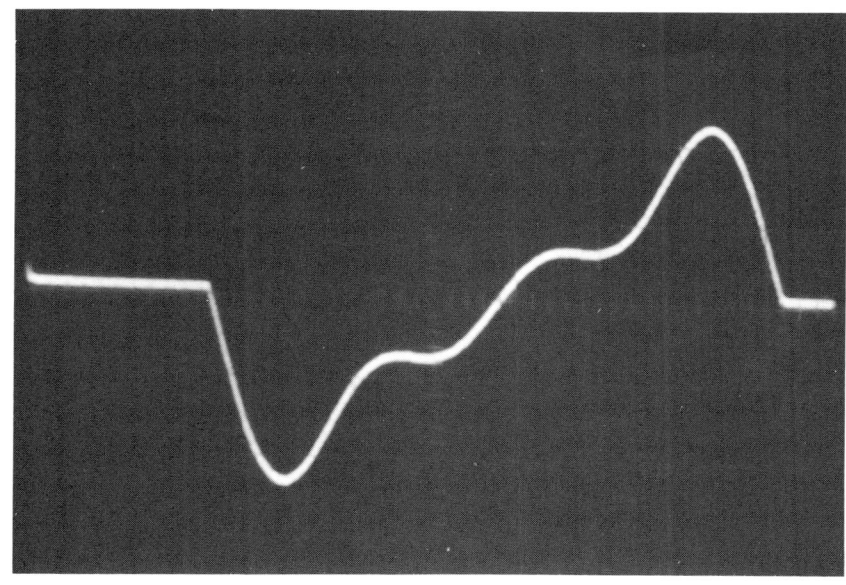

Photo 4: *An oscilloscope display of the waveform resulting from the synthesis of a typical complex waveform using the program in listing 5 and the digital to analog converter in figure 9. The waveform is the result of summing three terms of a Fourier series (see figure 11).*

```
90  PRINT "WAVEFORM BEING CALCULATED"
92  REM THIS PROGRAM CALCULATES THE COORDINATES
    OF A COMPLEX WAVEFORM
93  REM THE POINTS ARE IN PAGE 100 (OCTAL)
100 LET B=3.14/180*360/256
110 FOR A=0 TO 255
120 LET E=-((255/3.14)*SIN(A*B))
125 LET F=-((255/(2*3.14))*SIN(2*A*B))
130 LET G=-((255/(3*3.14))*SIN(3*A*B))
150 LET Y=INT(127.5+E+F+G)
160 PRINT A,Y
170 FILL 16384+A,Y
180 NEXT A
500 END
```

Listing 5: *An extended BASIC program which calculates sample points of the Fourier series illustrated in figure 11 and stores them in a table. Digital Group MaxiBASIC interpreter.*

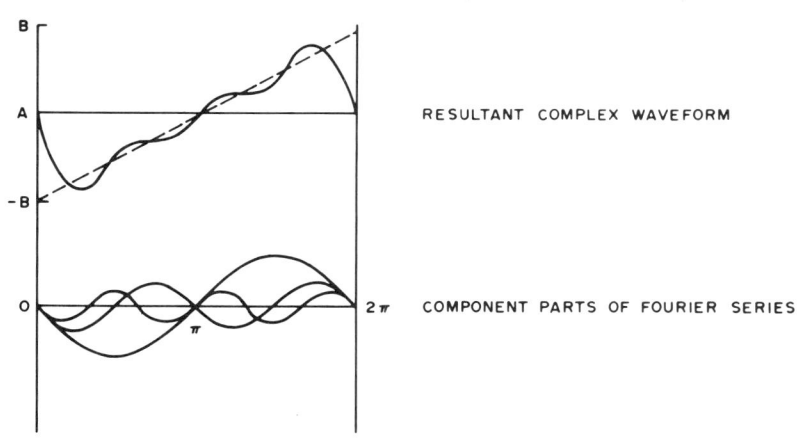

EQUATION:
$f(t) = A - B/\pi \sin WT - B/2\pi \sin 2WT - B/3\pi \sin 3WT$
WHERE $W = \pi/180$ DEGREES

Figure 11: *A typical complex waveform which is the sum of three terms of a Fourier series. These equations were used by the program in listing 5 to generate the oscilloscope trace of photo 4.*

INTERFACE ASSEMBLY AND CALIBRATION

1. Be sure to build the circuit with good quality sockets for all integrated circuits. With all components except integrated circuits wired in place, and presuming that there are no shorts, apply power to the interface. It should be noted that while the interface is shown with Altair (S-100) bus notation, there is no requirement that it be an S-100 configuration. The digital to analog conversion will work with any computer capable of providing an 8 bit data bus, 8 bit IO address bus, and an output enable strobe. Computer cycle time and architecture are irrelevant. For use with a Digital Group 8080 system, the address and data buses are connected to the equivalent DGS pin numbers, S-100 pin 77 on the interface board is grounded, and the DGS pin 17 IO write signal is used on pin 45 of the interface board in place of Sout.

2. Using a meter, check to see that the right supply voltages are on the appropriate integrated circuit pins and that V_{ref} on the digital to analog converter is approximately 6.2 V. If substituting parts, take care not to exceed 15 V between Vcc and Vee on the CMOS 4051.

3. Disconnect the power and attach the port decoding jumpers for the desired port addresses. Each of the six address lines, A7 thru A2, can be, by the appropriate placement of the jumpers, decoded as an inverted or noninverted signal. In building the circuit from scratch, an appropriate technique is to use a DIP socket with each pin, used as a jumper terminal. Selective wiring between the pins can then be done with wire wrap or Vector Slit-N-Wrap. The inverted choice is designated as a zero code, and the noninverted as a one. If all jumpers were set to the one position, channel 1's port address would be decoded as binary 11 111 100$_2$, or octal 374. If all jumpers were set to zeros, channel 1 would start at port address 0 and channel 4 would be 377 octal. If all jumpers were set to zeros, channel 1 would start at port address 0 and channel 4 would be port address 3 octal. Pick the binary code for whatever port assignment desired and wire the jumpers.

4. Insert integrated circuits IC1, 2, 3, 4, 5, 7 and 9. Apply the power, and with a short program which just outputs a value from the accumulator to an output port, output a binary 10 000 000 to the port address corresponding to channel 4 on the interface board. Using a meter to monitor the output of the LM301A, adjust the zero pot R2 until the output is 0 V. With the same programming technique, load a binary 11 111 111 (octal 377) to channel 4 port address and adjust the span pot R1 for a meter reading of +5.12 V. A binary setting of 00 000 000 should output −5.12 V. If you are unsuccessful at this point, with power off, remove the MC1408L-8 and the LM301A, and verify that the binary output of the scratch pad is correct. With the integrated circuits presently installed, the scratch pad is latched at an address of channel 4. Nine times out of ten, problems like this can be attributed to choosing an incorrect port code. Turn off the power.

5. Insert the clock generator IC6, reapply power, and using a scope or frequency counter, verify an approximate 200 kHz clock rate. Turn off the power.

6. Next, insert IC8, the CMOS multiplexer IC10, and the sample and hold op amps IC11 and 12. Be very careful in handling the CMOS integrated circuit. It is very easily damaged by static charges. Turn on the power and then using the same simple program, output a binary value to one of the channel addresses and note with a meter that it is in fact the correct voltage. Using the program, vary the output of each channel separately across the range and note that no other channel outputs should change. Sympathetic tracking usually indicates a bad multiplexer integrated circuit.

> A few cautions: Don't use op amps with a frequency response less than the LM301A and use only the L8 version of the MC1408-L8 (not MC1408-L7 or MC1408-L6) if you want a guaranteed eight bits of precision.

Tune In and Turn On!

Part 1: A Computerized Wireless AC Control System

In which a homebrew wireless AC control system foils Clarence's one-upmanship...

"Hi, Steve, you look lost in thought." Ken seated himself beside me on the front step of my house. "Your computer finally getting to you?"

I raised my head slightly and shook off the daydream appearance. "Oh, don't mind me. I'm just waiting for my neighbor Clarence to come over the way he usually does when he sees me sitting out here. No doubt he's going to tell me about the latest gadget he just bought or tantalize me with some new component in his kilowatt stereo system." The more I thought about Clarence's one-upmanship, the madder I became. "I go out and buy a lawn mower and he buys a tractor for his 1/4 acre lawn. I paint my trim and he paints his house."

"Don't get so upset. I've got a neighbor like that down at my end of the street, too. It's not that unusual." Ken's presence was beneficial. I was less likely to commit homicide with witnesses around. That kind of stuff was too messy anyway. I had something better planned for Clarence. In fact the more I thought about it the better I felt.

"Clarence doesn't have a computer yet, does he?", Ken asked.

"No. But I'm sure he's looking. The last time he was here he told me how he had found out about mine. Apparently someone showed him a copy of BYTE. He's looking for a computer now, I'm sure." Ken looked at me with a certain degree of skepticism. He also has a technical background and understands the uses and applications of computers.

"What would Clarence do with a computer?", he asked. I was sure he wanted to own one but resolved that he couldn't afford one in the foreseeable future. "He doesn't know the first thing about them."

"Knowing Clarence, he'd probably use it as a door stop. Use is unimportant to him. Ownership is the key. I really don't think I can keep him from buying one but I'm going to take advantage of the fact that Clarence always has to have something better." I had been scheming, devising and programming at a feverish pace ever since Clarence put me on notice that he was going to buy a computer.

"What are you planning?" Ken was becoming increasingly curious.

"Oh, nothing special. I'm just going to make Clarence think that my computer's capabilities are greater than they actually are. If he wants to buy one that does what I'm going to simulate, it'll cost him a hundred grand.

Ken smiled. He knows that deep down I am soft and gentle but also knows that I enjoy playing a practical joke.

"I know you have quite a system, but how are you going to make it appear like one costing $100 K?", he quizzed.

"Skulduggery and trickery, my friend." I was about to explain when Clarence suddenly appeared on my walk. I gave Ken a nudge and said, "Here he comes, right on time. Just play along."

"Hi, Steve, Ken. I just happened to notice you out here and thought I'd stop over for a chat. I've been giving that computer thing some thought. Dropped by the computer store today to ask them about... what did you call it...mass storage? Well anyway, they said I should get four dual density — I think it was — floppy disks. That should be adequate. You only have two, don't you, Steve? You must find yourself limited," Clarence continued. First it was the best 8 bit unit he could find; then he settled on a 16 bit system but was still trying to decide whether 64 K of memory would be adequate. "I looked at some printers, too. I think your DECwriter is adequate, but doesn't Digital Equipment sell something a little better? For more money, of course."

I was coming to a slow burn. Ken's expression seemed to say, "Is this guy for real?"

"I really don't know, Clarence. Why don't we go in and check with my computer."

Clarence's eyebrows rose a little as we got up to enter the house. I made a point of mentioning that he should check the mailbox beside the door since he was closest. As he opened it I said, "Never mind, I just remembered I gave the mail to the computer earlier today."

Clarence's mouth opened a bit, but he was not ready to argue the point. I gave Ken the elbow again to keep him from saying anything. "Just to be on the safe side, maybe I'd better check. Please close the door and come into the den."

As Clarence turned to close the door, I stepped into the den, reached behind the corner of one of the bookcases and pressed a button. This was the signal for the computer in the basement to go into action. I started counting silently down from 20. By the count of ten Clarence had entered the den. I motioned for Ken and Clarence to sit down and said, "We'll get the information you need later, Clarence. I'd better check on that mail first. It might be important." Six, five, four . . . . I stood up in the middle of the room and said, "Computer?" . . . Ken and Clarence looked at me as if I were crazy . . . two . . . one . . . zero . . . .

At the next instant the table lamp next

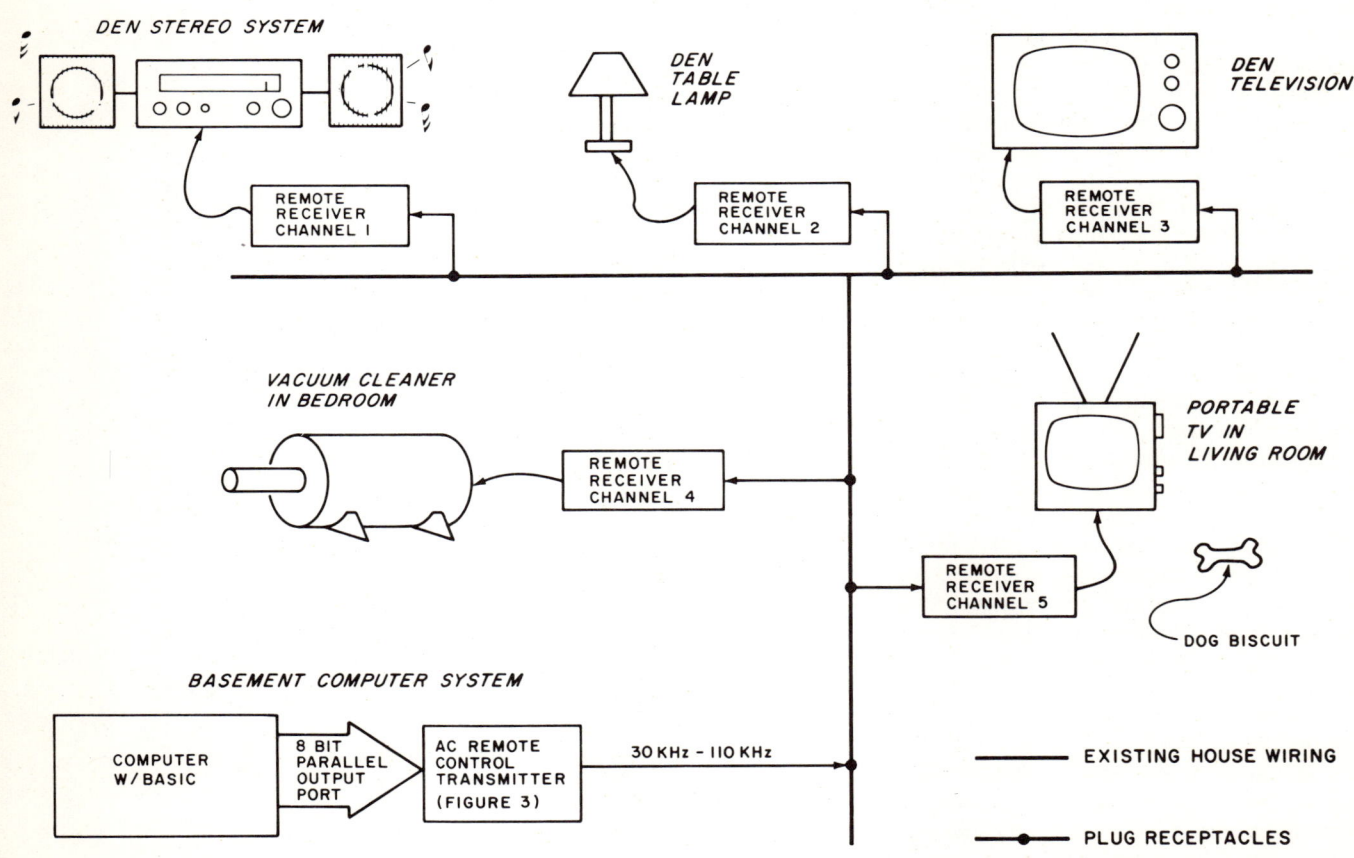

Figure 1: Block diagram of the author's wireless AC remote control system. An AC transmitter modulates the existing house wiring with high frequency signals. These signals are detected by special receivers (described in Part 2) which plug into any AC receptacle. Appliances or other electrical devices can be plugged into the receivers and controlled by the user's home computer. The setup shown is one application of a 4 receiver system. Applications include turning house lights on and off during the user's absence, automatically taping off the air from a stereo, etc.

to me seemed to turn on by itself. A second later the stereo turned on, though no music was heard. Presently, in a nonhuman voice that a Star Trek fan would appreciate, the speaker said, "Computer!" I started counting down mentally from 30 this time.

"WHAT!?", Clarence and Ken both said in unison. I put my forefinger to my lips and motioned to Ken to play along. Clarence was too engrossed in the current situation to notice. "How did you do that?", he said excitedly.

The 30 seconds were almost up as I stood and said, "Computer, did I give you the morning mail to process?" Two . . . one . . . zero . . . . The voice responded with the single word, "Affirmative."

I started to count ten seconds this time.

Clarence's eyes were wide open as I said, "Computer, give me a listing of the mail delivery."

"Mail Delivery Recorded ... Date 3-20-78 ... File N472 ... Magazine — Popular Science ... March 1978 ... Bill — Home Heating Inc ... $64.32 ... Due 30 days ... Bill . . . ." The somewhat metallic voice spoke in a monotone and at a constant rate. It was unmistakably synthetic and no one could dispute it. I listened to the computer speaking through the stereo system and waited for the key word (my next cue). ". . . Daily Newspaper . . . Hartford Courant . . . 3-20-78 . . . Major headlines as follows . . . ."

"Enough!", I shouted, and the voice stopped. It was actually programmed to stop anyway, and I started mentally counting to the next phase.

"What kind of computer is this? How big a system do you have?", Clarence exclaimed. I waved him back to his seat and decided to lay it on a little thicker.

At the right time I said, "Computer, have you finished the house work?"

"Negative ... Master Bedroom should be vacuumed . . . it shall be done . . . ."

A vacuum cleaner switched on upstairs and could be clearly heard in the den. Clarence jerked his head around when he heard the noise and nearly fell out of his chair. I turned toward the stereo and said, "No! Do it later!" Within a couple of seconds the noise of the vacuum cleaner stopped. This told me I had about two minutes.

Clarence and Ken were amazed. "Well Clarence, what do you think? The house is completely under computer control. It knows what I'm saying and does what I want."

"Will it respond to my voice?", Clarence asked weakly.

"Oh I'm sure it understands you, but it only responds to my voice ... obviously for security reasons. We wouldn't want someone telling it to do something bad, would we? I only use it for constructive purposes, like my checking account." The two minutes were up. I raised my arm and pointed to the TV set. It switched on apparently by itself.

A few seconds later a checking account statement appeared on the screen and started scrolling slowly up the screen. Clarence got up, walked over to the display and stared at it as though hypnotized. I grinned sadistically at Ken. He grabbed my arm and whispered, "How are you doing all this?"

"Shhh. It's done in BASIC. I have one of those new Votrax speech synthesizers feeding into the auxiliary input of the stereo. The TV is really a video monitor. It's wired to the computer system in the basement. Turning things on and off is simple with my new AC remote control receivers spread around the house. I just used the speak command in Zapple BASIC the same way other people use print commands. When the program is triggered, it starts a preprogrammed sequence. I know what it's going to say and how much time there is between statements."

"Oh, you're a nasty one, aren't you?" Ken smiled.

"So much for all this, Clarence; you must have better things to do. I have to go out soon. I hope you don't mind?" I glanced at my watch noticing it was nearing 7 PM, and motioned for him to follow me toward the front door. As we were leaving the den, the video monitor, stereo and lights extinguished as miraculously as they had come on. Clarence just shook his head and followed, muttering something about needing a drink.

At exactly 7 PM as Clarence was about to leave, we passed through the living room where he noticed a small TV sitting on the floor next to the couch. He was about to

Photo 1: AC remote receiver (shown in center of photo) enables author's Scottish terrier, Brenda, to watch Lassie reruns.

ask something when a bell sounded; my Scottish terrier Brenda came tearing into the room and sat in front of the TV. The TV came on instantly and a program flashed onto the screen. I waved my hand to Clarence and said, "Oh, don't worry about that. It's just a rerun of Lassie. The computer takes care of the dogs, too."

This last bit was obviously too much for Clarence. He just kept muttering as he left, saying something about maybe reconsidering his 16 bit decision and going to 32 bits. I never heard the rest as he left, still shaking his head.

Ken waited until Clarence was gone and then said, "I can understand how you staged the stuff in the den, but your dog?"

"Look Ken, if you're going to do something, you might as well do it right. As far as Brenda is concerned, she just heard a bell and came to sit and wait for a dog biscuit the same way she's been doing every night at 7 PM for weeks."

AC Remote Control

I don't expect everyone to build remote control devices like the ones presented here just to get back at the Clarences of the world, but I do see them as the next logical extension of the house computer system. Many experimenters have graduated from using the computer strictly for games and are now writing more sophisticated programs. They may be accounting, music, composition or straight number cruncher programs, but the key is evolution. The concept of a home management system is fine, but it is bound by the system peripherals.

The basic logic flow of any computer system is: input, process, output. The computer accepts data input, processes it based upon a fixed routine called a program, and outputs the results. This result can either be an alphanumeric response on a video display that allows the operator access to this processed information, or a logical result such as yes and no, or on and off. In the latter case, the single logical on or off value can also be used to control some device. A typical example is a furnace circulator pump. Temperature information is entered into the computer, which decides whether the heat is too high, in which case the pump should be off, or too low, in which case the pump should be on. This decision could be displayed at an operator console, instructing the operator to physically turn the pump on or off, but it would be far more efficient if the computer could perform the action as well as calculate the decision.

The concept of computer control is as old as the computer itself. Process control and data acquisition are the major applications of industrial computers. While the computer structure might be similar, the logistics are quite different. When a factory wants to add a computer to control a process, they automatically add 30 percent to the control costs for wiring! In the home application, even though the wiring cost might be less, the idea of stringing wires all over the house is abhorrent to most of us. No one wants to start punching holes in the walls.

The easiest alternative is wireless control. Such an approach uses the existing 115 VAC house wiring for both control power and signal transmission. This method is most cost effective in limited applications using fewer than a dozen channels, or in the case where the operations being controlled are not critical.

Carrier Current Systems

Simply stated, the carrier current method transmits a high frequency carrier (30 kHz to 500 kHz) similar to a standard radio transmission into the house wiring. It is superimposed on the 60 Hz, 120 VAC line and is broadcast throughout the house. This transmitted carrier, often referred to as carrier current, can be modulated to send music or digital information. In limited on and off control applications, though, the mere presence or absence of the carrier frequency is used to provide the control logic. The use of a modulated or unmodulated system depends ultimately on the number of parameters to be transmitted. If only one output is to be controlled, and it is going to be on or off (such as a desk lamp), a single frequency can be used. Detection of the frequency of transmission at the receiver turns the light on, and its absence turns the light off. Controlling two outputs requires two separate frequencies, one for each channel, and additional logic must be added in the receiver if the appearance of simultaneous output control is required. In cases where more than 20 channels are to be controlled or multiple settings are required at each controlled point, modulated transmissions are best employed. An example of this would be a 256 position level switch in some remote location. Rather than attempting to use 256 separate frequencies, a single frequency can be modulated and used to transmit an 8 bit code to the receiver. This is similar in format to the serial data presently used on cassette interfaces. The only difference is that the serial data stream is transmitted on a high frequency carrier and detected in a receiver before being converted for use. This method should only be

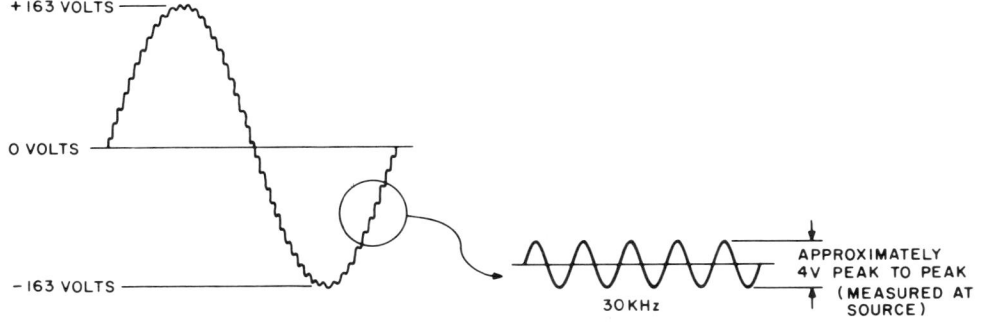

Figure 2: Example of carrier current transmission. The standard 60 Hz 115 VAC sine wave is shown being modulated by a 30 kHz carrier. Two different frequencies 4 kHz apart are used to turn devices on and off, respectively, in this design. (Note: drawing is not to scale.)

considered for extensive communications, since it is relatively expensive and the receivers are more complex.

The major consideration one should make when looking at a carrier current control system is the ultimate number of discrete points to be controlled. An output channel is defined as a single bit, ie: a 4 channel system would consist of four on/off control elements. In a single channel system, the simplest carrier/no carrier method is normally employed. For systems with the capability of two to ten channels, multiple frequencies with latching logic are usually considered. In cases where the minimum number of channels is 16, modulated carriers and serial data transmission are advised. There exists a gray area between ten channels and 20 channels. Both multiple frequency and serial data can be used in this range, but the cost difference must be considered.

Carrier Current Control Methods

There are four carrier current transmission methods that could be used on the standard home computer system:

1. **Single Channel On/Off.** Usually a high frequency carrier is transmitted through the house wiring. A tuned receiver turns on when the tone is transmitted, off when not.

> Advantages: Cheap. Less than $10 for both transmitter and receiver.
>
> Disadvantages: One channel only. Tone transmitter must remain on for output to remain on.

2. **Multiple Channel — Multiple Frequency.** Generally speaking, two high frequency carrier current signals are usually not transmitted simultaneously if they are from separate channels. The AC line is quite noisy and not exactly the best antenna. To avoid harmonics which could trigger unaddressed channels, single unique frequencies are used for each channel. In a multiple channel arrangement, no single channel is continually addressed, so some method must be incorporated to latch the logic output. The multichannel methods seen most often utilize pulsed transmission. A particular receiver's frequency is pulsed once or twice within a timed window. One pulse means "on," two mean "off." The desired control output is latched into a flip flop in the receiver.

> Advantages: Relatively inexpensive. About 20 different channels can be accommodated with a transmission bandwidth of 100 kHz. Only a single frequency receiver is required for each channel.
>
> Disadvantages: Pulsing the latch on or off requires external gating logic in addition to a tuned receiver. Multiple channel arrangements require considerable interchannel decoupling and narrow receiver bandwidths. Depending on the particular logic design, this can be inconsistent with "pulse window" techniques. Control pulses must be accurately timed using either hardware or software techniques. This method, while conceptually simple, requires considerable additional circuitry to make it glitch proof.

3. **Multichannel — Multifrequency — Dual Receivers.** This method is essentially the same as the previous one except that separate frequencies are used to turn the controlled output on and off. Either method would utilize the same transmitter.

> Advantages: Since separate frequencies are used for the set and reset functions, special constraints on timing are eliminated. Long time-constant input filtering techniques can be used to reduce glitches. No special software is necessary to drive the transmission device. This method combines the best features of methods 1 and 2.
>
> Disadvantages: Decreases the total number of possible control outputs.

Table 1: Power wiring table for figures 3a and 3b.

Number	Type	+5 V pin	−12 V pin	gnd pin	+12 V pin
IC1	MC1408	13	3	2	–
IC2	LM301A	–	4	–	7
IC3	MC4024	14	–	7	–
IC4	H11A1	no supply pins designated			
IC5	MC1403	1	–	3	–
IC6	741	–	4	–	7

Since two separate frequencies are required for each channel, only about ten total channels can fit in a 100 kHz bandwidth.

4. Single Frequency — Asynchronous Data Transmission. This type of carrier current transmission system can be used to transmit serial data rather than a discrete control signal which is on or off. This data, when received and decoded, can be effectively used to control a number of devices. The method is essentially an extension of the pulse window transmission concept stated earlier. Finer filtering methods are required though, since timing is more critical.

Advantages: A single frequency system can allow as many as 128 controlled outputs on a single frequency for each 8 bit data word.

Disadvantages: Expensive. Transmitter is serial and each receiver must incorporate logic for serial to parallel conversion, usually in the form of a universal asynchronous receiver-transmitter (UART) or its equivalent.

A Design with Expansion in Mind

Most likely, any experimenter interested in constructing a carrier current control system will want to start with one or two channels. In my own case I can see expansion to maybe eight channels. The most cost effective approach for me is to use either system 2 or 3 described above. The multi-frequency pulse transmission method has in my experience proven to be too unreliable in practice. Reliability is gained at the expense of considerable extra circuitry. In a system used to control the operation of 115 VAC appliances and lights when I'm not at home, I need as much reliability as I can get. For this reason my design relies on the use of two frequencies for each channel: one to turn the device on and a different frequency to turn it off. These frequencies will be grouped in pairs and referred to as a single channel. The bandwidth of each channel is about 8 kHz. In practical terms this means that, if the transmitter has a total frequency range of 30 kHz to 110 kHz, or 80 kHz, then 80 kHz divided by 8 kHz equals ten independent channels. Within this 8 kHz band, two separate frequencies are allocated. One turns the device on while the other turns it off. In the example illustrated in this article, channel 1 occupies 35 kHz to 43 kHz. The on and off frequencies are 35 and 39 kHz, respectively. The next channel, channel 2, occupies 43 to 51 kHz and the on and off frequencies are 43 and 47 kHz, respectively. There is no magic strategy for picking frequencies. Each remote receiver detects two frequencies 4 kHz apart. The only consideration is that all receiver frequencies be separated by at least 4 kHz. The fewer the channels, the further apart these frequencies can be. In a 2 channel system, choosing widely separated frequencies is safest.

Figure 3a: Precision ± 2.50 V source for use with the transmitter in figure 3b.

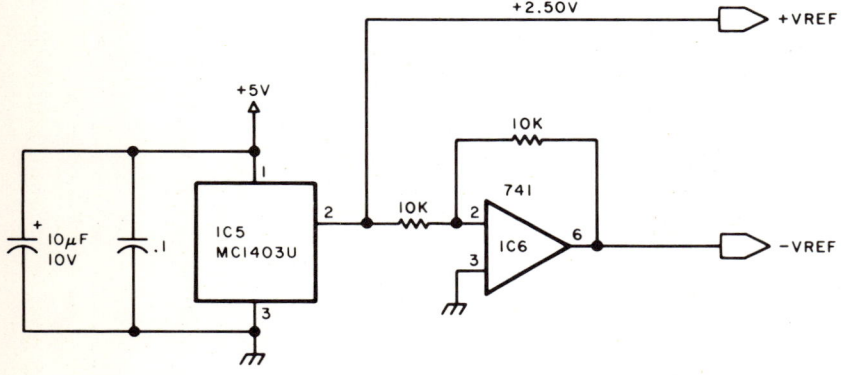

Figure 3b: AC remote control transmitter. The circuit consists of a digitally programmable frequency generator (IC1, IC2, IC3, IC5 and IC6). The output of IC1, a digital to analog converter, is converted from a current to a voltage by IC2 and sent to IC3, a voltage controlled oscillator. In this design, the voltage controlled oscillator can produce frequencies in the 30 kHz range. Opto-isolator IC4 keeps the computer circuitry from interacting with the house wiring (see CAUTION note!). The transmitter section consists of IC4, Q1, Q2, and Q3. The three transistors form a power amplifier which couples the signals through a capacitor onto the AC line. The .5 W output of the amplifier is sufficient to reach all areas of most home wiring systems.

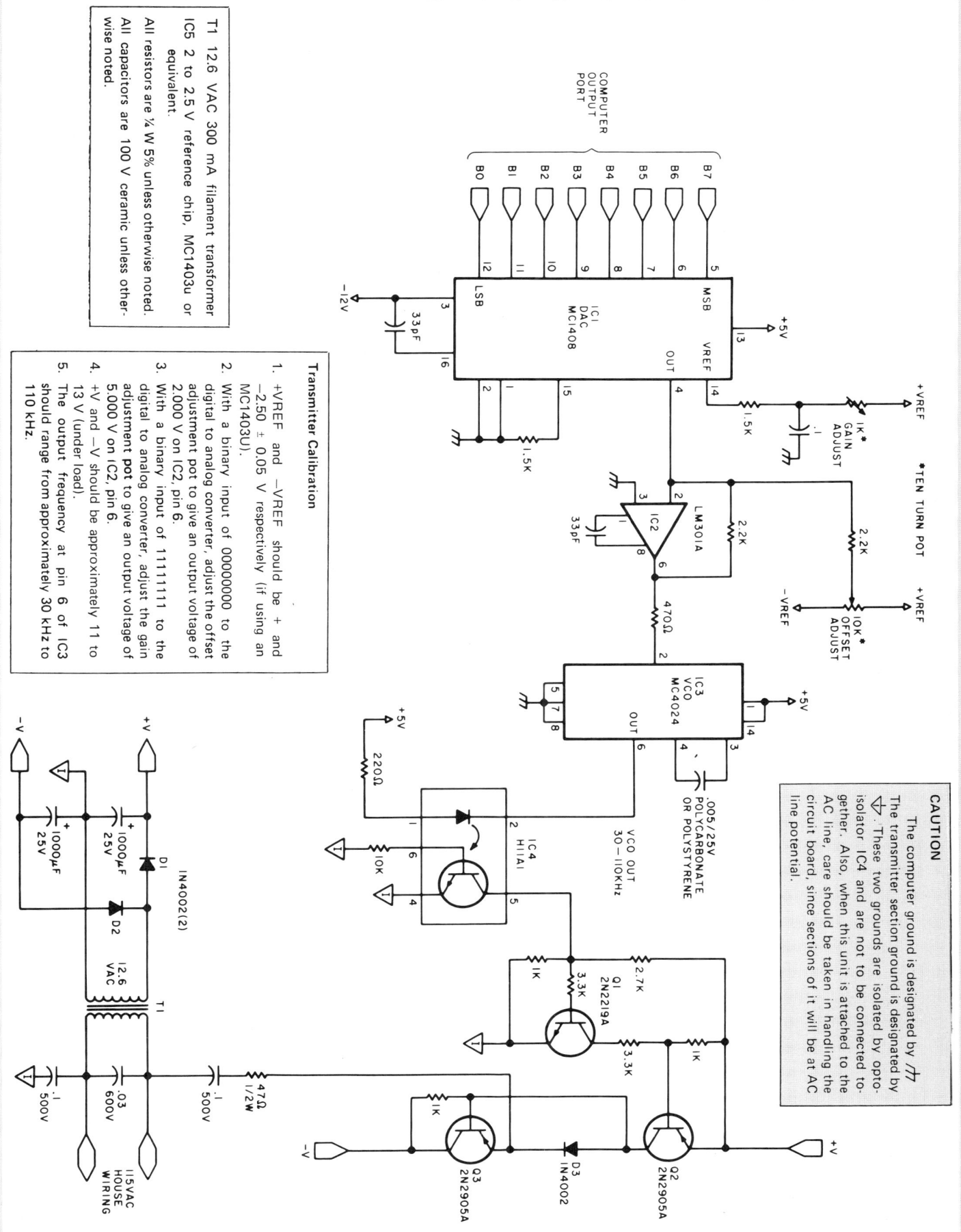

Photo 2: *Prototype boards of transmitter (at left) and one receiver board. Receiver unit is described in Part 2.*

Channel 1 could occupy 35 kHz to 43 kHz, and channel 2 could be between 83 kHz and 91 kHz (and transmit on 83 kHz and 87 kHz). Apportioning bandwidth to maximize the number of channels is a major consideration in a multifrequency system. (I will describe the receiver section next in Part 2.)

Figure 3 is the schematic of the AC remote transmitter. It consists of a digitally programmable frequency source and an optically isolated house wiring driver.

The programmable frequency generator, IC1, IC2, IC3, IC5 and IC6, forms a precision voltage controlled oscillator. IC1 is an 8 bit digital to analog converter (explained in greater detail in my article "Control the World" page 47), whose output current is proportional to the 8 bit data word impressed on its input lines. The current output is converted to a voltage through IC2 and presented to the input of IC3, voltage controlled oscillator (VCO). Its output frequency is proportional to input voltage.

Analog frequency sources such as this are usually avoided because of stability problems. The alternative involves programmable divided-by-N counters and a crystal frequency input, which would mean about 25 integrated circuits to produce the same range of selected frequencies. Therefore, it is important to overcome potential stability problems. The major error-producing components in such designs are usually the voltage references and oscillator timing elements. By using a precision voltage reference circuit, IC5 and IC6, and incorporating polystyrene low drift capacitors in the voltage controlled oscillator section, these problems are virtually eliminated.

The result is a digitally programmable oscillator. With the values chosen, the range is about 30 kHz to 110 kHz. Changing the output frequency is simply a matter of changing the code on the digital to analog converter. Within the 80 kHz range of the voltage controlled oscillator there will be 256 discrete increments of frequency. Presuming that the input and output characteristics are linear, each increment would be 80000/256 or approximately 300 Hz. This means that, if a digital input code of binary 0000000 produces an output of 30,000 Hz, then octal 00000001 would be 30,300 Hz. Further extrapolation gives an output frequency of 49.2 kHz for binary 01000000 (decimal 64). In reality, the voltage controlled oscillator is not perfectly linear, but the output frequency can be set empirically by using a simple BASIC program. This setup procedure will be covered in detail when I discuss the receiver calibration section in Part 2.

Once the oscillation frequency has been produced, the next problem is to transmit it through the house wiring. This transmitter section consists of IC4, Q1, Q2 and Q3. The oscillator output is optically isolated and coupled to the output driver stage through IC4. The three transistors form a power amplifier and pump about .5 watts onto the AC line. This amount of power is sufficient to reach all areas of your home and probably a few of your neighbors, but there should be no interference with any household appliances. [*As in all carrier current systems, the range is any AC wiring sharing the same final step down transformer. This might be two or three houses in suburbia, or one floor of an apartment house or dormitory ... CH*] Since the output driver is isolated from the computer, it cannot use the computer power supply as its power source, so components D1, D2 and T1 form a voltage doubler circuit

```
100 FOR X = 0 to 255
110 OUT 2,X
120 REM PORT 2 IS THE OUTPUT PORT ATTACHED
    TO THE DAC INPUT
130 FOR D = 1 TO 500
140 NEXT D
150 REM THIS IS A DELAY ROUTINE SO THAT THE PROGRAM
    DOESN'T SCAN TOO FAST TO SEE
160 NEXT X
170 GOTO 100
180 REM CONTINUE TO CYCLE INDEFINITELY
```

Listing 1: *A BASIC program to test the voltage controlled oscillator shown in figure 3. The program causes the output frequency of the oscillator to ramp up in fairly linear fashion and reset.*

to provide approximately + and − 13 V to run the driver. It is important to note that there are two separate grounds in the circuit. One is the computer ground and the other is the driver circuit ground. They are NOT to be connected together (see CAUTION note).

Building and Testing the Transmitter

Photo 2 shows the transmitter on the left and one of the receiver boards on the right. It is necessary to build the receiver to completely test the transmitter without the use of an oscilloscope to make sure everything is all right. Certain shortcut methods can be employed this time, though, to give you reasonable confidence about the circuit's operability.

Build the circuit as shown in figure 3 with the exception of the driver circuit and IC4. Add a 0.1 µF capacitor in parallel with the 0.005 µF capacitor already between pins 3 and 4 on IC3. This will effectively lower the output frequency range of the voltage controlled oscillator into the audio range. By putting a 100 Ω resistor between IC3 pin 6 and an earphone whose other terminal is connected to ground, this audio tone can be heard. It is a simple matter to change the tone. The astute experimenter will realize that we have constructed a programmable tone generator, possibly suitable for music applications.

Use BASIC to Run the Controller

As with most of my recent designs, this one is driven by a latched parallel output port, and update speed is of no particular importance. This makes it a natural for BASIC, which sets 8 bit output ports. This interface controller can be set to any frequency within its range under program control. BASIC can also perform a simple test to determine whether the voltage controlled oscillator works (see listing 1). This program causes the output frequency of the voltage controlled oscillator to ramp up in a roughly linear fashion and reset. With the capacitor values in the schematic, the range should be approximately 30 kHz to 110 kHz. Again, picking any larger capacitor value will allow this sawtooth tone generator to be heard in the audio range.

Actual control of a device comes after the receiver section has been built and mounted in an enclosure such as that shown in photo 3. While it is difficult to discuss the application without having discussed the method, I don't want to leave everyone hanging till Part 2. The simple program in listing 2 controls two remote channels, designated channel 1 and channel 2, from the computer keyboard. This is written in Micro Com Zapple BASIC.

In Part 2 I'll describe the design and construction of the receiver section as well as discuss more detailed applications. A natural for this project is to use a quantity of these remote receivers to control light and sound sources around the house to simulate occupancy when no one is home.■

Photo 3: Complete receiver package. Remote controlled appliance plugs into rear of box. Set and reset buttons allow appliance to be controlled locally as well as remotely.

Listing 2: A sample BASIC program used to control the circuit in figure 3.

```
100 PRINT "INDICATE CHANNEL TO BE CONTROLLED
        -1 OR 2-"
110 INPUT A
120 IF A ≤ 2 GOTO 150
130 GOTO 100
150 PRINT "DO YOU WANT TO TURN CHANNEL"; A; "ON OR OFF?"
160 INPUT B$
170 IF B$ = "ON" GOTO 300
180 REM THE REMOTE CONTROLLER IS ATTACHED TO OUTPUT PORT 2
190 REM THIS ROUTINE TURNS A CHANNEL OFF
200 IF A = 1 THEN OUT 2, 180
210 REM 180 IS THE DECIMAL OFF CODE FOR THE CHANNEL 1
        PROTOTYPE
220 IF A = 2 THEN OUT 2, 118
230 REM 118 IS THE DECIMAL OFF CODE FOR THE CHANNEL 2
        PROTOTYPE
240 GOTO 100
300 REM THIS ROUTINE TURNS A CHANNEL ON
310 IF A = 1 THEN OUT 2,162
320 REM 162 IS THE DECIMAL ON CODE FOR CHANNEL 1
        PROTOTYPE
330 IF A = 2 THEN OUT 2, 96
340 REM 96 IS THE DECIMAL ON CODE FOR CHANNEL 2
        PROTOTYPE
350 GOTO 100
```

Tune In and Turn On!

Part 2: An AC Wireless Remote Control System

In Part 1 I outlined the transmitter section of a wireless AC remote control system that can be easily attached to any computer with an 8 bit parallel output port. As previously stated, it will allow remote on and off control of up to ten AC powered devices. Now I will cover the design of a typical receiver section.

Figure 1 shows the schematic of a single channel receiver station and photos 1 and 2 illustrate a typical layout of a constructed receiver. (A photo of the completed receiver is shown in Part 1.) The receiver consists of three basic sections: input filter and power supply, on and off tone detectors, and output latch. Except for minor component value differences necessary to change the channel frequencies, all receivers will have the same configuration.

Input Filter and Power Supply

Each receiver, designated as a single channel, receives two transmitted frequencies from the computer. One is used to turn the AC device on and the other to turn it off. These two tones must be close enough to be passed through the same filter section but not close enough to interfere with each other. For this reason, a channel bandwidth has been designated to be 8 kHz, and no two tones are closer than 4 kHz.

The function of the input filter is to reject the 60 Hz line frequency and all other frequencies except the 8 kHz band of a specific channel. While this may appear true in theory, it is not quite the result. Instead, the amplitudes of various frequencies will be affected as they pass through the filter. 60 Hz will be virtually nonexistent, and if the passband is from 35 kHz to 43 kHz, that frequency range should be the highest amplitude. This amplitude variation across the spectrum can be facilitated somewhat

Photo 1: The finished prototype receiver board.

Photo 2: Internal view of finished prototype receiver chassis.

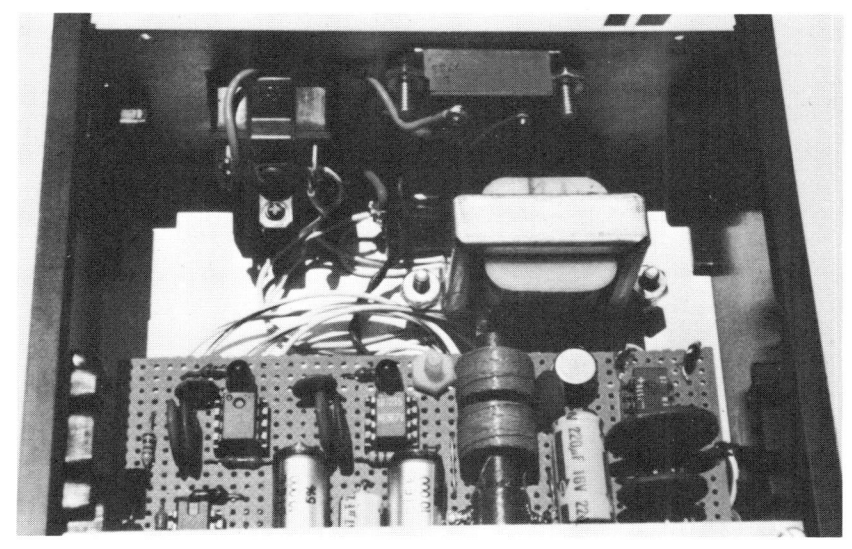

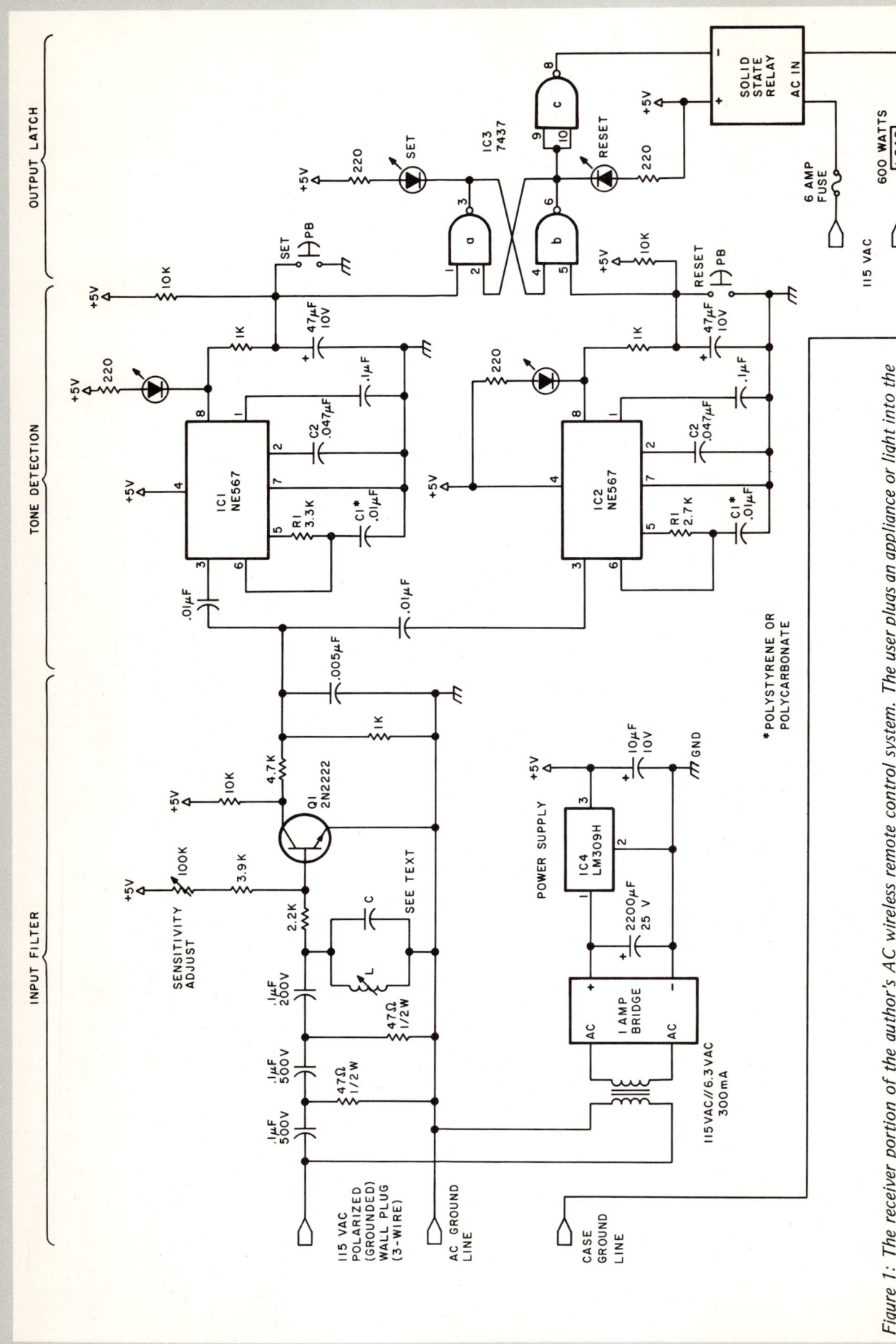

Figure 1: The receiver portion of the author's AC wireless remote control system. The user plugs an appliance or light into the receiver, which in turn is plugged into a wall socket. One of two frequencies is sent at a time through the house wiring by a separate computer controlled transmitter (described in Part 1). The receiver responds to these frequencies by turning its device on or off, respectively. A specially designed tuned bandpass filter amplifies only that pair of frequencies dedicated to its receiver, attenuating all other frequency pairs. After some amplification, the signal is sent to two tone decoders (IC1 and IC2) which respond to the two frequencies independently. Two buttons are also present on the receiver so the user can operate the device locally. Note that the use of a 3 wire grounded plug to connect to the AC line is highly recommended.

by the addition of a tuned inductance and capacitance (LC) circuit, called a bandpass circuit. The center frequency of the LC circuit should be set for the center of the particular passband desired. In the case of 35 to 43 kHz, the inductor and capacitor are chosen to produce a resonance at 39 kHz: the result is a passive filter. As the RC section passes frequencies close to 39 kHz, the LC combination starts to resonate (which increases the overall amplitude seen at the base of Q1). In practice, a low Q slug-tuned 1 to 10 millihenry coil salvaged from an old TV set will work well. By using this LC circuit, the fundamental frequency of the transmitted waveform is sufficiently high in level to be differentiated from the second and third harmonics also present. A sensitivity adjustment on the base of transistor Q1 aids in the detection process by allowing only signals of sufficient amplitude through the next amplifier filter section of Q1.

The use of an LC filter does require some component value changes to cover the 30 kHz to 110 kHz range of the transmitter. Figure 2 is the schematic of the LC combination in question and includes the formulas required to make this calculation. Again, calculations are only part of the answer and are acceptable only in 2 or 3 channel applications. For optimum tuning, the component values should be chosen according to the equation. Then using an oscilloscope, measure the voltage across the LC circuit and slowly adjust the slug-tuned coil to peak at the desired frequency. A voltmeter on the AC setting will not respond sufficiently; only an oscilloscope with high impedance inputs should be used.

The power supply section is a standard rectifier and 3 terminal regulator supply. The circuit requires less than 100 mA and values are not critical. The LM309 voltage regulator is the plastic TO-5 packaged version of the standard LM309K, which is a TO-3 metal can. Either can be used and no heat sink is required.

Tone Detectors

The heart of the receiver is in the two tone detectors, IC1 and IC2. Each is tuned

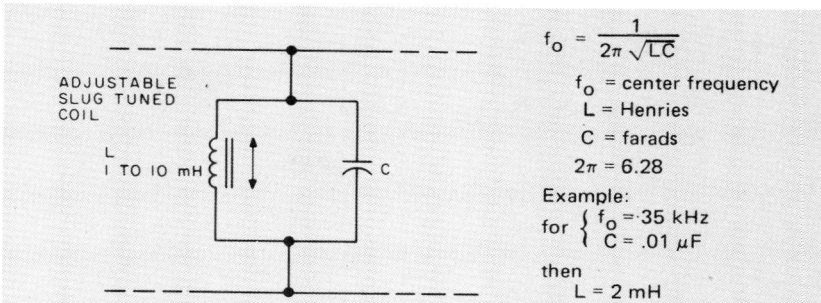

Figure 2: Calculation of inductor and capacitor values for the tuned bandpass filter used in the reciever's input section.

$$f_o = \frac{1}{2\pi \sqrt{LC}}$$

f_o = center frequency
L = Henries
C = farads
2π = 6.28

Example:
for $\begin{cases} f_o = 35 \text{ kHz} \\ C = .01 \ \mu F \end{cases}$
then
$L = 2$ mH

to a specific frequency or tone within its respective channel bandwidth. For the channel 1 frequencies I have chosen (35 kHz to 43 kHz), IC1 would be set for approximately 35 kHz and IC2 would be set 4 kHz higher at 39 kHz. IC1 is considered the set frequency receiver and IC2 is the reset receiver. LEDs are attached to their outputs to facilitate tuning. These lights will light only when the correct frequency is present at the respective pin 3.

As with the input filter, these are tuned circuits and they require component value changes for the different channels. Figure 3 shows an individual receiver and outlines the equations used to select components. The values I have chosen are standard and could be set closer with the addition of trim pots, etc. In practice, this won't be necessary unless all ten channels are to be constructed.

Output Latch

The outputs of the set and reset tone detectors go to the set and reset flip flop made from two NAND gates (IC3a and IC3b). If either the set pushbutton is pushed or IC1 receives the proper signal, the flip flop goes into the set state and the output device is activated. It will stay in the "on" condition until either the reset pushbutton is pushed or a reset signal is received through IC2.

Although the 7437 is quite capable of driving a silicon controlled rectifier (SCR) directly, turning on a triac is a bit more involved. When the parts necessary to perform this function cost more than a

Table 1: Power wiring table for figure 1.

	IC Type	+5 V	Gnd
IC1	NE567	4	7
IC2	NE567	4	7
IC3	7437	14	7
IC4	LM309	3	2

The solid state relay noted in the schematic can be either a Sigma 226 RE1-5A1 as shown in photo 1 or the homebuilt unit of photo 3 and figure 4. Minimum current rating should be 6 A.

1. All resistors 1/4 W carbon 5% unless otherwise noted.
2. All capacitors are 100 V ceramic unless otherwise noted.
3. The values of L and C in the tuned filter are computed for the particular center frequency chosen (see figure 2). In general L should be an adjustable slug tuned in a range of 1 to 10 mH. C will range from .001 to .01.
4. If this receiver is used on AC lines which also power many inductive devices such as motors and pumps, voltage surge protection may be required on the input.
5. A 7400 can be substituted for the 7437 if the set and reset LEDs are eliminated.

Figure 3: Selection of components for the tone decoder.

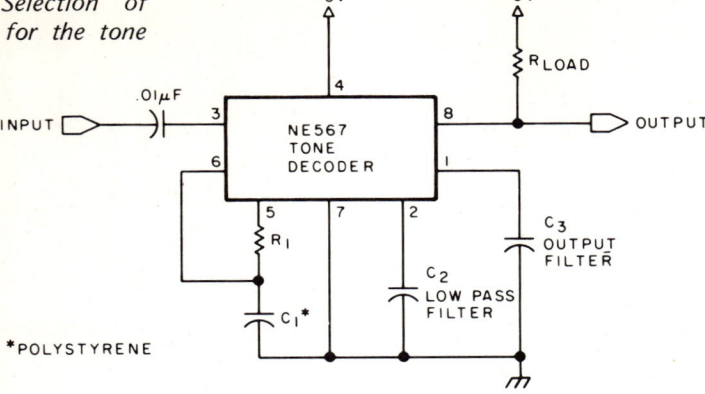

Example:
for $R_1 = 3.3\ k$ and $C_1 = .01$
$f_0 = 33.3\ kHz$
with $C_2 = .047\ \mu F$
Bandwidth $\cong 1600\ Hz$
$C_3 = .1\ \mu F$

1. Select R_1

   $f_0 \cong \dfrac{1.1}{R_1 C_1}$

   f_0 = detection frequency (Hz)
   R_1 = ohms ($1\ k \leqslant R_1 \leqslant 20\ k$)
   C_1 = farads

2. Select bandwidth of less than 2 kHz for each frequency. For input amplitude $\geqslant 200\ mV$

   $BW \cong \sqrt{\dfrac{f_0}{C_2}}$

   f_0 = detection frequency (Hz)
   $C_2 = \mu F$
   BW = bandwidth (Hz)

   and:

3. $C_3 = 2\ C_2$ minimum

commercial solid state switch, it's time to go commercial. There are experimenters who will want to use SCRs because they have them, though.

Figure 4 is a schematic of an alternate 1000 W solid state relay; photo 3 is the prototype I constructed as an example. It is important to note that, while both the SCR and homebrew device in figure 4 are opto-isolated devices, the AC remote receiver itself is not isolated, and care must be taken when probing into a plugged-in unit. In this case, the only advantage of the opto-isolator is that it provides the required current to drive the SCR or triac; a 7437 by itself may not. SCR gate currents have a wide variation (1 to 100 mA for various SCRs all rated for 8 A) and a 7437 does not have unlimited drive capability. For some less current consuming applications, a standard 7400 can be used instead of a 7437.

System Checkout

There are two ways to calibrate this system: trial and error (good for one or two channels only); or with the proper test equipment (necessary for three or more channels). I prefer the latter and will discuss that technique.

The first thing to do after building the transmitter is to determine what frequencies are being transmitted. Using the program in listing 1 and a frequency counter attached to pin 6 of IC3 on the transmitter board will aid calibration. The frequency output of the transmitter described in Part 1 will have 256 possible values but not all are required at this time. A program could be written to scan slowly across all frequencies and stop when the receiver picks it up. This method involves trial and error. I prefer to tune the transmitter to a known frequency, then tune in the receiver.

Once the transmitter is set up, the next project is the receiver. For reasons I'll describe later, it is best to plug the transmitter and receiver into the same wall socket initially (use an extension cord if necessary). Using the previous program, set the transmitter to continually transmit one tone in the center of a channel, such as for channel 1 (39 kHz). Choose component values from figure 3 (figure 1 is configured for channel 1) and adjust the coil slug until the maximum voltage appears across the LC circuit in the filter section. Reset the frequency transmission for the set frequency (35 kHz) and adjust the sensitivity pot until the LED at pin 8 of IC1 comes on. Failure of the LED to light indicates any of the following:

1. Insufficient transmission amplitude: check transmitter output.
2. Wrong frequency transmitted or wrong components chosen for the receiver: check program action and recheck calculations.
3. Sensitivity pot misadjusted: attach scope to collector of Q1 and note that sensitivity pot turns signal on or off.
4. Bad tone decoders.

Once this phase is completed, set the transmitter frequency to the reset frequency (43 kHz) by entering the appropriate number when running the program of listing 1. Then check to see that the LED on IC2 lights. The sensitivity pot may require adjustment. The key is to find a setting that works for both set and reset frequencies simultaneously. This same procedure is repeated for any other channel.

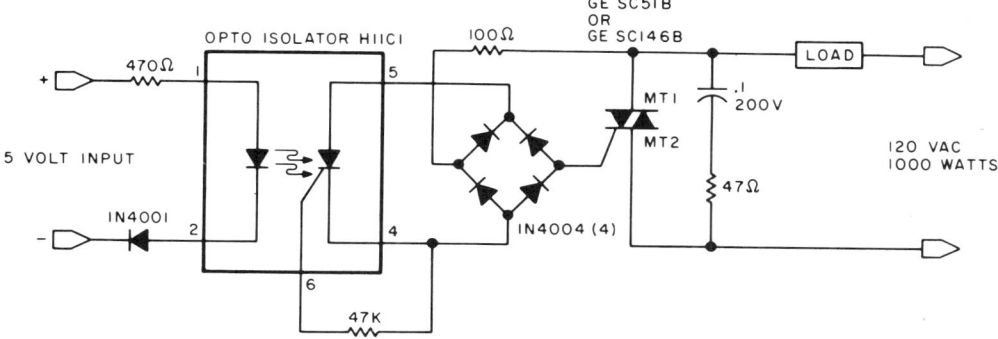

Figure 4: 10 A solid state relay suitable for use in a TTL to 115 VAC application.

Using the System in the Home

The transmitter is plugged into any 110 VAC outlet in the vicinity of the computer. Depending on the home, it may or may not transmit to all outlets in the house. Most homes have 220 V service which consists of two independent 110 VAC lines. A frequency transmitted into one line may not pass over into the other line with sufficient power to be detected at all receiver locations. It may be necessary to take one of the receivers and plug it into a number of different outlets to determine which are on the correct circuit. This potential problem is not unique with this particular design and is a factor to be considered in all carrier current designs. In most cases, if there are sufficient 220 VAC loads in use, such as heaters and stoves, etc, the carrier frequency will pass easily through the loads from one line to the other and the whole house will be covered.

The most obvious application of such a computer control system is a home lighting system used in conjunction with a burglar alarm. The major problem with conventional timer activated light controllers is that their consistently repeated on and off periods are an immediate tip-off that no one is home. With this system and either a real time, time of day clock, or timing loop functioning as a clock, the on and off periods of a number of lights can be altered dynamically. The program which accomplishes this function can be implemented as easily in BASIC as any of the test programs used to check out the AC remote controller described in this article.■

Photo 3: Homemade solid state relay (see figure 4).

```
100  PRINT "WHAT IS THE OUTPUT PORT NUMBER OF THE TRANSMITTER"
110  INPUT N :REM N IS IN DECIMAL
120  PRINT "OUTPUT UPDATE VALUE"
130  INPUT X
140  OUTPUT N, X :REM X is sent to the transmitter DAC
150  GOTO 120
```

Listing 1: A simple BASIC program to aid the user in calibrating the transmitter. A frequency counter is attached to pin 6 of IC3 in the transmitter in order to check the actual output frequency versus a typed in value.

Add a Voice to Your Computer for $35

Talk to Me!

"Talk to me! Talk to me!"

"OK! I'll talk to you if you need it that much!" Ken called out as he descended the stairs into my cellar workshop. "You sure you aren't going a little buggy?"

I looked up from the video monitor and parted the piles of cassette tapes and printouts. Ken was a good neighbor and I knew his comment was only in jest. I hit the carriage return and the speaker said, "Talk to me!"

Ken smiled when he realized I was just exercising the voice synthesizer option I had previously added to my system.

"This synthesizer is part of the reason I'm here this evening," he said.

"What's the problem?" I asked.

"No problem really. We just got a microcomputer in my company's R and D lab and I've been playing with it lately. It's pretty sophisticated and has plenty of memory space. What would it cost to put that type of synthesized voice on our computer? I can probably raise $50 among the technicians for it. They'd get a kick out of it."

"Well, depending on the manufacturer and the particular interface, they usually run from $400 to $800 and up." I looked at the startled expression on Ken's face. It was what I normally call "peripheral face," the look you get when you tell someone that it'll cost $1100 for a video terminal to communicate with the computer he just bought for $250.

"So much for that idea. How's the weather been lately?"

"Wait!" I interjected. "How much memory do you have on your lab microcomputer?"

"40 K, I believe. Why?"

"How much of a vocabulary do you need?"

"I suspect we'd only need the numbers 0 through 9 and a few letters. We want to monitor data and verbally record channel number and input value. But at that price it's far too expensive to justify."

"How about digitized speech? You probably have enough memory for that."

"What's that?"

"It's a process to record speech digitally. For all practical purposes it's like a tape recorder, but instead of magnetic tape for the storage medium it uses the computer's programmable memory. The tape recorder uses an analog storage method while the computer stores the information digitally."

"If it's that simple why don't more people use it?"

"It's mostly because it's not very memory efficient. A voice synthesizer is an analog voltage generator that creates the speech phoneme sounds through a hard wired circuit. In its most advanced form a single 8 bit byte can be used to tell the synthesizer what discrete sound it should make. By sending it a series of byte codes, words can be made from the discrete sounds. That's the way my Votrax synthesizer works." I pulled out a pad to sketch my explanation. "In digitized speech the analog voice input is sampled very quickly with a high speed analog to digital converter, and the samples are stored in memory. To reconvert to analog or "say" the words, the stored digital data is sent to a digital to analog converter at the same rate and in the same order the samples were taken. The concept of digitized speech has been around for a long time, but up until recently the cost of a system dedicated to this was prohibitive. You already have the computer and enough memory for limited applications. All you need is the high speed analog to digital and digital to analog converters and the knowledge to do it."

"And what is that going to cost me, $500?" Ken was still skeptical.

I opened a drawer under the bench. It was my "junk box" (in my case one corner of my cellar is a junk *room*). I rummaged through the prototype boards from previous experiments and pulled out a particular one. "Ah, here we are. You remember when I designed that 8 channel digital voltmeter (pages 13 and 25). I needed it to troubleshoot this board. This is all you need for

77

Figure 1a: Block diagram of a digital speech recording system. Speech is picked up as sound waves by the microphone and is amplified and processed through a high speed analog to digital converter which samples the analog sound waveform several thousand times a second. These samples are stored in the computer's programmable memory.

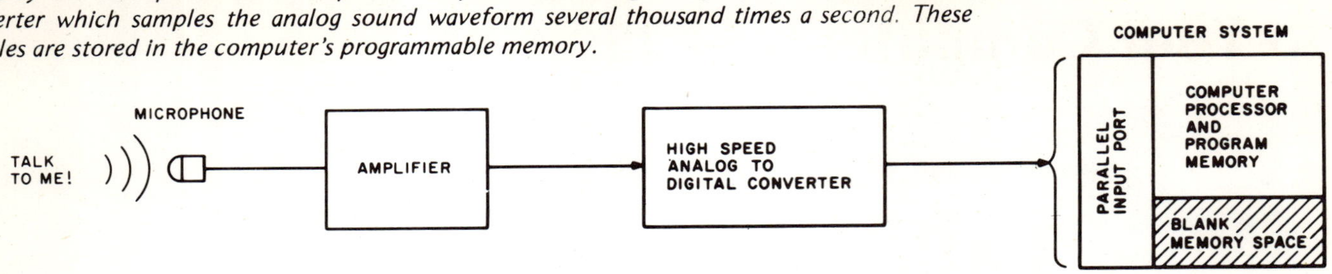

digitized speech." I tossed the board to Ken. "It contains a 100,000 sample per second 8 bit analog to digital converter and an equivalent speed digital to analog converter. And now the beauty part: It cost less than $35 to build."

"Great! Tell me how to use it. How much memory does it need? What kind of program does it use? Can you tell me how to use it so I can borrow it for work tomorrow?"

"Well, let's go over the concept in more detail. . . ."

What is Digitized Speech?

Digitized speech is simply a standard data acquisition technique with a new definition. For years people have been using computers to scan analog to digital input converters and store the results in memory. Often, in high speed applications such as wind tunnels and nuclear experiments, the sample rates can exceed thousands of samples a second. In cases where the critical event is of short duration, these thousands of samples are stored directly into memory to increase system throughput capabilities. When the event has passed and sampling has stopped, the computer memory contains a record of that event in discretely timed intervals. The stored data is now available to be reduced, analyzed or listed. It's often listed in "slow motion." This technique employs an analog pen recorder and a digital to analog converter. Each sample is successively processed through a digital to analog converter at a slow rate to the pen recorder. The result is an expanded view of a short event.

An alternative method for utilizing this stored data is to play it back in real time. In this case the computer outputs the stored data to the digital to analog converter at the same rate the data is taken. The output of the converter would then exactly duplicate the values of the event previously recorded (at the times the samples were taken).

Digitized speech is a specific application of this type of data recording technique. Your voice, when applied to a microphone and amplifier, creates a fluctuating analog voltage that varies at the frequency rate of the sound. If this analog signal is applied to the input of a high speed (greater than 10,000 samples per second) analog to digital converter and stored in memory, the computer won't care whether the source is speech or a nuclear reaction. The analog fluctuations are "digitized" at discrete sampling intervals and stored (figure 1a). If the stored memory table is sent to a digital to analog converter at the same rate it was initially sampled, the speech is reproduced exactly. Of course there are trade-offs and limitations that have to be considered to produce a usable system (figure 1b). We will consider them in detail later.

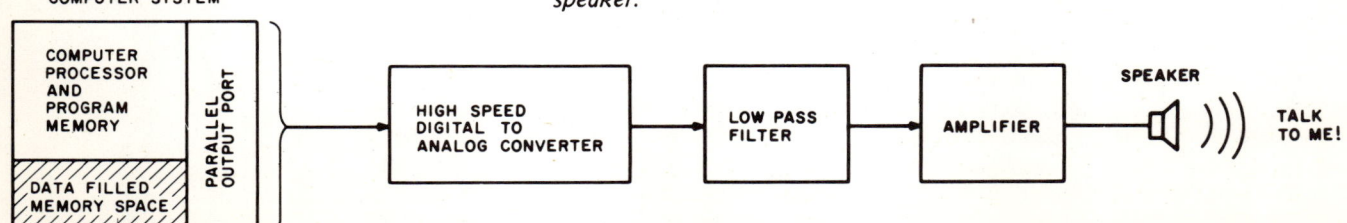

Figure 1b: Block diagram of a digital speech playback system. Digital sample points stored by the system in figure 1a are converted by a high speed digital to analog converter into an analog speech waveform. A low pass filter is used to smooth the signal, which is then amplified and played back through a speaker.

A digitized speech system creates its output waveform by digital to analog conversion rather than by completely analog generation as in the case of a voice synthesizer. The major consideration that limits the usefulness of digital speech is the vast quantity of data which must be stored to reproduce a single spoken word.

Choosing the Correct Sampling Rate

The 8 channel digital voltmeter mentioned earlier has a maximum sampling rate of 25 conversions a second. A slow speed analog to digital converter of this type is of no value in this application. The normal human voice occupies a bandwidth of 4000 Hz, and taking

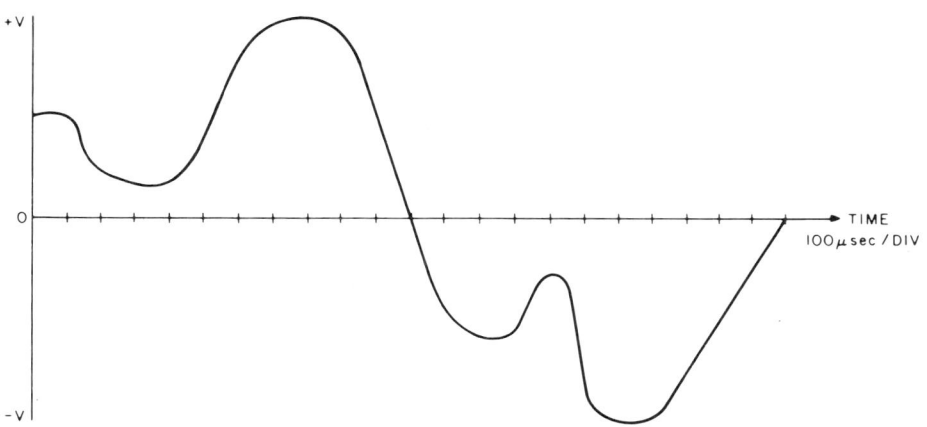

Figure 2a: A waveform (considerably simplified) which is characteristic of the voice.

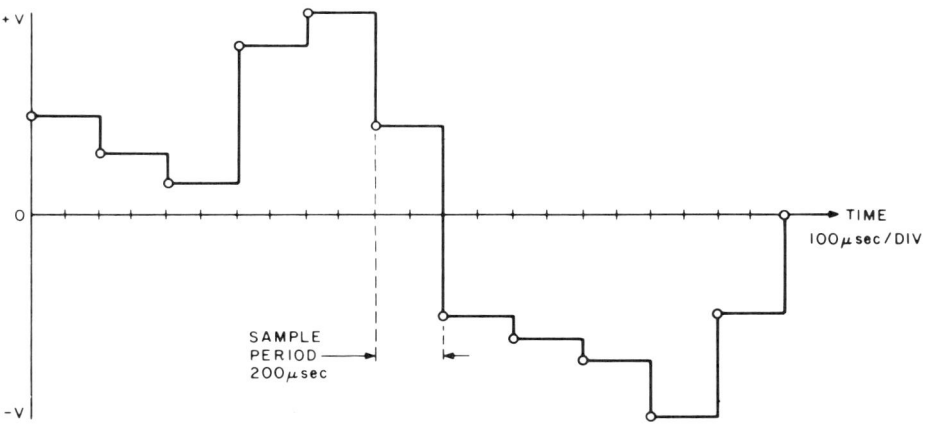

Figure 2b: Waveform in figure 2a after being processed through a digital to analog converter at a sample rate of 5000 samples per second.

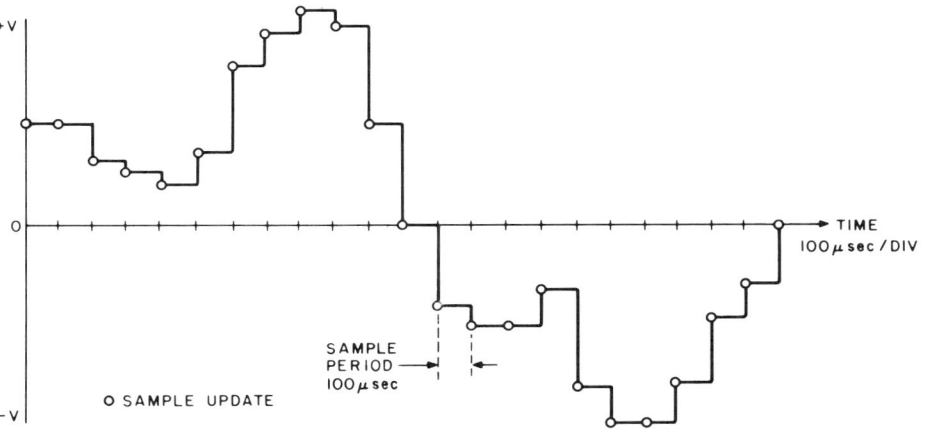

Figure 2c: Waveform in figure 2a after being processed through a digital to analog converter at a sample rate of 10,000 samples per second.

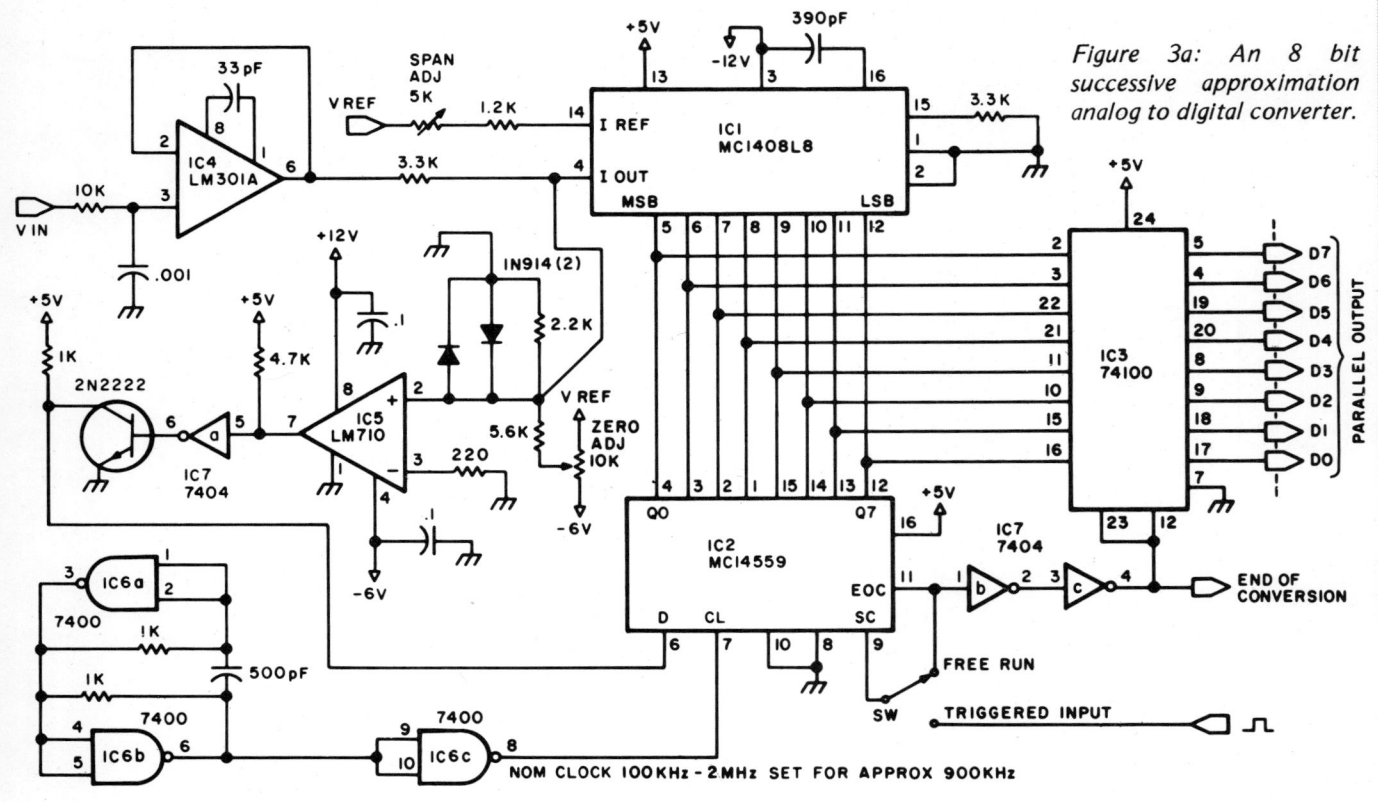

Figure 3a: An 8 bit successive approximation analog to digital converter.

Table 1: Power wiring table for figures 3a and 3b

IC Number	Type	+5 V	Gnd	+12 V	−12 V	−6 V
IC1	MC1408L8	13	1		3	
IC2	MC14559	16	8			
IC3	74100	24	7			
IC4	LM301A			7		4
IC5	LM710			8		4
IC6	7400	14	7			
IC7	7404	14	7			
IC8	MC1408L8	13	1		3	
IC9	LM301A			7	4	

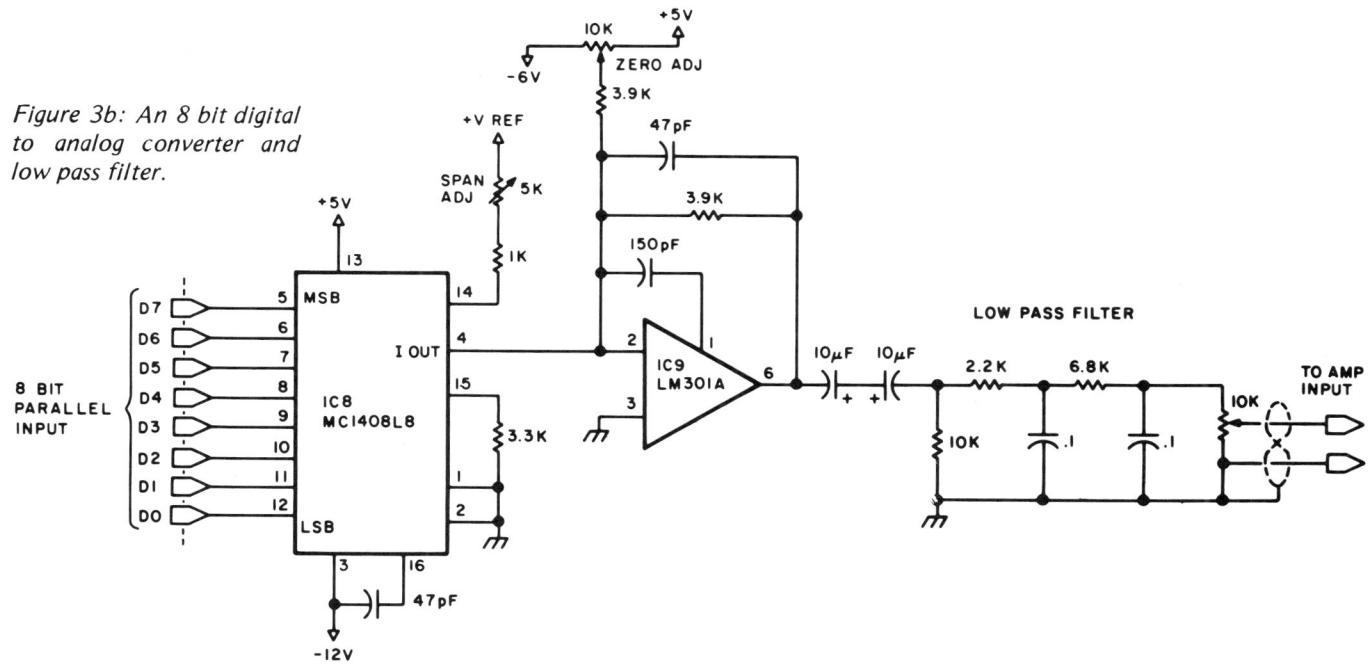

Figure 3b: An 8 bit digital to analog converter and low pass filter.

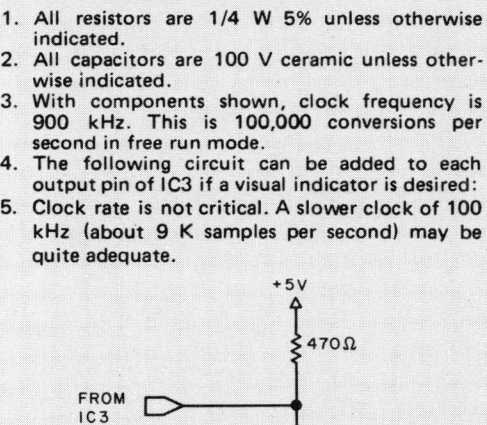

Notes for Figures 3a, 3b and 3c:

1. All resistors are 1/4 W 5% unless otherwise indicated.
2. All capacitors are 100 V ceramic unless otherwise indicated.
3. With components shown, clock frequency is 900 kHz. This is 100,000 conversions per second in free run mode.
4. The following circuit can be added to each output pin of IC3 if a visual indicator is desired:
5. Clock rate is not critical. A slower clock of 100 kHz (about 9 K samples per second) may be quite adequate.

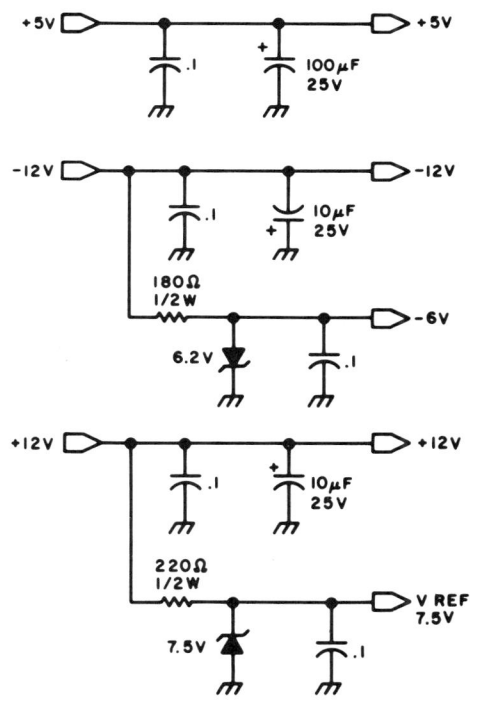

Figure 3c: Power supply circuitry for figures 3a and 3b.

25 samples within a period of one second could not effectively record the event. At what sampling rate should audio speech be digitized?

There is a specific law used to determine this rate, called the Nyquist criterion. It states that, at the very minimum, the sampling rate of the digitizer must be twice the maximum frequency of the input sample. If human voice extends to 4 kHz, the minimum sample rate should be 8 kHz. This presumes that there is an ideal low pass filter on the output of the converter. Ideal filters are something like perpetual motion, impossible to attain. In reality the sampling rate should be three or four times the highest input frequency. This means that to digitize voice fully you need a sample rate of from 12 to 16 kHz.

It is easier to explain the digitization process visually. Figure 2 illustrates an expanded view of a typical speechlike waveform. Voice waveforms are complex: the majority of the voice sounds exist below 1500 Hz, but intonation and accent occupy the higher frequencies. It is these added harmonics and inflections that make one voice different from another, and capturing and recording them is an important consideration. The waveform in figure 2 has been digitized at two different rates for comparison. Figure 2a is the original waveform which consists of a fundamental frequency of approximately 500 Hz and some added components of higher frequency. If this waveform is "digitized" or sampled at a 5000 samples per second rate and the stored values are sent to a digital to analog converter, the resultant waveform would be that shown in figure 2b. It is easy to see that only a vague representation of the original waveform would be recorded. Even though this output is filtered before being amplified, the higher frequency components of the original input would be lost. Increasing the sampling rate to 10,000 samples per second as in figure 2c gives a better record of the higher frequencies. The addition of a good low pass filter would eliminate the sharp transitions between samples.

Tradeoffs to be Considered

The benefits associated with the reduced cost of the voice input and output circuitry are counteracted by the increased memory requirements. Digitized speech uses a lot of memory. In the previous example, if the voice input is sampled at 10,000 samples per second, the table in memory needed to store one second of data would be 10,000 bytes long (presuming an 8 bit analog to digital converter). If increased fidelity is required and the sampling rate is set for 16 kHz, the table would fill up at a rate of 16,000 bytes per second.

Obviously, systems like my own, which already have considerable amounts of programmable memory, would be easy to use for experimenting with digital speech. I do not recommend buying additional memory just to store a few words, but, if you have it, you'll be surprised at the results.

Building a Voice Digitizer

To experiment fully with digitized speech, it is necessary to have a high speed analog to digital converter to store the analog input and a high speed digital to analog converter to reconstruct the analog output.

Figure 3a shows the schematic of an 8 bit analog to digital converter capable of sample rates in excess of 200,000 samples per second. With an 900 kHz clock rate it will run at a modest 100,000 samples per second. Figure 3b shows an 8 bit digital to analog converter and low pass filter with similar capabilities. The estimated total cost for parts is $35.

The analog to digital converter is a general purpose high speed 8 bit converter that can be used for any data acquisition application requiring high speed. The technique used to attain this speed is called successive approxi-

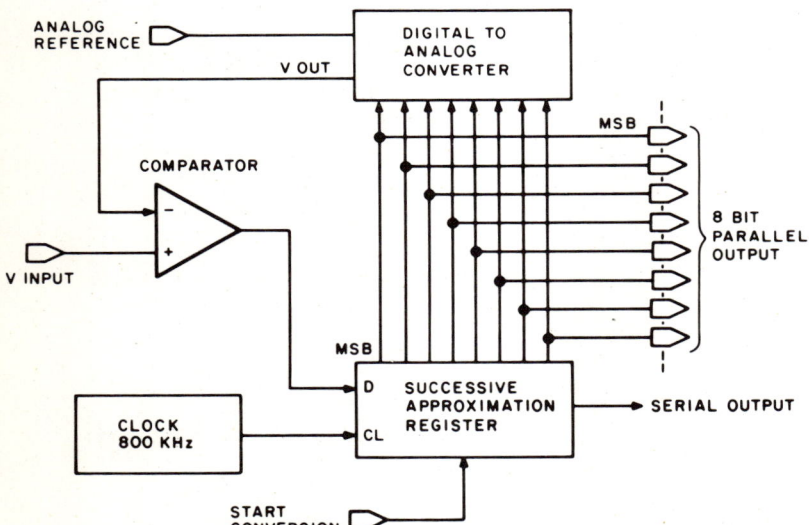

Figure 4: Block diagram of a typical successive approximation analog to digital converter. The device uses a digital to analog converter to perform its function. The successive approximation register is initially set to 0. After a start conversion pulse, the register enables the output bits one at a time, starting with the most significant bit (MSB). As each bit is enabled, the comparator gives an output signifying whether the amplitude of the input signal is greater than or less than the amplitude of the digital to analog converter. If the converter output is greater, the bit in question is set equal to 0. Otherwise it is set to 1. The process continues for the remaining bits until the conversion is complete.

mation. The circular logic of successive approximation is best explained in a block diagram (see figure 4).

Initially, the output of the Successive Approximation Register (SAR) and mutually connected digital to analog converter is at a zero level. After a start conversion pulse, the register enables the output bits one at a time starting with the most significant bit (MSB). As each bit is enabled, the comparator gives an output signifying whether the amplitude of the input signal is greater than or less than the amplitude of the converter. If the converter output is greater, that particular bit is set equal to 0; if less than, it is set to 1. The register moves successively to the next least significant bit (retaining the setting on the previously tested bit or bits) and performs the same test. After all the bits of the converter have been tested, an EOC is output and then the conversion cycle is complete. The entire conversion period takes only nine clock cycles, and another conversion begins on the next clock pulse when in free run mode. To retain the 8 bit value between conversions, an 8 bit register (IC3) has been added (see "Control the World," page 47 for a complete description of MC1408 digital to analog converter operation).

Assembly and Testing

1. Component types and values are chosen to allow high speed operation. Substitution of slower devices may compromise overall performance.
2. Assemble components on a prototype board as neatly as possible. Keep wires between components short and direct. The MC14559 is a CMOS device and it should be handled carefully. Sockets are suggested for all integrated circuits.
3. Check power supply voltage before inserting integrated circuits. Then insert clock oscillator IC6. The clock frequency should be around 900 kHz.
4. Insert the rest of the integrated circuits and ground the V input connection of IC4. Slowly rotate the zero adjust pot until the parallel output of IC3 reads binary 10000000. This output can be read either through a computer program which scans and displays this value or with LEDs attached to the output pins. In practice, the LEDs are easier in the long run.
5. Remove the short on V input and apply a voltage of +2 V. Adjust the span adjust pot until the displayed output is 11111111. The result of this procedure is an analog to digital converter with an input range of −2 to +2 V represented by binary 00000000 and 11111111 patterns respectively. 0 V is represented by 10000000. Any voltage span between + and −5 V can be set on this circuit using this method.
6. The digital to analog converter section should be assembled with the same care. Insert all ICs. With all parallel input pins at a logic zero level, adjust the zero pot until IC9 pin 6 reads 0 V.
7. With all parallel input pins at a logic 1 level, adjust the span pot until the output at IC9 pin 6 equals the +V setting of the analog to digital converter, or as in the example (2 V).
8. The low pass filter in the schematic is optimized for the speech samples in the text, but can be experimentally determined. The optimum cut off frequency of the low pass filter should be the sampling rate frequency. (ie: 10 kHz cut off for 10 kHz sample rate).
9. The easiest way to test the entire unit is to attach the analog to digital converter output to the digital to analog converter input. What goes in should come out! Since both units would be running continuously at the 100,000 samples per second rate, this will give the experimenter firsthand knowledge of the ultimate fidelity of the system. Don't expect miracles with an 8 bit unit; 12 bit units would be far superior, but 8 bit precision is more than adequate. A standard cassette recorder in the record mode serves as a handy amplifier. The amplified output is available at the earphone jack on most recorders.

Using the Interface with a Computer

Not everyone will want to add a voice to their home computer but the concept is none the less intriguing. Once you have built the analog to digital converter and digital to analog converter of figure 3 you are ready to digitize the spoken word. Listing 1 is a simple program that reads the analog to digital converter output and puts the values sequentially in a memory table. Hardware for the experiment should be arranged as in figure 1b. When the program is executed it will scan the input port containing the analog to digital converter information and will compare this value to hexadecimal A8 (when speech is started, the audio level will presumably exceed this trigger level). The amplifier should be adjusted to eliminate false triggering because of background noise.

When the input level is attained, the digitization process begins. The program sets the beginning address of the memory table and sequentially reads the input port and stores the value. The rate at which the sampling occurs is determined by the value of a constant, "SAMP." A value of hexadecimal 38 is approximately 3 kHz on my Z-80 system. When the table is filled, the program stops. All programs in this article, while written on a Z-80, use only 8080 instructions.

Once the table is filled with digital values corresponding to a voice input, we are ready for the next phase: voice output. The hardware is configured as in figure 1b, and the output program shown in listing 2 should be used. The same values as those of the input program should be used for START, END and SAMP. When the program is executed, the recorded data gives a speech output.

As with most computer experimenters, hearing is believing. To allow people to try out the concept without having to construct the analog to digital converter I have included a predigitized listing of a few words. This 2000 byte listing (listing 3), will say "Talk to me" when read out using the program of listing 2. Since I could not presume that everyone had the patience to hand load a 10,000 byte table with good fidelity, a compromise was in order. The sample rate on this table is only 3 kHz, but the speech will still be understandable. It should also be realized that since this example of digitized speech is actually recorded sounds, the words "Talk to me" will be in my voice. The fact that I have a fairly low voice allows understandable speech even at these very low sample rates.

More Advanced Applications

I don't want you to finish this article and think that digitized speech is as limited as I have represented it so far. It is possible to totally simulate the capabilities of an analog speech synthesizer with more involved software. If you realize that the analog synthesizer works by connecting strings of distinctly independent phonemes, it is not hard to consider that the same can be true for the digital method. Each phoneme could be recorded separately and would occupy approximately 2 K bytes. As in the analog situation, a separate control program determines how these individual phonemes are to be connected together. Besides determining the type of phoneme to be used, the processor must also create the waveform. Such a system uses significantly more memory and processing time than something like the Votrax, but it is equally as versatile.■

Listing 1: An 8080 assembler program that reads the 8 bit parallel output of the analog to digital converter and stores the samples sequentially in memory. This assembly uses octal notation for machine codes.

```
120000                  0100 *
120000                  0110 *
120000                  0120 * VOICE TO MEMORY TABLE TEST PROGRAM *
120000                  0130 *          S.CIARCIA
120000                  0140 *
120000                  0150 *
120000                  0160 START  EQU  010000 MEMORY TABLE START HL ADDRESS
120000                  0170 END    EQU  110    MEMORY TABLE END H ADDRESS
120000                  0180 TRIG   EQU  250    INPUT START CONVERSION LEVEL
120000                  0190 IPORT  EQU  020    A/D INPUT PORT NUMBER
120000                  0200 SAMP   EQU  070    SAMPLE RATE TIME CONSTANT
120000                  0210 *
120000                  0220 *
120000                  0230 *
120000 333 020          0240 INP    IN   IPORT  READ A/D INPUT VALUE
120002 376 250          0250         CP   TRIG   COMP. INPUT TO CONVERT TRIGGER LEVEL
120004 302 000 120      0260         JP   NZ,INP LOOP AGAIN IF NOT SUFFICIENT LEVEL
120007 041 000 010      0270         LD   HL,START LOAD TABLE START ADDRESS
120012 333 020          0280 AGAIN  IN   IPORT  TAKE A SAMPLE
120014 167              0290         LD   (HL),A STORE SAMPLE IN MEMORY
120015 315 030 120      0300         CALL DELY   SAMPLE TIME DELAY
120020 043              0310         INC  HL
120021 174              0320         LD   A,H
120022 376 110          0330         CP   END    TEST TO SEE IF AT END OF TABLE
120024 302 012 120      0340         JP   NZ,AGAIN IF NOT TAKE ANOTHER SAMPLE
120027 166              0350         HALT
120030                  0360 *
120030                  0370 *
120030                  0380 * SAMPLE RATE TIMING LOOP *
120030 006 070          0390 DELY   LD   B,SAMP
120032 005              0400 DCR    DEC  B
120033 302 032 120      0410         JP   NZ,DCR
120036 311              0420         RET
```

Listing 2: An 8080 assembler program designed to output digital speech samples to the digital to analog converter at the correct rate. This assembly uses octal notation for machine codes.

```
120000                    0100 *
120000                    0110 *
120000                    0120 * MEMORY TABLE TO VOICE OUTPUT TEST PROGRAM *
120000                    0130 *           S.CIARCIA
120000                    0140 *
120000                    0150 *
120000                    0160 START  EQU  010000  MEMORY TABLE START HL ADDRESS
120000                    0170 END    EQU  012     MEMORY TABLE END H ADDRESS
120000                    0180 OPORT  EQU  022     D/A OUTPUT PORT NUMBER
120000                    0190 SAMP   EQU  070     SAMPLE RATE TIME CONSTANT
120000                    0200 *
120000                    0210 *
120000                    0220 *
120000 041 000 010        0230        LD   HL,START  LOAD TABLE START ADDRESS
120003 176                0240 AGAIN  LD   A,(HL)    TABLE VALUE TO ACCUMULATOR
120004 323 022            0250        OUT  OPORT,A   OUTPUT BYTE TO D/A
120006 315 021 120        0260        CALL DELY      SAMPLE TIME DELAY
120011 043                0270        INC  HL
120012 174                0280        LD   A,H
120013 376 012            0290        CP   END       TEST TO SEE IF AT END OF TABLE
120015 302 003 120        0300        JP   NZ,AGAIN  IF NOT OUTPUT THE NEXT SAMPLE
120020 166                0310        HALT
120021                    0320 *
120021                    0330 *
120021                    0340 * SAMPLE RATE TIMING LOOP *
120021 006 070            0350 DELY   LD   B,SAMP
120023 005                0360 DCR    DEC  B
120024 302 023 120        0370        JP   NZ,DCR
120027 311                0380        RET
```

Listing 3: A listing of the digital samples making up the phrase, "Talk to me" spoken by the author. This somewhat bandwidth limited signal allows interested readers to reproduce the message through an 8 bit digital to analog converter without having to build the analog to digital converter.

```
THE FOLLOWING LIST HAS THE ADDRESS LOCATION IN DECIMAL
ALL MEMORY BYTE VALUES ARE GIVEN IN OCTAL NOTATION
32768    277    307    320    250    177    140    077    037    001    000
32778    000    000    000    027    101    220    274    303    300    260
32788    213    210    174    147    100    054    007    001    014    007
32798    003    030    047    040    050    037    050    060    077    140
32808    170    234    203    170    156    117    060    037    047    060
32818    034    003    040    076    077    140    150    127    053    060
32828    037    040    077    137    113    060    077    117    060    057
32838    043    060    076    067    120    077    157    200    174    137
32848    160    140    077    107    077    067    060    070    057    041
32858    044    037    041    034    017    027    040    037    023    060
32868    070    043    060    054    047    060    056    037    040    070
32878    047    045    074    037    060    074    077    140    077    037
32888    377    370    004    123    220    274    127    000    136    047
32898    000    000    000    000    000    077    377    260    000    100
32908    176    377    107    000    077    357    240    017    000    240
32918    130    000    000    000    000    000    377    377    000    000
32928    177    263    320    000    000    240    357    133    000    036
32938    227    020    000    017    000    000    227    377    130    000
32948    101    240    317    061    000    077    377    120    057    043
32958    140    077    000    020    007    000    000    377    377    000
32968    000    277    300    220    000    000    330    314    000    077
32978    137    067    040    016    023    000    000    000    377    377
32988    000    000    344    257    120    000    000    363    174    000
32998    147    140    037    027    030    017    000    000    077    377
33008    240    000    067    340    224    047    000    076    377    040
33018    000    177    063    050    017    003    010    000    000    377
33028    377    000    000    277    237    150    000    000    311    274
33038    000    140    170    037    040    034    017    000    000    037
33048    377    300    000    107    320    230    043    000    137    377
33058    000    056    157    040    074    007    020    004    000    000
33068    377    377    000    050    316    227    140    000    027    370
33078    074    057    101    077    077    000    054    003    000    000
33088    377    377    000    017    221    260    234    000    030    356
33098    147    060    034    147    060    000    067    000    000    000
33108    377    377    000    017    210    237    213    000    077    303
33118    140    037    047    140    014    007    074    000    007    040
33128    000    377    245    000    237    067    220    117    013    200
33138    016    113    060    017    047    020    077    017    074    077
33148    017    140    177    157    141    130    137    120    120    077
33158    047    070    057    057    060    057    047    070    077    073
33168    076    077    107    120    134    117    100    077    077    060
33178    064    027    020    036    037    040    074    067    120    120
33188    077    120    076    137    061    130    077    067    120    077
33198    107    100    077    077    120    130    200    120    120    136
33208    103    130    077    077    120    077    077    071    077    077
33218    100    077    077    100    076    077    070    074    067    060
33228    070    057    061    070    057    060    070    057    060    070
33238    057    061    074    077    100    076    077    077    076    077
33248    073    074    077    067    070    077    067    074    077    067
33258    100    077    077    100    077    077    100    077    077    073
33268    076    077    101    076    077    101    120    077    077    100
33278    077    077    100    077    077    075    076    077    101    077
33288    077    101    077    077    075    076    077    077    076    077
33298    073    070    077    067    074    077    067    074    077    073
33308    074    077    077    074    077    077    073    077    077    075
33318    077    077    073    076    077    071    076    077    070    076
33328    077    077    061    074    077    057    061    076    067    067
33338    063    074    077    063    074    077    067    076    077    067
33348    074    077    067    074    077    074    077    073    077    100
33358    077    077    100    077    077    100    077    077    101    077
33368    077    101    076    077    101    076    077    077    110    077
33378    077    110    077    077    101    077    077    101    077    077
```

Listing 3, continued:

```
33388   101   077   077   077   076   077   073   076   077   077
33398   076   077   077   074   077   077   074   077   077   074
33408   077   073   074   077   077   074   077   077   071   077
33418   077   070   076   067   070   076   067   070   076   067
33428   060   074   067   061   076   067   063   074   067   063
33438   074   067   063   074   077   071   074   077   067   074
33448   077   067   074   077   067   074   077   067   074   077
33458   073   074   077   077   100   072   077   100   077   077
33468   101   076   077   101   076   077   101   120   077   077
33478   120   077   077   103   077   077   103   077   077   077
33488   110   077   077   110   077   077   076   077   077   076
33498   077   077   074   077   077   071   076   077   071   076
33508   077   071   076   077   071   076   077   071   076   077
33518   065   074   077   067   074   077   065   074   077   063
33528   074   077   063   074   077   063   070   077   063   074
33538   077   063   074   077   063   074   077   067   074   077
33548   067   074   077   067   070   077   067   070   077   073
33558   100   077   077   100   077   077   101   077   077   073
33568   120   077   077   110   077   077   110   077   077   120
33578   077   077   110   077   077   103   077   077   077   110
33588   077   077   100   077   077   100   077   077   100   077
33598   077   100   077   077   073   077   077   071   076   077
33608   073   076   077   071   077   077   061   140   217   143
33618   076   057   053   140   077   013   040   077   063   020
33628   074   057   060   077   077   101   057   027   020   060
33638   027   060   077   143   120   077   077   120   130   077
33648   107   070   076   067   120   137   147   140   077   077
33658   120   134   077   140   130   077   120   074   077   063
33668   077   077   027   060   077   123   074   074   021   030
33678   057   007   070   037   027   040   077   127   140   137
33688   137   200   150   077   060   040   037   020   030   017
33698   013   060   057   063   100   077   107   140   137   137
33708   140   144   147   140   134   077   063   074   047   040
33718   036   037   043   074   077   100   074   077   100   140
33728   137   137   140   134   077   070   074   047   070   077
33738   117   111   120   077   121   140   137   161   174   156
33748   117   074   076   047   040   037   017   020   003   000
33758   000   277   317   320   174   077   010   040   077   121
33768   076   017   073   070   077   051   070   027   000   000
33778   002   000   000   017   147   370   276   147   040   077
33788   077   200   140   117   000   040   017   121   140   167
33798   043   060   017   023   000   000   000   000   157   243
33808   360   260   107   010   134   157   200   130   077   000
33818   030   037   101   077   157   133   074   057   073   060
33828   007   000   000   000   027   220   277   227   103   077
33838   067   140   160   147   043   040   017   040   060   077
33848   073   150   137   127   060   077   043   020   007   001
33858   000   034   147   200   230   177   140   130   117   127
33868   077   077   053   050   037   041   060   076   101   130
33878   077   107   120   077   067   060   056   037   040   037
33888   057   100   150   147   147   160   137   121   120   077
33898   073   070   074   043   060   057   053   100   077   117
33908   120   120   077   061   070   037   040   054   037   071
33918   134   137   153   160   137   127   140   077   077   070
33928   074   047   060   070   057   074   077   117   121   134
33938   077   073   074   047   041   050   037   040   060   077
33948   120   160   157   133   140   077   077   100   077   057
33958   060   060   043   060   074   067   100   077   117   121
33968   077   077   061   064   037   040   050   037   041   076
33978   077   140   150   154   127   120   077   077   070   076
33988   057   040   060   047   060   076   077   120   134   137
33998   111   077   077   047   070   037   041   060   057   067
34008   120   137   143   144   154   137   120   077   077   071
34018   074   057   051   064   057   060   076   077   120   140
34028   077   103   076   076   057   060   037   041   040   057
34038   067   120   137   147   140   140   117   120   077   077
34048   063   070   057   047   070   057   061   074   077   117
34058   140   077   077   074   076   057   060   056   037   060
34068   057   067   120   137   137   140   140   117   107   120
34078   077   063   070   057   041   060   057   057   074   077
34088   107   120   077   077   100   076   057   060   056   037
34098   040   037   077   120   154   137   141   150   077   123
34108   120   077   063   060   037   040   060   076   057   076
34118   077   147   140   134   077   063   060   037   040   034
34128   007   001   020   077   140   230   176   167   120   137
34138   077   140   077   067   040   054   033   060   077   067
34148   100   077   147   140   140   077   063   060   037   040
34158   040   027   005   020   037   160   174   237   167   160
34168   137   077   120   077   077   040   056   007   041   074
34178   057   070   076   117   140   150   077   073   074   057
34188   047   050   037   023   020   034   027   170   177   207
34198   200   136   137   100   130   077   067   070   037   041
34208   060   067   061   074   077   105   140   137   117   076
34218   074   057   060   037   033   040   017   007   040   170
34228   163   201   174   137   140   077   077   077   074   076
34238   041   060   057   053   074   077   101   120   136   143
34248   120   077   067   060   070   047   041   057   027   040
34258   034   047   140   160   177   200   140   137   101   076
34268   077   067   070   057   033   060   057   063   074   077
34278   103   140   140   127   100   076   067   060   070   047
34288   040   054   037   040   070   077   140   170   157   141
34298   140   077   117   110   077   077   060   070   057   060
34308   077   067   074   077   117   121   130   077   063   070
34318   057   041   070   047   043   077   047   061   074   077
34328   121   160   176   141   120   077   077   100   077   067
34338   060   070   047   060   076   077   100   077   117   121
34348   120   077   063   070   047   043   070   057   061   060
34358   057   061   120   137   147   160   137   107   120   077
34368   077   074   076   057   060   057   047   060   077   077
34378   121   120   077   073   074   077   060   070   057   053
34388   070   057   061   074   077   133   160   154   127   120
34398   077   077   100   077   077   070   074   057   060   077
34408   077   077   120   120   077   070   074   060   070   057
34418   047   070   057   061   074   077   063   140   137   133
34428   140   130   077   100   077   077   071   077   077   063
34438   076   067   060   074   057   060   070   047   040   070
34448   077   140   140   156   137   130   077   077   100   077
34458   067   060   057   043   060   076   067   100   077   077
34468   100   077   077   063   076   057   060   070   067   061
34478   074   077   100   077   077   103   120   077   117   120
34488   077   077   107   077   077   075   076   077   067   074
34498   077   065   074   077   067   076   077   063   120   137
```

Listing 3, continued:

```
34508    123    140    136    107    100    077    067    070    074    057
34518    060    074    057    060    076    057    060    077    067    070
34528    076    067    070    076    077    100    077    077    107    077
34538    077    077    100    077    077    070    077    067    070    076
34548    063    070    076    057    070    076    067    100    077    067
34558    070    077    077    100    076    077    100    077    077    100
34568    076    077    073    077    077    077    100    077    073    074
34578    077    073    100    077    077    110    077    077    100    077
34588    077    077    077    077    077    100    077    077    110    077
34598    077    100    077    077    074    077    077    100    077    077
34608    101    077    077    075    076    077    065    074    077    063
34618    074    077    067    076    077    071    076    077    067    074
34628    067    061    070    077    061    074    077    063    074    077
34638    063    074    077    067    070    077    067    070    077    063
34648    070    077    067    074    077    077    100    077    077    101
34658    077    077    100    076    077    067    074    077    071    076
34668    077    077    076    077    077    100    077    077    100    077
34678    077    103    120    077    101    120    077    103    120    077
34688    077    120    077    077    100    077    077    100    077    077
34698    100    077    077    075    077    077    077    076    077    073
34708    074    077    067    074    077    073    074    077    071    074
34718    077    067    074    077    063    070    076    053    070    077
34728    063    070    077    067    074    077    067    074    077    067
34738    074    077    067    070    077    067    070    076    067    070
34748    076    077    070    076    077    100    077    077    073    077
34758    077    073    074    077    073    076    077    077    120    077
34768    077    110    077    077    101    077    077    103    120    077
34778    103    110    077    077    110    077    077    110    077    077
34788    100    077    077    100    077    077    075    077    077    075
34798    076    077    075    076    077    073    076    077    073    074
34808    077    067    070    077    067    074    077    073    155    014
```

Build a Keyboard Function Decoder

"Dear, when you go downstairs would you turn the printer on for me?"

My wife Joyce was on her way to the basement with an armload of photographic supplies. "And could you see if I turned the video display off as well?"

I was reclining in an overstuffed chair with the keyboard in my lap. Joyce stopped at the doorway and said, "Who was your last servant?"

"Please do it for me, honey," I said, chastened. "I have papers all over my lap and you wouldn't want me to spill my martini, would you?"

"Hey, kid, I thought computers were supposed to make life easier for us poor folk."

"They do! It's the peripherals that don't."

The next logical question I asked myself was: why shouldn't turning the printer or recorder on and off be as easy to do as any other computer transaction? A couple of quick solutions came to mind. One is to install an intercom system and station a person next to the computer while the remote terminal is in operation.

A second and more practical alternative is to put long extensions on the power lines of your peripherals and apply power to them from a remote location, but this means rewiring your house if the computer is downstairs and the terminal is upstairs (as in my case).

The third and probably best approach is to use some of the unused functions on your keyboard to control peripherals remotely. There are a number of unprinted characters on a keyboard such as: end of transmission, end of text, or device control codes. By attaching an ASCII decoding circuit to monitor the line between the keyboard and the computer, these functions can be isolated and utilized as peripheral device control signals — more about this later.

The ASCII Code

Most keyboards use ASCII coding, a 7 bit binary code with an eighth bit sometimes added for parity checking. (Here we ignore the proposed extensions to the officially defined ASCII code which makes it a true 8 bit code or nine bits with parity.) A complete list of ASCII codes is outlined in "Complete ASCII" by Dave Ciemiewicz (February 1978 BYTE, page 19). When your computer program is executing and awaiting data from the keyboard, a special keyboard input routine is usually activated in the program. The subroutine first determines whether a key has been pressed by checking for a key-pressed strobe signal. On systems that do not check parity (and thus use only 7 bit ASCII), the eighth bit of an input port is often set as the strobe bit. The other seven bits are not considered unless this strobe bit is "true." When this is the case, the seven bits are compared to a valid entry table within the program to determine what to do with the input. If there is no valid comparison, the input key does nothing.

The software read and compare routine is analogous to a hardware address decoder. For a particular ASCII code like CONTROL R hexadecimal 12, a circuit such as that in figure 1 could be used to decode and identify only this particular code. For routine uses such as a hardware reset, this is the way many computer experimenters decode an ASCII code. This basic circuit can be duplicated many times to decode other codes. Figure 2 illustrates how this approach can enable a CONTROL R to turn on a device

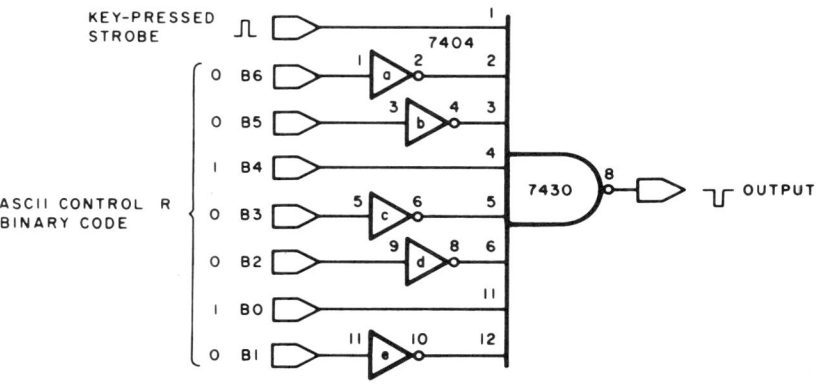

Figure 1: Sample hardware circuit to decode a single control code (in this case, CONTROL R). The pulse output width is the same as that of the key pressed strobe.

Figure 2: Printer on and off control designed with discrete logic elements. Pressing CONTROL R causes a logic signal to activate an external relay in series with the printer power line. Pressing CONTROL T resets this circuit and turns the printer off.

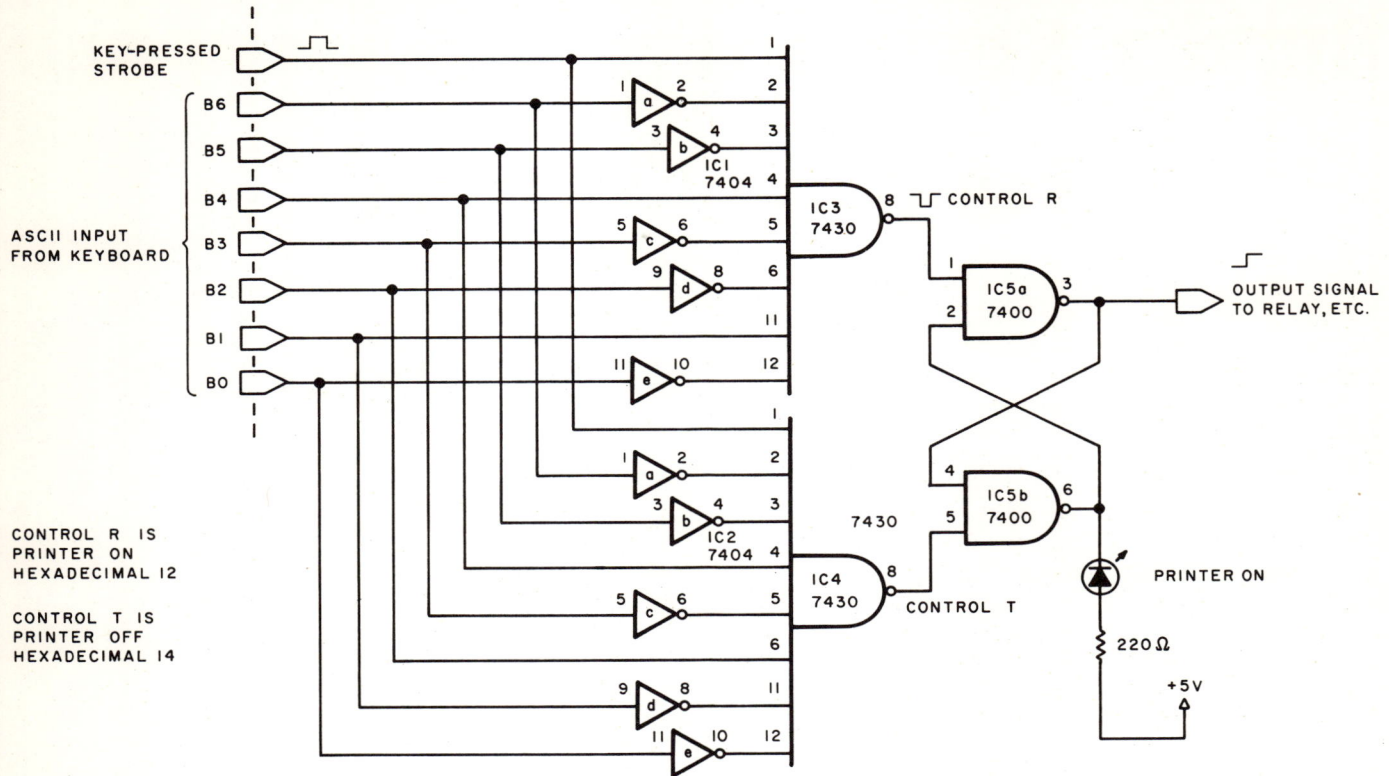

such as a printer, and a CONTROL T to turn it off. The method reaches a point of diminishing returns when more than one device is to be controlled, though.

Another disadvantage of this handwired decoding is that it is difficult to change the decoded value. I recently received a letter from a reader who needed a remote reset button. He built a circuit similar to the one in figure 1, and it worked fine for the software he was using at the time. But when he changed from MaxiBASIC to Zapple BASIC, he found that the control code he had chosen for reset was necessary for use in the BASIC, so out came the soldering iron and in went another integrated circuit. Then came the expansion of more software from other manufacturers, and the circuit had to be changed again. His complaint was concerned not with the method of decoding the signal but rather with the difficulty in changing its particular address.

I, of course, wanted to have a hardware reset and peripheral device controller. I could build a combination of the circuits in figures 1 and 2 and hope that the next piece of software I get doesn't use one of the control codes I used, but a concept this simple shouldn't require that much wiring or make it that hard to change addresses.

Since I like the idea of using the keyboard to control the peripheral devices and don't like to solder any more than necessary, the best alternative for me is a programmable read only memory board control code decoder.

Consider how a programmable read only memory works: a binary code is impressed on the address input lines and, in the case of

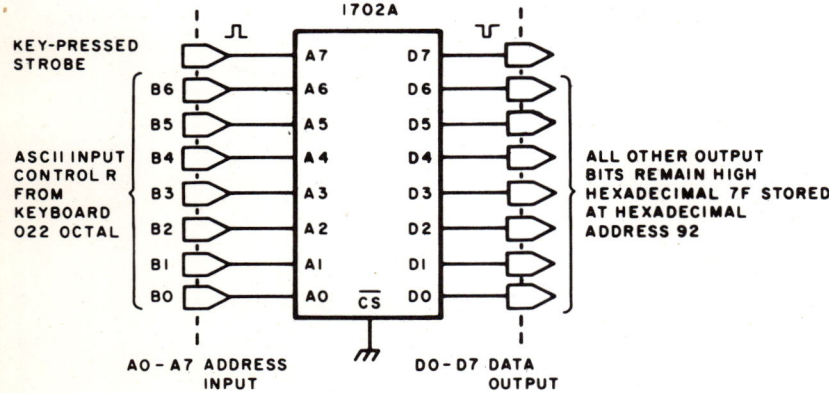

Figure 3: 1702A erasable read only memory used as an 8 bit address decoder. When CONTROL R is depressed on the keyboard, the output at D7 goes low (or true) for a period equal to that of the key-pressed strobe. This circuit can replace up to eight of the circuits shown in figure 1.

Hexadecimal	Octal	Parity	Character	Control Keyboard Equivalent	Alternate Code Names
00	000	EVEN	NUL	@	NULL, CTRL SHIFT P, TAPE LEADER
01	001	ODD	SOH	A	START OF HEADER, SOM
02	002	ODD	STX	B	START OF TEXT, EOA
03	003	EVEN	ETX	C	END OF TEXT, EOM
04	004	ODD	EQT	D	END OF TRANSMISSION, END
05	005	EVEN	ENQ	E	ENQUIRY, WRU, WHO ARE YOU
06	006	EVEN	ACK	F	ACKNOWLEDGE, RU, ARE YOU
07	007	ODD	BEL	G	BELL
08	010	ODD	BS	H	BACKSPACE, FE0
09	011	EVEN	HT	I	HORIZONTAL TAB, TAB
0A	012	EVEN	LF	J	LINE FEED, NEW LINE, NL
0B	013	ODD	VT	K	VERTICAL TAB, VTAB
0C	014	EVEN	FF	L	FORM FEED, FORM PAGE
0D	015	ODD	CR	M	CARRIAGE RETURN, EOL
0E	016	ODD	SO	N	SHIFT OUT, RED SHIFT
0F	017	EVEN	SI	O	SHIFT IN, BLACK SHIFT
10	020	ODD	DLE	P	DATA LINK ESCAPE, DC0
11	021	EVEN	DC1	Q	XON, READER ON
12	022	EVEN	DC2	R	TAPE, PUNCH ON
13	023	ODD	DC3	S	XOFF, READER OFF
14	024	EVEN	DC4	T	TAPE, PUNCH OFF
15	025	ODD	NAK	U	NEGATIVE ACKNOWLEDGE, ERR
16	026	ODD	SYN	V	SYNCHRONOUS IDLE, SYNC
17	027	EVEN	ETB	W	END OF TEXT BUFFER, LEM
18	030	EVEN	CAN	X	CANCEL, CANCL
19	031	ODD	EM	Y	END OF MEDIUM
1A	032	ODD	SUB	Z	SUBSTITUTE
1B	033	EVEN	ESC	[	ESCAPE, PREFIX
1C	034	ODD	FS	/	FILE SEPARATOR
1D	035	EVEN	GS	]	GROUP SEPARATOR
1E	036	EVEN	RS	^	RECORD SEPARATOR
1F	037	ODD	US	—	UNIT SEPARATOR

Note: To transmit any control code, depress the CTRL key while pressing the character key on the same line under Keyboard Equivalent.

Table 1: ASCII code of control characters.

the 1702A, an 8 bit binary word stored at that location appears at the output. By selectively storing specific values at designated locations in the programmable read only memory, a single 1702A can be structured to perform the functions of eight separate decoders like the one in figure 1. For example, if a CONTROL R code were impressed on the address lines of the 1702A, and hexadecimal 7F (binary 01111111) is stored in hexadecimal address 12, the most significant output bit will go low whenever this pattern appears. All other output lines will remain at a high level. The same method can be used for eight different ASCII codes. The function of the circuit shown in figure 1 can be performed by an erasable read only memory (EROM) as shown in figure 3.

To use an EROM for this purpose, first choose eight different ASCII codes which are available on your keyboard and which are not used as software control codes. By convention, CONTROL Q, CONTROL R, CONTROL S and CONTROL T have been set aside to represent Reader On, Punch On, Reader Off and Punch Off, respectively. The other four control codes could be CONTROL W, X, Y and Z, etc. Table 1 shows the ASCII control codes.

An unprogrammed (erased) EROM has all bits set to the 1 state. This is true for the 1702A, the 2708 and the 2716. Next, choose eight control codes and make a list such as the one in table 2.

Store the binary word listed at the respective address location equivalent to the ASCII code with the eighth bit (the strobe bit) set high. For a CONTROL R, a hexadecimal 14 code, this would become an address of hexadecimal 94. When one of these particular keys is pressed, a particular output bit of the EROM goes low for the duration of the keypressed strobe. Obviously, if only a short pulse is necessary for your control applica-

Table 2: Hexadecimal values to be stored in EROM to decode eight control codes.

Keyboard	Hexadecimal Code	Hexadecimal EROM Address*	Hexadecimal Value to be Stored in EROM
CTL Q	11	91	7F
CTL R	12	92	BF
CTL S	13	93	DF
CTL T	14	94	EF
CTL W	17	97	F7
CTL X	18	98	FB
CTL Y	19	99	FD
CTL Z	1A	9A	FE

Note: All other address locations should have hexadecimal FF (fully erased data) stored in them.

*The EROM address is the 7 bit ASCII code with the eighth bit set high.

tion, no further logic is necessary. In my application it is necessary to "hold" the state of three devices and pulse two of them. This requires latches made from external gates to maintain the control output after the initiating pulse. One method is to trigger an RS flip flop on and off with two separate codes. In this way, CONTROL R and CONTROL T can be used to turn the printer on and off, respectively. Figure 4 illustrates the completed keyboard function decoder utilizing a 1702A EROM. It allows latched on and off control of three devices and pulsed control of two more. I chose a 1702A because of its cost advantages: at $3.50 it is more appealing than a $12.50 2708; but the 2708 may be more easily programmed for most people (see "Program Your Next EROM in BASIC," page 39). It can be used instead of the 1702A with the appropriate pin assignment changed. Since the 2708 is a 1 K EROM and the 1702A is 256 bytes, the two extra address lines A9 and A10 should be grounded on the 2708. If you decide to use the method of figure 2 and not use an EROM to make the circuit of figure 4, it will take 14 TTL chips just to create the logical equivalent of the EROM.

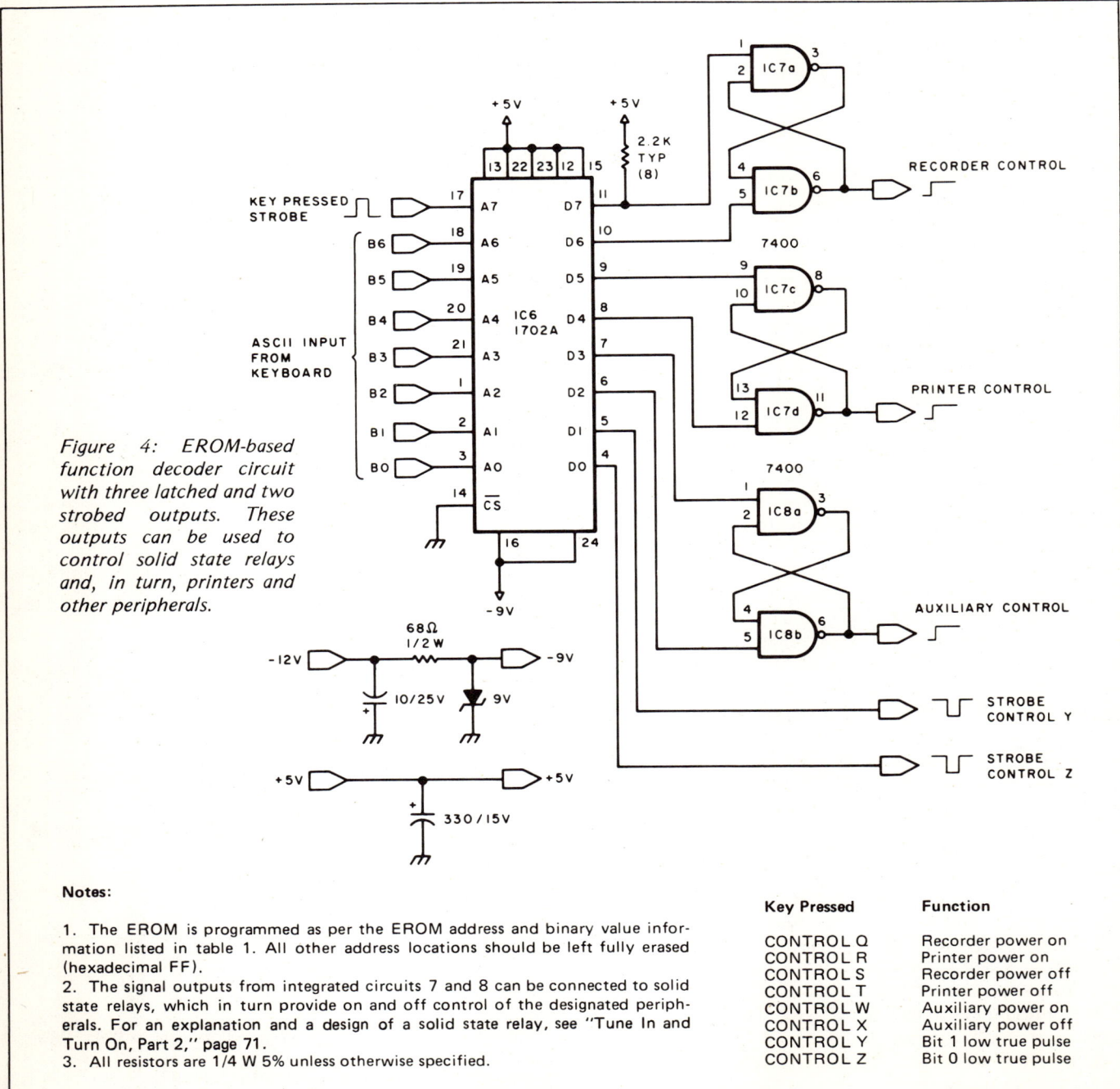

Figure 4: EROM-based function decoder circuit with three latched and two strobed outputs. These outputs can be used to control solid state relays and, in turn, printers and other peripherals.

Notes:

1. The EROM is programmed as per the EROM address and binary value information listed in table 1. All other address locations should be left fully erased (hexadecimal FF).
2. The signal outputs from integrated circuits 7 and 8 can be connected to solid state relays, which in turn provide on and off control of the designated peripherals. For an explanation and a design of a solid state relay, see "Tune In and Turn On, Part 2," page 71.
3. All resistors are 1/4 W 5% unless otherwise specified.

Key Pressed	Function
CONTROL Q	Recorder power on
CONTROL R	Printer power on
CONTROL S	Recorder power off
CONTROL T	Printer power off
CONTROL W	Auxiliary power on
CONTROL X	Auxiliary power off
CONTROL Y	Bit 1 low true pulse
CONTROL Z	Bit 0 low true pulse

Table 3: Power wiring table for figures 2 and 4.

Number	Type	+5 V	Gnd
IC1	7404	14	7
IC2	7404	14	7
IC3	7430	14	7
IC4	7430	14	7
IC5	7400	14	7
IC6	1702A	see schematic	
IC7	7400	14	7
IC8	7400	14	7

Some Final Thoughts

I guess I don't have to worry about finding someone to be my peripheral "slave" any more. The uses of this remote control system can be extended beyond the ones I've outlined; my horizons were limited at the time. Once I sit back in that chair with a keyboard in my lap, it takes an earthquake to move me. ∎

> **NOTE:** Realize, of course, that there are many other equally simple methods for decoding ASCII. These circuits are presented to illustrate one such method and discuss the use of programmable read only memory as an address decoder and driver.

Let Your Fingers Do the Talking

Part 1: Add a Noncontact Touch Scanner to Your Video Display

"Thanks for coming, Steve. I'm glad we were finally able to schedule this meeting. This problem we have is driving us crazy." Fred scurried over to me in the waiting room and shook my hand.

"Let's get you signed in at guard headquarters and then I'll introduce you to Ted."

This was the first time Fred and I had ever met. But his look of relief told me he thought I was some kind of engineering whiz kid. I picked up my briefcase and we walked to the guard's desk. The place was the prototype for a blue chip company waiting room. Decked out with numerous perfectly blended chairs and sofas, it gave the impression of slick tastefulness, and above all *money*. Current issues of various news and business magazines were arranged neatly on the highly polished end tables. I imagined somewhere within the inner depths of the company walls a heavy walnut grained office door with a brushed brass plate reading "Customer Coordinator for Waiting Room Impressions."

My "life in a big company" fantasies were interrupted as I signed my name to the guest card. Signing my name and title was the least significant thing they had me do. There were questions of citizenship, social security number and sex, statements that I represented an equal opportunity employer, and a list of subversive organizations to which I might belong. The urge to check them all and watch the bells and whistles go off was curtailed by my basic marketing instincts.

I passed the card, which ultimately revealed more information than even my wife knew about me, to the guard. He frowned and scrutinized the card carefully. The delay was agonizing as he examined every detailed answer.

"I'll have to inspect that briefcase, buddy," he said.

Surely I'm no buddy of yours, sir, I thought to myself. I fully expected the frown I usually receive when my briefcase is inspected at airports. The inspectors thumb through the piles of paperwork and, upon discovery of an issue of BYTE, quickly cover up this unusually titled magazine and gulp an embarrassed "Next!" Much to my surprise the guard seemed uninterested.

"OK, here's your visitor's badge. Remember, you have to be escorted at all times," he said, and whisked me away with a sweep of his hand.

Fred appeared relieved. I was now on the inside and hoped I could help alleviate his urgent problem.

"OK, Fred, what's your problem and how can my company help you?" This was a basic marketing question for our type of business which specializes in technical solutions through custom electronics — which really means providing engineering consulting to companies who have become embroiled in political debate over the latest in-house technical fiasco.

"We'll get to Ted's office in a few seconds and I'll let him explain. Basically we need a black box."

Before I could get the functional requirements from Fred, we arrived at Ted's office. Being introduced to Ted as "director of marketing" elicited a certain degree of respect, because in his company this was a vice-presidential position. Ted motioned me to a seat at his mahogany conference table near the window overlooking the company golf course. After asking how we wanted our coffee, he stated in a very businesslike manner, "I presume Fred has filled you in on the problem?"

Fred jumped in before I could answer, "I'm sorry, Ted, I haven't had a chance to."

Ted stood up, rotated his body 90 degrees and pointed to the video display terminal in the corner. "That's my problem! Or rather the computer types downstairs who program it!"

I looked at the display. It was a standard graphics terminal similar to those available from several manufacturers.

Ted continued, "Programmers program computers for other programmers! They never think of the user. I drag that terminal to board meetings so we can review marketing figures, and I spend half my time entering 8 digit passwords, hitting escape and control keys to select options, and answering endless quantities of mindless interrogation." Ted was getting a little hot under the collar. "Time is money in those meetings and here in my office. I don't want to spend all day playing true confessor with a computer! Its function is to display information and that's all the interaction I want."

Ted's problem was not unusual. Where a program requires that the next entry be a control R, one had better type a control R. In higher level systems operators need all kinds of cross reference manuals to communicate in the different languages.

"Look," Ted turned on the display and typed the log-on password and terminal identification. Various options were displayed. "This is what I mean. If I want one of these options, I have to type a 5 digit code, wait to give a particular file number and then some other code."

As displays flashed on the screen I couldn't help but offer the obvious question, "Ted, why can't your programmers just change the software to allow single or 2 digit entry?"

"That would be fine if the software weren't already written. We're talking about millions of dollars worth of software and I'm using only a small portion within a large operating system. I want to be able to choose what I want simply."

Ted needed a "black box" and he knew exactly what he wanted.

"I want something to replace this keyboard for the limited specific application of menu selection and display. Put a log-on button on it. When I press log-on it will send whatever information is necessary. The user should know only that he or she has to log into the system—that's all. Next, give me a key that will send the necessary message to get into the menu programs I use and then I can select the options by number. You send any other messages that are necessary."

Ted was not discussing the usual black box. He was promoting the idea of intelligent rather than dogmatic communication with the computer. A person at this level in the corporate structure could not be expected to maintain the code word and syntax library of the average programmer downstairs. What he wanted was only logical. I left the meeting with the feeling that here was a man who also realized it was time to fight rather than conform.

Perhaps if computers were programmed less for interaction with computer peripherals and more with the human operator in mind, people would be less afraid of them. Ted's application was specific and repetitive but he was still burdened with the general system protocol. In a company that probably had a thousand programmers generating software, his cry to change everything to allow simple input and output (IO) for his application would be fighting an uphill battle. He knew this and also realized that it was easier to change it at his end.

We would make Ted's black box for him and it would solve his immediate problem, but what of the future?

Do your computer input devices limit you? Many personal computer systems have this problem.

Consider a simple program to teach your child mathematics. Such a program in its least complicated form might involve a multiple choice and printout something like this:

$$4 \times 8 = 28, 30, 31, 32, \text{ or } 35$$
The right answer is?

Most BASICs would require typing 32 and a carriage return. Don't forget the carriage return! Remember, you have to conform to the input protocol of the BASIC.

Now, before I explain what I'm driving at, let me give another example. Say you want to use your system for a home management application, such as putting together a shopping list. You could list out the following on the screen:

```
1. Milk          6. Peanut butter
2. Butter        7. Dog biscuits
3. Margarine     8. Cheese
4. Eggs          9. Coffee
5. Rice         10. Tomatoes
      control P for next page
```

Obviously, the number and a carriage return could be entered to choose the items that would be ultimately listed out as a shopping list. A few pages along in the listings, though, the entry data will get more complex strictly from the sheer volume of possible choices. Most homemakers would tire of the complexity of such a system even though the concept of just choosing items from a list sounds simple.

The solution is to watch the way our young mathematics student might react when we display the expression 4 X 8 on the screen. The natural response is to *point* to the answer!

The homemaker would appreciate using a system that communicates in straightforward terms. Display a list of groceries and let the user point to the desired items.

A New Data Input Device

How do you point to a particular selection on a video display generated menu? The computer needs to know how to interpret your response regardless of the input device. The ASCII keyboard is strictly an input code to the computer. There are unique codes for each switch on the keyboard. The computer doesn't know the location of the particular key that prints an R or a Q. It recognizes only a 7 bit code for these letters. If you don't have a keyboard on your computer, but want to check out some software that needs very little typed entry, you could use seven toggle switches. It would be very slow, but the computer wouldn't care. All it's concerned about is that you present the code it wants.

The same goes for any device attached to a computer. The most obvious way to point to a video display screen and have the computer understand it is to use a light pen. Such units have been described before in BYTE so I won't go into too much detail here (see the references at the end of the article). All a light pen interface does is present to the computer, usually in the same manner as a keyboard input, a code representing a position on the video display screen. This code has to be translated by the program from a position into an action. More on this later.

But, why use a light pen? This again makes the operator conform more than necessary.

Fingers Came Before Light Pens!

Though not capable of the same positional resolution as the light pen, it is possible to design an interface that allows a noncontact data input. Photo 1 is a picture of the prototype designed to illustrate such a technique. It is an infrared scanning system that serves as a low resolution noncontact digitizer. In this particular case it is mounted on the front of a video display to approximate the function of a light pen, but it could just as easily be laid over a typed sheet of

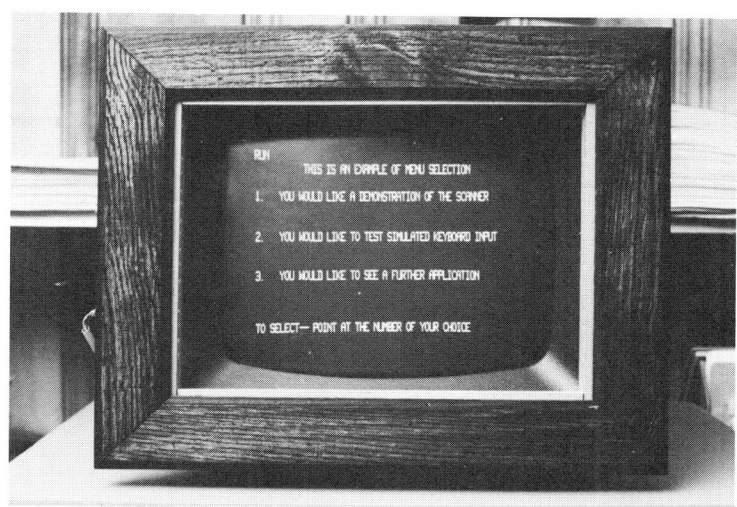

Photo 1a: Noncontact scanning digitizer in action with a BASIC program.

Photo 1b: Side view of the video monitor showing circuitry mounted on two printed circuit boards on either side of the picture frame.

Photo 2: Display showing locations of the 256 points of the array.

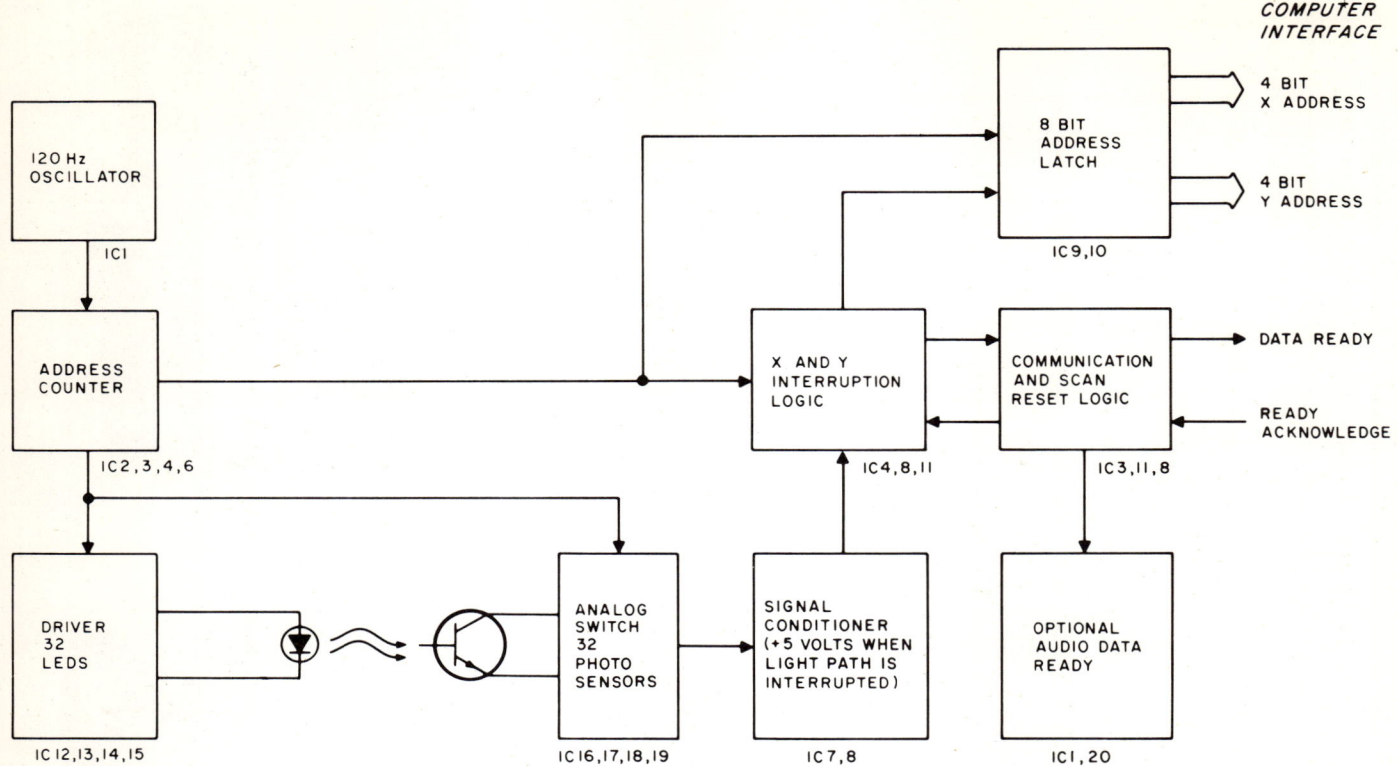

Figure 1: Block diagram of the noncontact scanning digitizer. Two rows of 16 pairs of LEDs and phototransistors are placed opposite each other in front of a video display. When the user breaks the infrared light beams with a finger or other object, a signal is sent to the computer giving the coordinates of the point in question.

paper in which position coordinates could be translated into usable relationships. I refer to it as a touch panel or touch scanner for lack of a better word.

Build Your Own Touch Panel

The touch panel is an elaborate infrared scanner. There are 32 pairs of infrared light emitting diode (LED) transmitters and receivers mounted around the perimeter of the screen. There are 16 on the X (or horizontal) axis and 16 on the Y (or vertical) axis. The resolution of such a device is therefore 16 by 16, and there are 256 individual points. Photo 2 shows this grid system.

Figure 1 is the block diagram of the system, and figure 2 shows the detailed schematics of the system. The noncontact digitizer is basically a hardware stepping circuit that turns on each transmitter/receiver pair sequentially and checks to see if anything (like a finger or a pencil) is blocking the beam. The transmitters and receivers are on opposite sides of the board, as illustrated in figure 3. The lower left corner is position (0,0) in a Cartesian coordinate system. The upper right is location (15,15).

The hardware first turns on the pair D_0 and Q_0 and then sequences down the line along the horizontal (X) axis to D_{15} and Q_{15}. Only one pair is energized at any one time. If any of the beams within these 16 pairs is obstructed, the 4 bit binary code for that location is loaded into IC9. The scan continues in the Y direction in a similar manner and the 4 bit Y position is loaded into IC10. If the hardware senses that something is obstructing an X and Y beam within one scan around the perimeter, it sets a data ready flag and stops the scanner.

The data presented to the computer is an 8 bit word representing a 4 bit X coordinate and a 4 bit Y coordinate. These lines are simply tied to a parallel input port, in the same manner as all the other devices I design. The data ready bit can be read either as a single bit input on another port, or as a control line on a more intelligent interface. When the program senses that the data ready is high, it reads the scanner data and momentarily pulses the ready reset line low to start the scan cycle again.

Use a Picture Frame

The heart of the system is the LEDs and phototransistors shown in photo 3. The device on the left is a General Electric LED 56 and the photodarlington detector used with

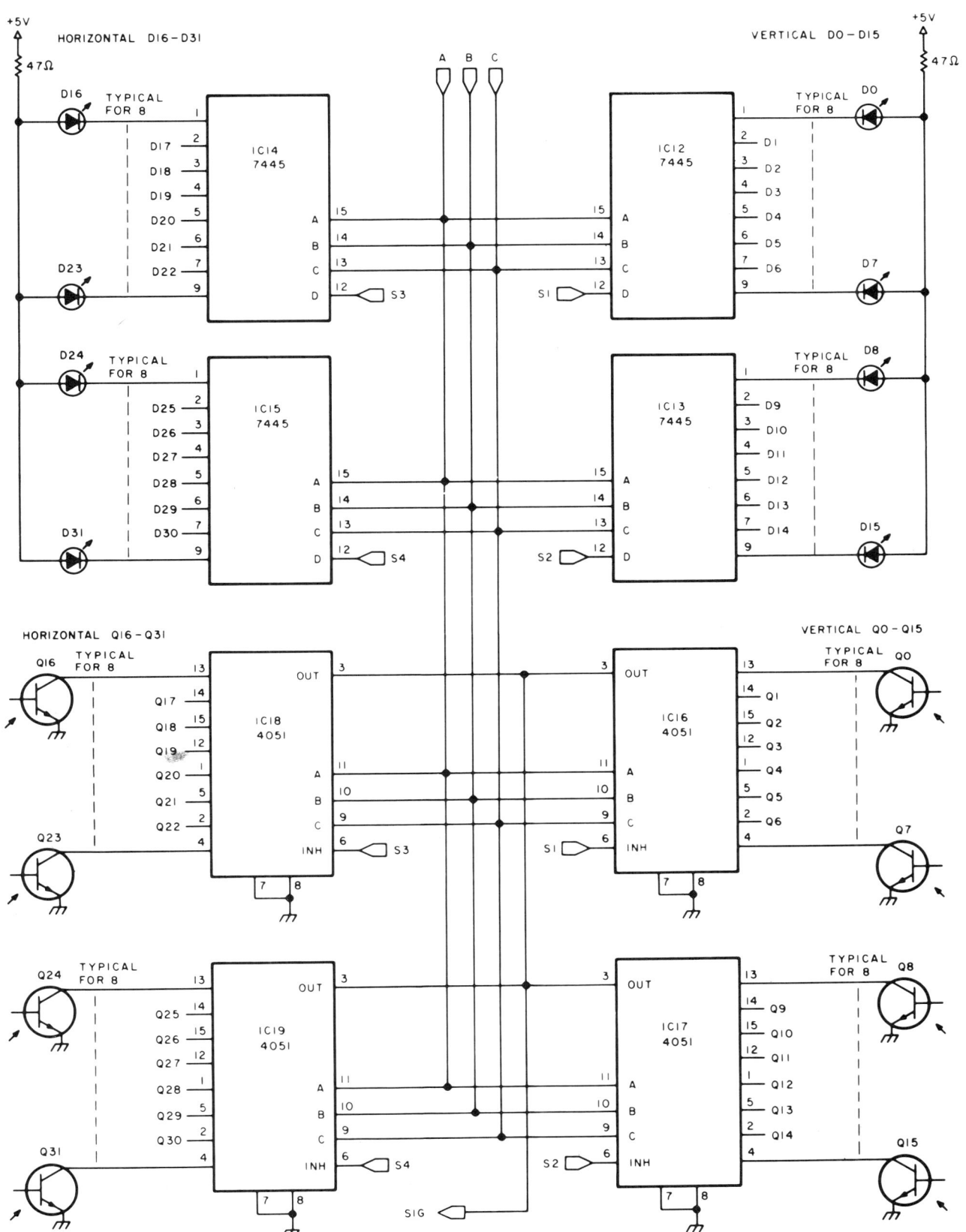

Figure 2a: LED driver and optical receiver circuitry for the noncontact digitizer. Each transmitter/receiver pair (consisting of an LED and phototransistor) is activated sequentially via lines A, B and C. D0 and Q0 are turned on first, and the sequence continues down the horizontal axis to D15 and Q15. If any of the beams is broken, the 4 bit binary code for that location is loaded into IC9 (see figure 2b). The scan continues in the Y direction and the 4 bit Y position is loaded into IC10. Any obstruction causes the data ready flag to be set and the scanner to be halted.

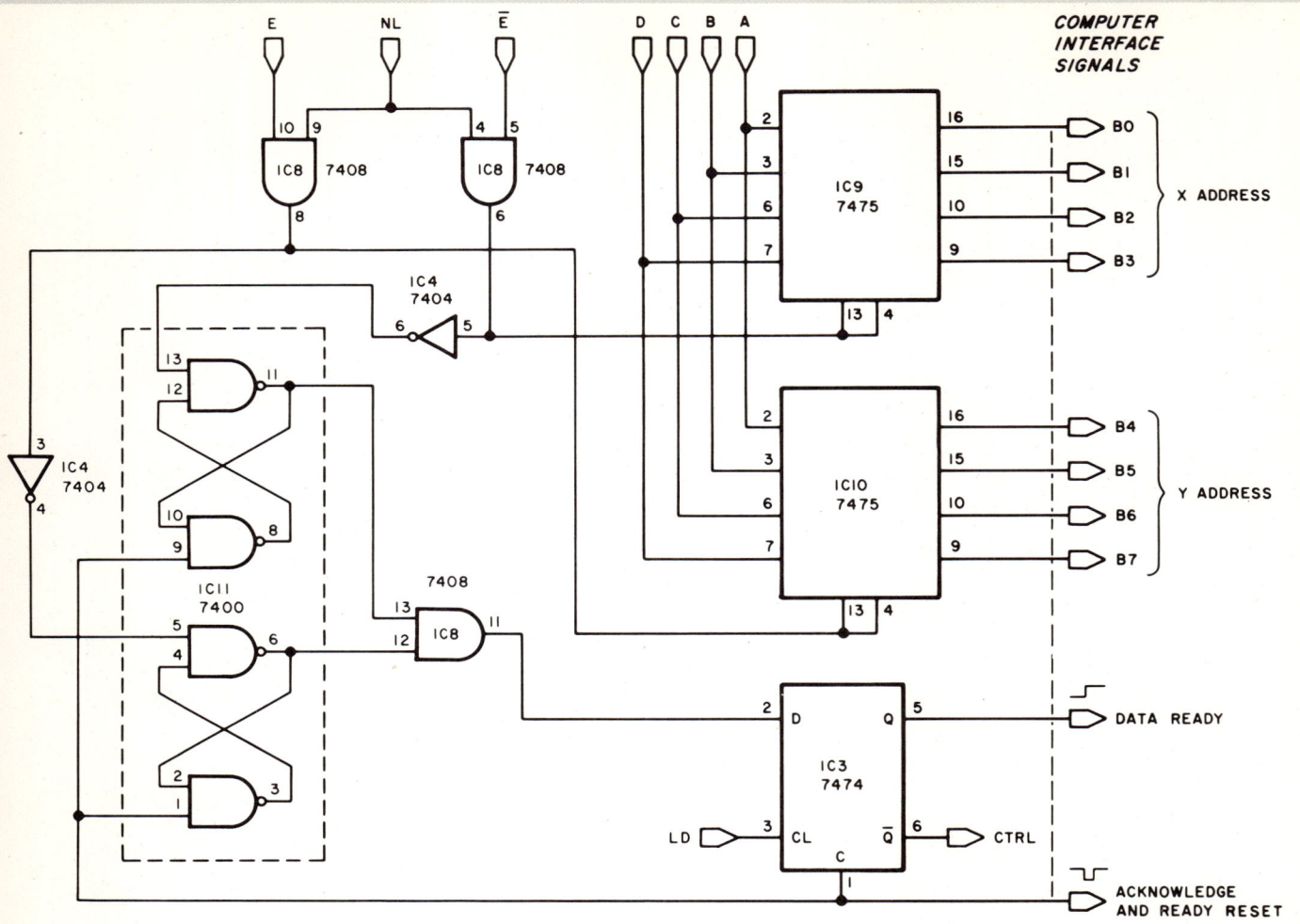

Figure 2b: Interface circuitry for the noncontact digitizer. Data presented to the computer is in the form of an 8 bit word representing a 4 bit X coordinate and a 4 bit Y coordinate. These lines are tied to the parallel input port of the computer.

NOTE: Any one building a unit from these designs should be advised that they are covered by a number of patents by the University of Illinois and may not be sold for profit.

Notes on figure 2

1. All capacitors are 25 V ceramics unless otherwise specified.
2. All resistors are ¼ W 5 percent unless otherwise specified.
3. ╱┬╱ denotes signal ground.
4. ICs 16 thru 19 are CMOS devices and should be handled carefully.
5. Additional LEDs on prototype unit are for testing purposes only.
6. Q0 thru Q31: GE LED56 infrared emitter.
   D0 thru D31: GE L14F2 photodarlington infrared detector.

IC	Type	+5 V	Gnd
1	7400	14	7
2	7493	5	10
3	7474	14	7
4	7404	14	7
5	74155	16	8
6	74123	16	8
7	LM311	8	1
8	7408	14	7
9	7475	5	12
10	7475	5	12
11	7400	14	7
12	7445	16	8
13	7445	16	8
14	7445	16	8
15	7445	16	8
16	CD4051	16	8
17	CD4051	16	8
18	CD4051	16	8
19	CD4051	16	8
20	74121	14	7

Table 1: Power wiring table for the noncontact digitizer.

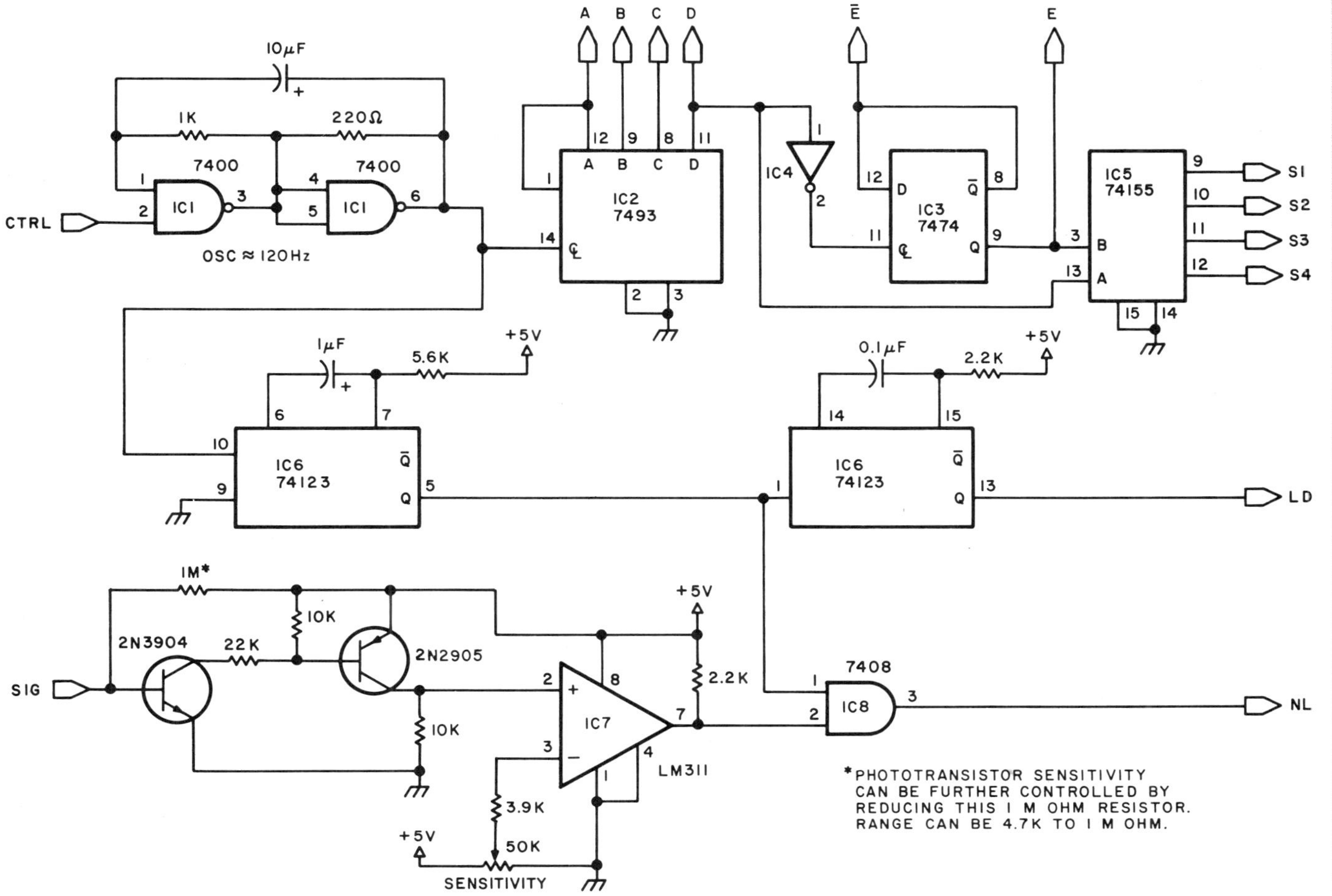

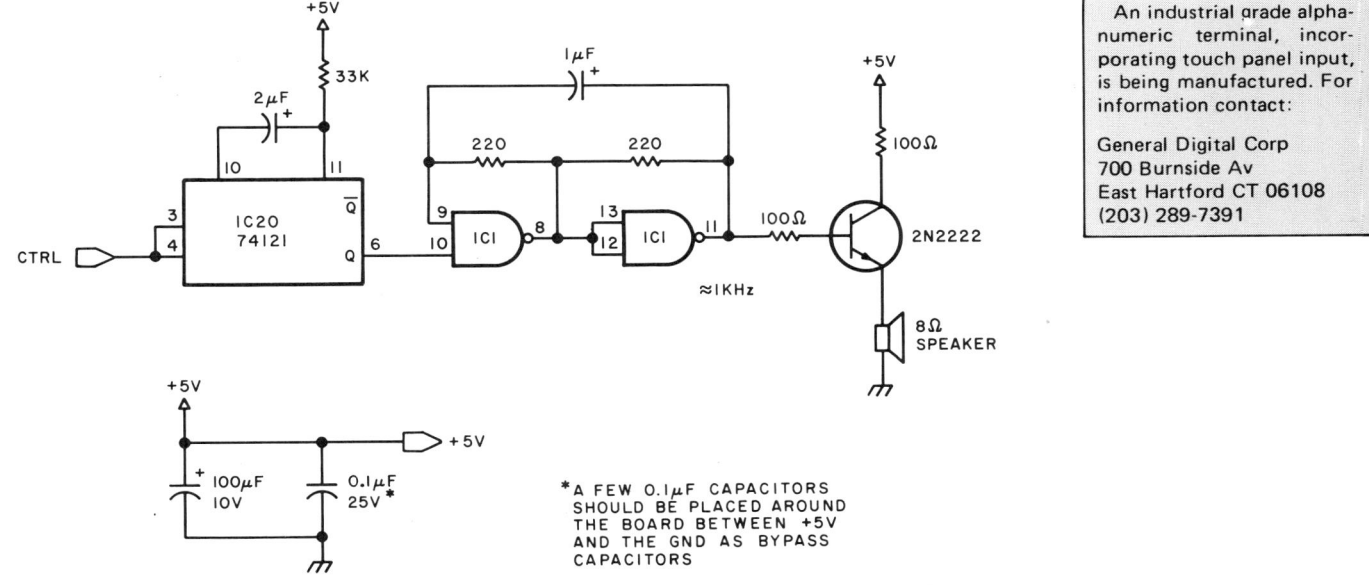

Figure 2c: Address decoder and phototransistor signal conditioning circuitry for the noncontact digitizer. IC2 is a counter driven by the oscillator at upper left. When a phototransistor is activated, the SIG line goes high, activating line NL, which stores the 4 bit address of the interrupted beam (see figure 2b). The scanner is finally halted via the CTRL line. The computer then reads the coordinates and reactivates the scanner.

An industrial grade alpha-numeric terminal, incorporating touch panel input, is being manufactured. For information contact:

General Digital Corp
700 Burnside Av
East Hartford CT 06108
(203) 289-7391

Figure 2d: Optional audio data ready signal circuit, which causes an audible beep on a speaker whenever a pair of beams is obstructed and sets the data ready signal.

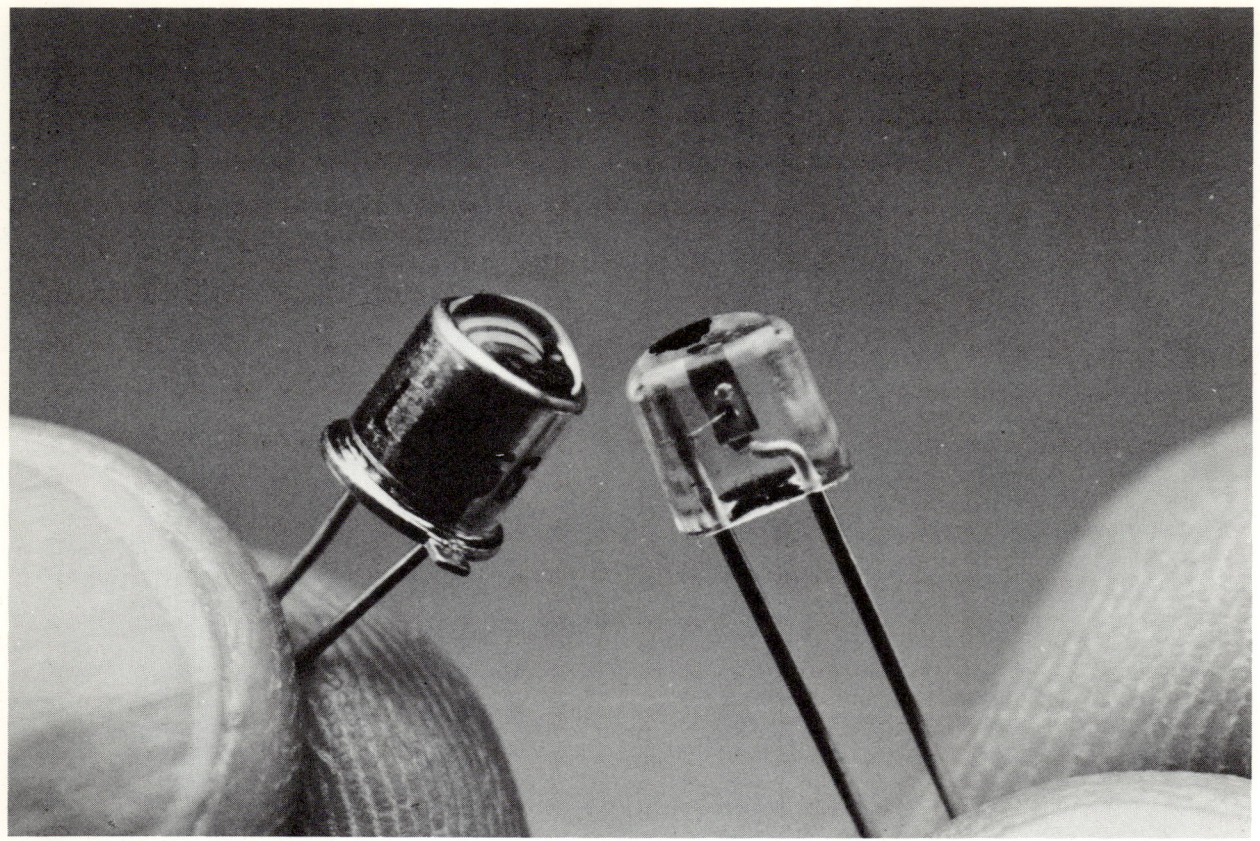

Photo 3: Lensed type GE LED56 light emitting diode (left) and nonlensed H17B1 photodarlington infrared detector. Pairs of either type can be used to transmit and receive infrared light, respectively, for use in the noncontact scanning digitizer.

it is the L14FZ. These units have built-in glass lenses and are very sensitive. A much less expensive though equally capable optoelectric pair is the H17B1 shown on the right in photo 3. Because it has no lens, it requires considerably more shielding from ambient light, but it will work if properly aligned. I have checked the operation of both devices and recommend the lensed type if you intend to use the touch scanner in high ambient light environments. The prototype described here used LED56s and L14F2s.

The frame that holds all the electronics is a $4 discount store wooden picture frame. Half inch (1.27 cm) wooden strips glued around the edges hold the phototransistors and LEDs in evenly spaced, recessed, ¼ inch (0.63 cm) holes. This technique is shown in photos 4a and 4b.

The entire assembly is attached to the picture frame and can be secured to the front of a video display. The display in these photos is a 12 inch (30.76 cm) surplus Phase 4 monitor.

One further addition to the hardware to aid users of the scanner is audio feedback to confirm that a position coordinate has been selected. The data ready strobe triggers a 0.1 second beep on a small speaker.

Calibration and Testing

There is virtually nothing to calibrate or test on this unit. The only adjustment is the

Photo 4a: Mounting the photodarlington detectors.

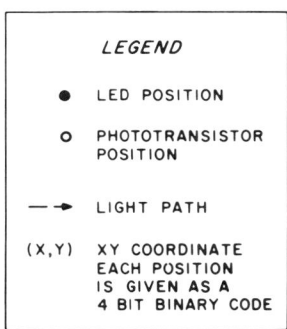

Notes for figure 3

1. Scan is sequential from D0 thru D31.
2. Only one LED is on at any one time.
3. Scan rate is approximately four samples per second.
4. Total detectable points = 256.

LEGEND

● LED POSITION
○ PHOTOTRANSISTOR POSITION
-→ LIGHT PATH
(X,Y) XY COORDINATE EACH POSITION IS GIVEN AS A 4 BIT BINARY CODE

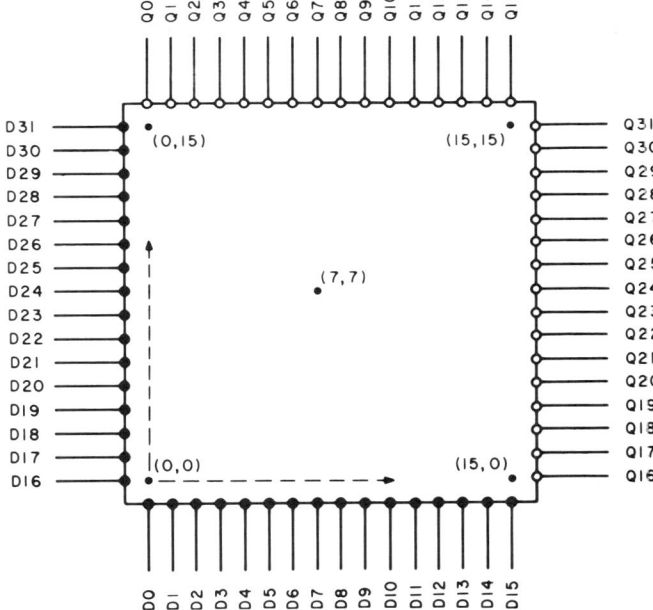

Figure 3: LED and phototransistor placement for the 16 by 16 Cartesian coordinate noncontact digitizer.

sensitivity control on the phototransistor amplifier. Direct sunlight or incandescent lights will cause saturation of the input and disable the scanner. The only other important consideration is mechanical alignment: the LED and phototransistor constituting each pair must be exactly opposite and in direct alignment.

The program in listing 1 is a simple BASIC program to exercise the scanner and provide the operator with an indication of its operational integrity. It is written in Micro Com 8 K Zapple BASIC. The decimal coordinates of X and Y will be output as your finger is moved across the scanned area. This is the only routine that has to be added to any BASIC program to exercise the scanner. If set up as a subroutine by changing line 210 to a RETURN statement, the routine will turn the scanner on when called and return to the main program with a value in variable D representing the coordinates to which you pointed. The main program then responds appropriately.

Obviously the scanner would be more efficiently driven by a machine language program, but I feel most users will be interested in utilizing this device with a high level language. The relatively slow scan rate allows considerable leeway.

In Part 2 I'll pursue the software (in BASIC) necessary to drive this scanner effectively. The major emphasis will be the use of menus and keyboard substitutions.■

REFERENCES

1. Loomis, Sumner S, "Let There Be Light Pens," January 1976 BYTE, page 26.
2. Webster and Young, "Add a $3 Light Pen to Your Video Display," February 1978 BYTE, page 52.

```
100     REM **RESET DATA READY BIT TO START SCANNER**
110     OUT 16,0 :OUT 16,255 :REM THIS IS A 10 MSEC STROBE
120     REM **TEST DATA READY BIT**
130     T=INP(2) :REM READ INPUT PORT 2
140     T=T AND 1 :REM MASK ALL BUT LSB
150     IF T <> 1 THEN GOTO 130
160     REM ** READ DATA **
170     D=INP(16) :REM SCANNER IS ATTACHED TO PORT 16
180     X=(D AND 240)/16 :REM MASK AND SHIFT TO OBTAIN 4 BIT X
190     Y=D AND 15 :REM MASK TO OBTAIN 4 BIT Y
200     PRINT"X=";X,"Y=";Y
210     GOTO 110
```

Listing 1: Program written in 8 K Zapple BASIC to exercise the scanner.

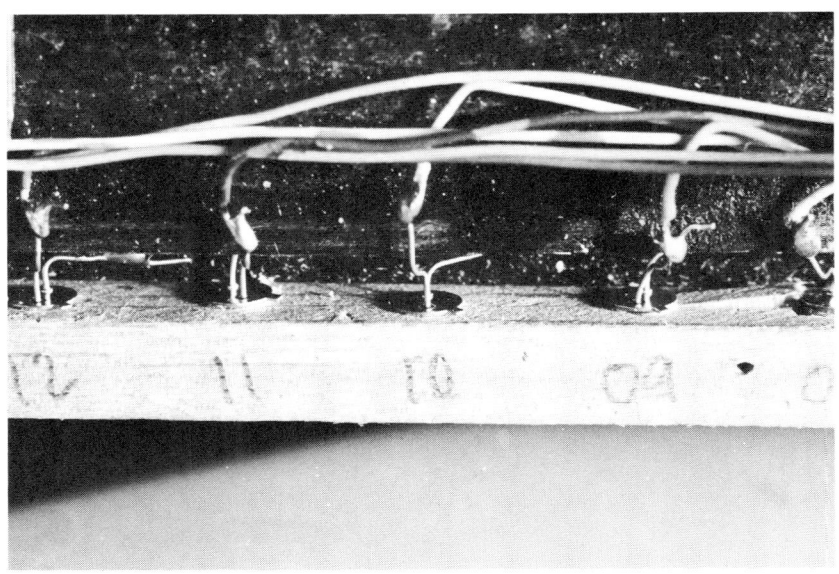

Photo 4b: Mounting the LEDs.

Let Your Fingers Do the Talking

Part 2: Scanner Applications

In "Let Your Fingers Do the Talking, Part 1: Add a Noncontact Touch Scanner to Your Video Display" page 95, I detailed the hardware design of a noncontact touch scanner which sits over a conventional video screen. This system, though lower in resolution, allows a fingertip to simulate the function of a light pen and with proper programming can become as important a peripheral as the common ASCII keyboard.

Quick Hardware Review

The scanner consists of 32 pairs of infrared light emitting diode transmitters and photo transistor receivers arranged around the perimeter of a picture frame. There are 16 pairs on the X axis and 16 pairs on the Y axis. The hardware logic sequentially activates the 32 pairs, first in the X direction (horizontal) then in the Y direction (vertical). If a physical obstruction is placed in the plane of the scan, one X and one Y beam are interrupted. The corresponding X and Y beam addresses are stored when this happens. Since there are 16 pairs per axis, each coordinate can be represented by a 4 bit code and both the X and Y addresses can be packed into one data byte.

The end result of the hardware logic is a very simple scanner to computer interface. The scanner output is one 8 bit byte containing the 4 bit X and 4 bit Y addresses. The only other signals are a little something often referred to as hand shaking. A data ready line is set to a high level output when the scanner has sensed an obstruction.

This data ready signal can be tied to a parallel input port and scanned as I have done, used as a control line on a peripheral interface circuit, or used directly to generate a processor interrupt. If the touch panel is to be exercised in BASIC, the first method will prove to be easiest. The latter method, normally used with a machine language program rather than BASIC, will be the most efficient from a memory utilization standpoint.

I continue to use BASIC wherever the interface data processing speed allows it. In this way I can write illustrative program examples which are not tied to a particular processor. Of course, the speed advantages of machine language may be useful if your programs using the touch panel have a lot to do; so feel free to strike out on your own using these BASIC programs as a model.

Whatever the software method utilized to recognize the data ready bit, the program action must be the same. After the data ready bit goes high, the data byte is stored and the data ready is reset by momentarily pulsing the ready reset line low. In BASIC, the easiest way to do this is to tie the ready reset line to one bit on a parallel output port (it need only be a strobe rather than a latched output) and then sequentially execute two OUT instructions. The 10 ms pulsewidth I get on my machine is the result of the time it takes for BASIC to respond. The program examples presented in the listings use the following port allocations (in decimal):

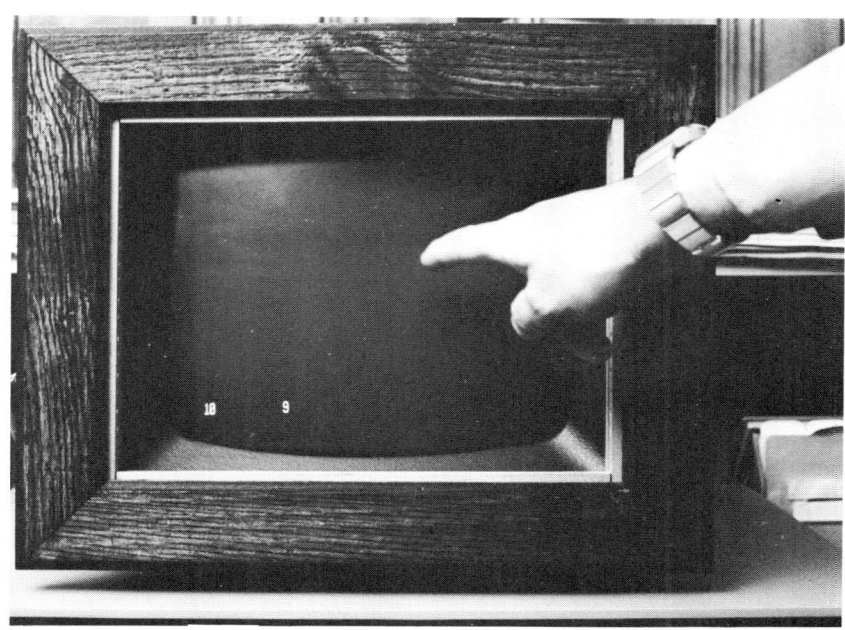

Photo 1: The basic information returned from the touch panel is a coordinate pair for one of 256 possible finger sized locations on the video display's face. Here, using the program in listing 3, the displayed coordinates 10 and 9 correspond to the point just touched on the screen.

Data Ready — Input Port 2
(least significant bit)

Ready Reset — Output Port 16
(least significant bit)

X, Y Coordinate — Input Port 16
(b_7-b_4 is X address)
(b_3-b_0 is Y address).

```
100  REM THIS IS THE ONLY SOFTWARE NECESSARY TO EXERCISE THE
     SCANNER
110  REM *** RESET SCANNER ***
120  OUT 16,0 : OUT 16,255 : REM THIS WILL GIVE A SHORT RESET PULSE TO
     PORT 16
130  REM *** TEST DATA READY ***
140  T=INP(2) : REM THE DATA READY SIGNAL IS BIT 0 OF PORT 2
150  T=T AND 1 :REM MASK ALL BUT BIT 0
160  IF T<>1 THEN GOTO 140 :REM TEST TO SEE IF DATA READY IS SET
170  REM *** READ DATA ***
180  D=INP (16) :REM SCANNER IS ATTACHED TO PORT 16
190  D1=(D AND 240)/16 :REM MASK AND SHIFT RIGHT 4 BITS
195  REM D1 IS THE X COORDINATE
200  D2=D AND 15
205  REM D2 IS THE Y COORDINATE
210  RETURN :REM RETURN IS ONLY NECESSARY IF CALLED AS A
     SUBROUTINE
```

Listing 1: Subroutine used to determine activated coordinates on the scanner.

```
10   PRINT "MY SCREEN ITCHES!! PLEASE SCRATCH IT!"
20   GOSUB 100 :REM ACTIVATE SCANNER
30   PRINT "OH!! THAT FEELS SO GOOOOOOOD!!!"
40   END
```

Listing 2: Example of using the entire video screen as a push button.

```
100  S=USR(255) :REM THIS IS A SCREEN CLEAR FOR DG Z-80
110  PRINT"THIS IS A TEST OF TOUCH INPUT"
120  PRINT"THE SCREEN IS CURRENTLY BEING SCANNED BY AN ARRAY"
130  PRINT"    INFRARED LEDS AND OPTICAL SENSORS"
140  PRINT
150  PRINT"POINT AT THE SCREEN SOMEPLACE "
160  GOSUB 1000 :REM GOTO THE SCANNER SUBROUTINE AND RETURN WITH COORDINATES
170  PRINT"              THANKYOU"
180  PRINT
190  PRINT
200  PRINT"THE SCANNER HARDWARE SAYS THAT YOU TOUCHED LOCATION"
210  PRINT"       X-";D1,"AND  Y-";D2,"   ON A 16X16 GRID"
220  GOSUB 2500 :REM CALL SLIGHT DELAY TIMER
250  S=USR(255) :REM CLEAR SCREEN
260  PRINT"LET ME DEMONSTRATE THE COORDINATE SYSTEM"
270  PRINT"POINT YOUR FINGER AT THE SCREEN AND I'll PRINT OUT (X,Y)"
280  PRINT"TO EXIT JUST POINT TO LOCATION (15,15) ---UPPER RIGHT"
290  GOSUB 1000 :REM CALL SCANNER
300  S=USR(255) :REM CLEAR SCREEN
310  IF D1=15 THEN 320 ELSE 330
320  IF D2=15 THEN END
330  PRINT
340  PRINT D1,D2; :REM PRINT COORDINATES
350  GOTO 290
1000 REM *** RESET SCANNER ***
1010 OUT 16,0 :OUT 16,255
1050 REM *** TEST DATA READY ***
1060 T=INP(2)
1070 T=T AND 1
1080 IF T<>1 THEN GOTO 1060
1090 REM *** READ DATA ***
1100 D=INP(16)
1110 D1=(D AND 240)/16 :REM THIS IS THE X VALUE
1120 D2=D AND 15 :REM THIS IS THE Y VALUE
1130 RETURN
2500 FOR W=1 TO 2000
2510 NEXT W
2520 RETURN
```

Listing 3: This program outputs the coordinates of the point you are touching on the screen. The output of the program can be used at a higher level to indicate some object that is printed on the screen.

Using the Touch Panel

Using the touch panel in any BASIC program, whether it be game or instructional, will necessitate having a subroutine to read and reset the scanner placed somewhere within the BASIC program. The total software necessary to exercise the touch panel is shown in listing 1.

If a GOSUB 100 command is encountered, BASIC vectors to this subroutine and begins execution. This subroutine will not return until someone touches the screen. Variable D1 would contain the X coordinate and D2 would contain the Y value. Each call to this subroutine results in returning to the main program with the X, Y address of a single touched point. To obtain ten touch inputs would require calling this routine ten times.

The simplest program utilizing the scanner would be one which sensitizes the entire screen to act as one giant push button. Such a program is similar to a press any key option on a keyboard.

The program in listing 2 prints "MY SCREEN ITCHES!! PLEASE SCRATCH IT!" on the video screen, waits for someone to touch any place on the screen and then responds with the message in line 30. Notice that we did not use the coordinate information from the scanner because we only needed to take advantage of the fact that the subroutine returns only if data is *ready*.

Test the Coordinate System

If one builds the touch panel, the first program written should be one that illustrates the coordinate system dynamically, such as the program in listing 3. (All BASIC programs in this article are written in Micro Com 8 K Zapple BASIC.)

After printing an opening comment on the video screen, the program calls the scanner subroutine as before. This time when it returns, it prints out the X and Y coordinate which was touched as shown in photo 1. The rest of the program is a repeat of this basic cycle with one exception. The values of D1 and D2 are both compared to 15 after each scan. Should you point at coordinate position (15,15) the program ends.

Converting Position to Function

So far we have displayed only the raw output of the scanner and have not used it in its true application. Telling you that you are pointing to location (4,2) illustrates that the touch panel functions, but does no use-

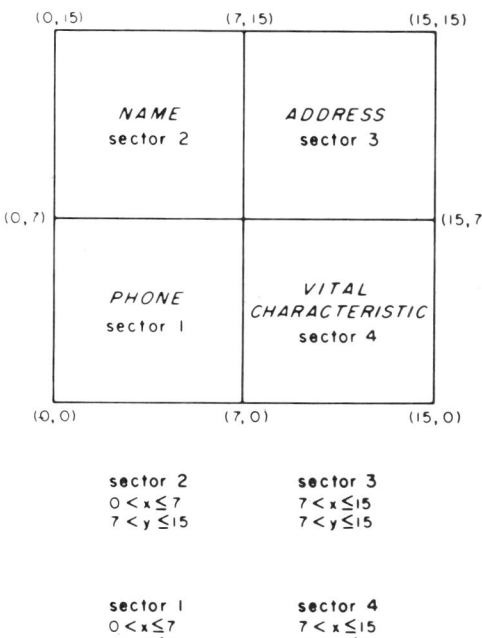

Figure 1: Physical arrangement of sectors on the screen as used by program in listing 4.

An industrial grade alphanumeric terminal incorporating touch panel input is being manufactured. For information contact:

General Digital Corp
700 Burnside Av
East Hartfort CT 06108

ful work. If instead some letter or word were at (4,2) and the program used this higher function output rather than just the numerical coordinate, we'd have something.

Fortunately it isn't all that difficult. By dividing the scanner system into fields and having each field represent a function, we can do useful work. A 2 level program must be written. First, it should have the capability of formatting the screen so that the printing is beneath the proper touch coordinate. Then, after returning from the scanner subroutine, it must translate this position value into the function designated by the printing on the screen.

A simple program which divides the screen into four fields or sectors and performs a function dependent on which sector is touched is shown in listing 4. Figure 1 describes the mathematical relationship between the coordinate system and the BASIC program of listing 4.

After printing the opening lines on the screen the program calls for the data from the scanner. The X coordinate (D1) is first tested to see if it is greater than 7. If it is, then either sector 3 or 4 must have been chosen. If D1 is less than 7 then it must be sector 1 or 2. After choosing whether it is the right or left half of the screen the test is repeated with the Y coordinate. In theory, this binary search method would require no more than eight such tests if all 256 points were designated as separate fields.

A further extension of this binary search

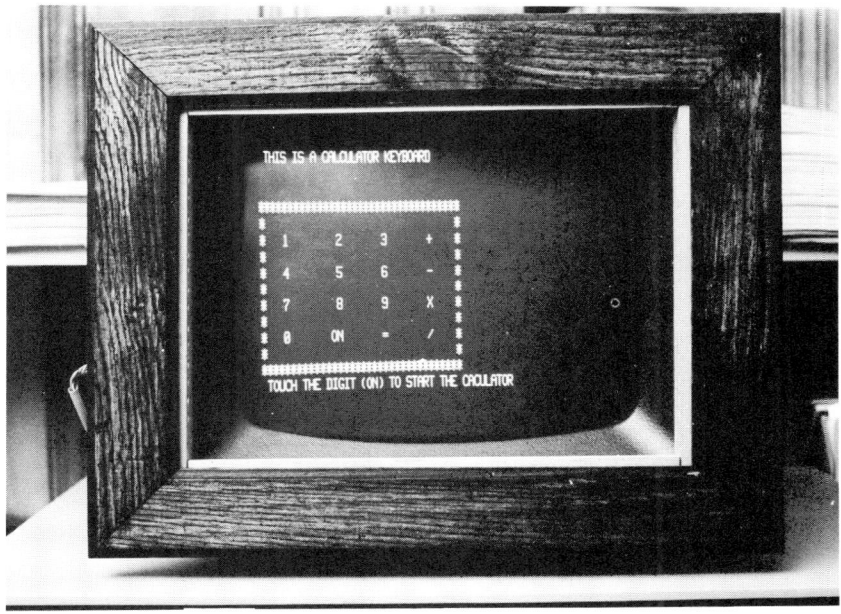

Photo 2: Here is a picture of an experiment which was backed up by a fairly long BASIC program: using the screen as the input device for a simulation of an ordinary 4 function calculator. The imagination of the user, to use a well-worn cliche, is the only limitation upon trying experiments with special purpose keyboards and interactive sequences on the screen. Use of the video display behind the touch panel area makes easily altered software the determining factor — rather than physical tools in the workshop.

```
100  S=USR(255)
110  PRINT"NAME                              ADDRESS"
120  FOR L=1 TO 12
130  PRINT
140  NEXT L
150  PRINT"PHONE                             VITAL CHARACTERISTIC"
160  GOSUB 1000
170  IF D1>7 THEN GOTO 300 ELSE GOTO 200
200  REM THIS ROUTINE DECIDES IF YOU ARE POINTING TO
202  REM SECTOR 1 OR 2
210  IF D2<7 THEN PRINT"UNLISTED NUMBER" :GOTO 2000
220  PRINT"BRENDA (THE LITTLE WOOFER) CIARCIA"
230  GOTO 2000
300  REM THIS ROUTINE DECIDES IF YOU ARE POINTING TO
302  REM SECTOR 3 OR 4
310  IF D2<7 THEN PRINT"SCOTTISH TERRIER -- FOUR LEGGED BURGLAR ALARM" :GOTO 2000
320  PRINT"BOX 582    GLASTONBURY,CONN. 06033"
330  GOTO 2000
990  REM
992  REM SCANNER SUBROUTINE
1000 OUT 16,0 :OUT 16,255
1010 T=INP(2)
1020 T=T AND 1
1030 IF T<>1 THEN GOTO 1010
1040 D=INP(16)
1050 D1=(D AND 240)/16
1060 D2=D AND 15
1070 RETURN
2000 FOR N=1 TO 2000
2010 NEXT N
2020 GOTO 100
```

Listing 4: Illustration of a BASIC program which simulates a 4 function calculator menu. The program inputs the screen coordinate position of a specific menu function.

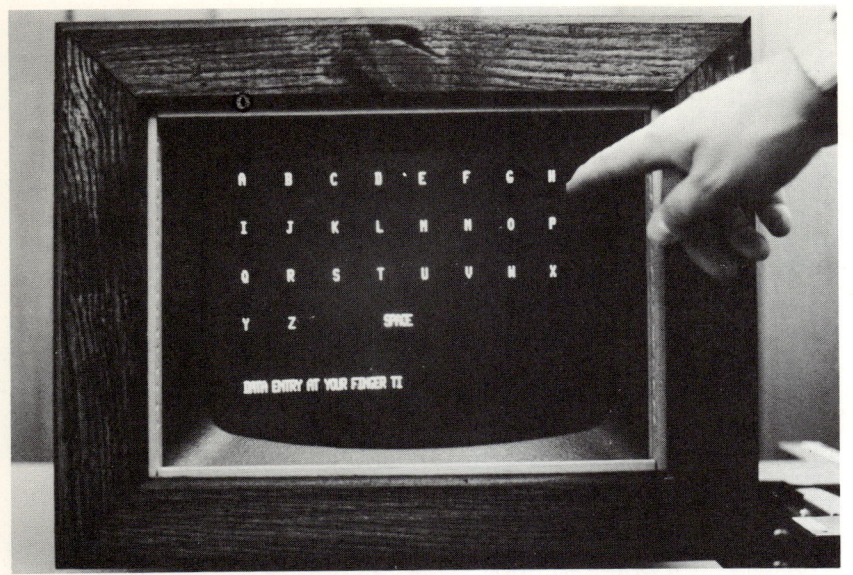

Photo 3: Touch panel input using the program of listing 5. The line of text at the bottom of the display was entered by touching the index finger to each letter in turn. The photo is shown with the letter P about to be pressed.

concept is used in the calculator of photo 2. While never meant to replace the hand held calculator it uses a routine similar to the previous example to determine the action of each of the 16 possible entries. The picture is included to present the reader with one of the many possible applications of the scanner. The program, however, is quite long and difficult to explain in an introductory article such as this.

Simulated Keyboard

One use of the touch panel would be the simulation of direct keyboard entry. Obviously this technique is valuable only where limited data entry is required. Large menu selection programs with numerous choices displayed may not always have the particular item of interest. By having one of the available selections be a keyboard display and entry routine such as photo 3 and listing 5, the miscellaneous entry could be accommodated. The program of listing 5 displays a keyboard on the video screen and allows one to *type* by pointing to the individual characters. The example does not include punctuation and a carriage return, but they could be easily accommodated.

One final note. Using the touch panel need not eliminate the standard ASCII keyboard as an input device. By using the BASIC INPUT command, keyboard entry is still available to the user as is the scanner through a callable subroutine. A program could be written where some entries come from the touch panel and others from the keyboard. A more versatile program would allow input from either device at any time.

Listing 6 is a simple program which demonstrates how BASIC can scan two input devices simultaneously and provide appropriate response.

I hope that this touch panel design will spark the creative interests of other computer enthusiasts. In a field where technology advances by leaps and bounds and product obsolescence can be described in months, innovative ideas are necessary to extend the concept of creative home computing. By adding advanced peripherals and high level languages, system obsolescence is delayed considerably.■

```
100 REM THIS PROGRAM DISPLAYS A KEYBOARD ON THE CRT SCREEN
110 REM AND ILLUSTRATES DATA ENTRY WITHOUT A PHYSICAL KEYBOARD
120 REM JUST POINT AT THE LETTERS AND IT WILL 'TYPE' YOUR MESSAGE
200 PRINT"A      B      C      D      E      F      G      H"
210 PRINT
215 PRINT
220 PRINT"I      J      K      L      M      N      O      P"
230 PRINT
235 PRINT
240 PRINT"Q      R      S      T      U      V      W      X"
250 PRINT
255 PRINT
260 PRINT"Y      Z              SPACE"
261 PRINT
262 PRINT
263 PRINT
264 PRINT
265 GOSUB 2500
268 GOSUB 1000
270 IF D2>=12 THEN PRINT CHR$(D1/2+65);:GOTO 265
280 IF D2>=10 THEN PRINT CHR$(D1/2+73);:GOTO 265
290 IF D2>=8 THEN PRINT CHR$(D1/2+81);:GOTO 265
300 IF D2>=5 THEN 302 ELSE 310
302 IF (D1/2+89)>91 THEN PRINT CHR$(32);:GOTO 265
303 PRINT CHR$(D1/2+89);:GOTO 265
310 IF D2=0 THEN GOTO 320 ELSE 330
320 IF D1=15 THEN 330 ELSE GOTO 265
330 S=USR(255) :REM CLEAR SCREEN
340 PRINT"TO RETRY EXERCISE----TOUCH SCREEN"
350 GOSUB 1000
360 GOTO 200
1000 OUT 16,0 :OUT 16,255 :REM LINES 1000-1070 READ THE SCANNER DATA
1010 T=INP(2)
1020 T=T AND 1
1030 IF T<>1 THEN GOTO 1010
1040 D=INP(16)
1050 D1=(D AND 240)/16
1060 D2=D AND 15
1070 RETURN
2500 FOR A=0 TO 500 :REM THIS IS A SHORT DELAY
2510 NEXT A
2520 RETURN
```

Listing 5: Keyboard simulation program.

```
100 REM THIS IS A SIMPLE PROGRAM TO ILLUSTRATE SIMULTANEOUS
110 REM DATA INPUT FROM EITHER THE TOUCH PANEL OR THE KEYBOARD
120 Q=INP(0) :REM KEYBOARD IS ATTACHED TO PORT 0
130 REM MSB IS KEYBOARD STROBE   --- BITS 0 TO 6 ARE 7 BIT ASCII
140 IF Q>0 THEN GOTO 220 :REM CHECK KEYBOARD STROBE
150 T=INP(2) :REM SCANNER DATA READY IS PORT 2 LSB
160 T=T AND 1
170 IF T<>1 THEN GOTO 120
180 D=INP(16) :D1=(D AND 240)/16 :D2=D AND 15 :REM READ SCANNER COORDINATE
190 PRINT"PANEL TOUCHED AT LOCATION (";D1;D2;")"
200 GOSUB 240
210 GOTO 120
220 PRINT"KEYBOARD KEY ";CHR$(INP(0));" PRESSED"
230 GOTO 120
240 OUT 16,0 :OUT 16,255 :REM RESET SCANNER HARDWARE
250 RETURN
```

Listing 6: Method for scanning two input devices simultaneously on a Digital Group Z-80 system.

Come Upstairs and Be Respectable

For those of you who remember about Walt and Ralph in "Having a Private Affair With Your Computer" *[April 1977 issue of BYTE]*, I suppose I can say that with friends like that I am not in any great need of enemies. What may have appeared as a losing situation on my part did have some beneficial side effects — namely, the remote terminal which I installed in my den to accommodate the comings and goings of people using my system.

This remote terminal is nothing more than a serial data link incorporating a universal asynchronous receiver-transmitter (UART) attached to a keyboard and a coaxial extension cable for a direct plug-in monitor. Any computer system which can be directly operated by a keyboard can be converted for remote input exactly as I will describe. The components are readily available and total cost should be less than $30.

The major application for a remote interface is to be able to describe and demonstrate your computer without having to clean up your shop before letting people in or worrying about what they'll touch. Often, when I have large parties, I will put a Kingdom game on the computer and let people play to their hearts' content in the den. Obviously, trying to do this in the basement where the computer is located would require constant attendance. All it would take is one drunk to lean on the processor card, or say, "What does this do?", as he flips the memory clear switch. I will have to admit though that what had originally started as a purely defensively initiated design has become an enjoyable addition to my system. If just writing software, I'll do it upstairs now, with the family, rather than appearing to isolate myself in the cellar every night, getting moldy, as my wife says.

A simplified block diagram of this remote terminal link is illustrated in figure 1. For the keyboard inputs to the computer both transmitter and receiver interfaces utilize an interesting device called a universal asynchronous receiver-transmitter. The internal structure of this device consists of a separate parallel to serial transmitter and serial to

Photo 1: The Remote Receiver Assembly. This is only one of the circuit layouts possible. Placement of parts is not crucial. The receiver is built so that it can be plugged directly into the microprocessor's main board.

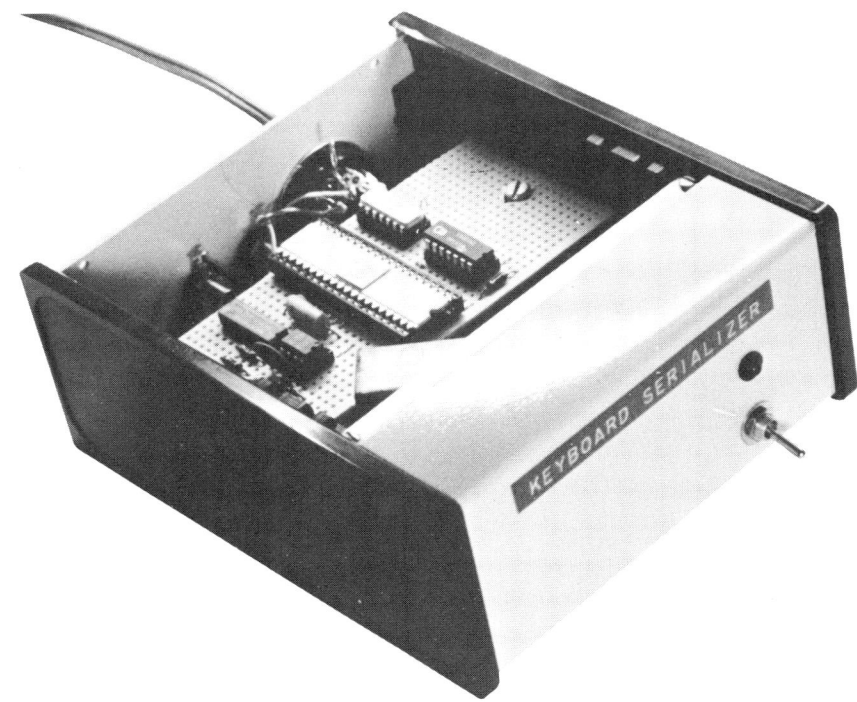

Photo 2: The Remote Transmitter Assembly. The transmitter also needs a power supply, contained within this box, for both itself and the keyboard. With a stylish cabinet such as this, you can be proud to display your newest addition to your friends.

parallel receiver joined by common programming pins. What this means, in fact, is that the two sections can be used independently provided they adhere to the same bit format which is selectable through the wiring of the device.

The transmission from the den to the basement is done asynchronously and in one direction only. As far as the computer is concerned, this input device appears as any other parallel input such as a keyboard. The other part of the system is a monitor to display computer generated video. The monitor in the den uses direct video signals and is attached to the video display electronics through a 200 foot coaxial cable, and thus does not require the computer to respond via the serial line.

Actual data transmission to the computer follows an asynchronous serial format illustrated in figure 2. When no data is being transmitted, the data line is sitting at a mark or 1 level waiting for a key pressed strobe from the keyboard. A key pressed strobe is a 1 to 5 ms positive pulse indicating that a keyboard key has been pressed and that an ASCII code of that key is available for transmission. This key pressed strobe, which is attached to the data strobe of the interface, causes the ASCII data to be loaded into a parallel storage buffer, and starts the transmission cycle. The serial output will then make a transition from a logical 1 to 0. This start bit transition indicates the beginning of a serially transmitted word. Following the start bit, up to eight bits of data follow, each data bit taking 16 clock periods. At the conclusion of the data bits, parity and stop bits are generated by the interface to signify the end of transmission.

If another key is pressed, the process will repeat itself. On the receiving end, the receiver section of the UART is continuously monitoring the serial input lines for the start bit. Upon its occurrence the eight bits of data are slipped into a register and the parity checked. At the completion of the serial entry, an output signifying data available is set which can be used as an input strobe to the computer. The interface will not process additional serial inputs unless the data available flag is acknowledged and

Figure 1: A simplified block diagram of the remote transmitter and receiver circuit. With a 1760 Hz oscillator driving the circuit, a data transmission rate of 110 bps will be attained. Although the exact frequency is not important, the two oscillators must be accurate in respect to each other or the circuit will not function correctly.

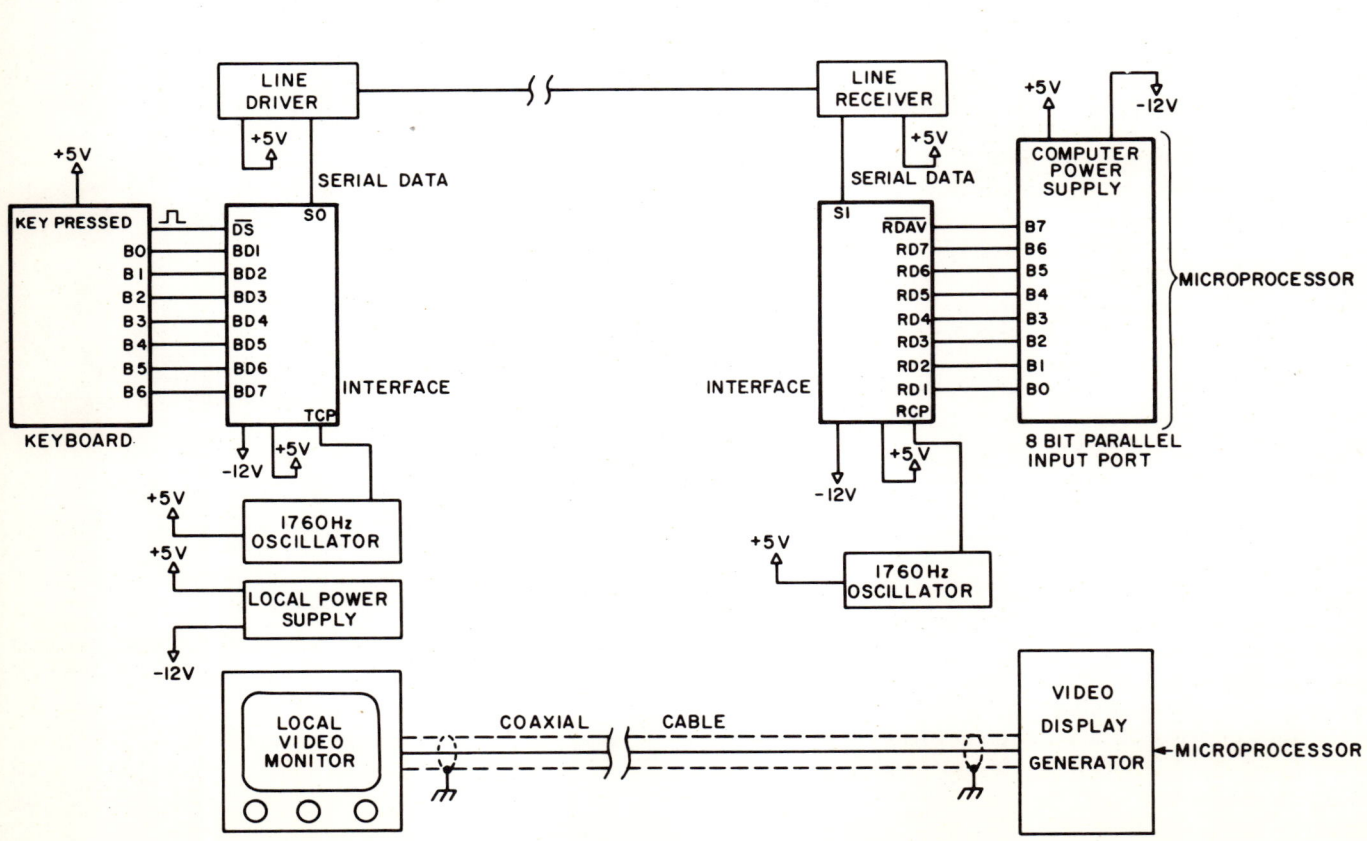

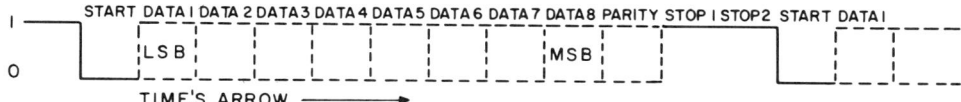

Figure 2: Diagram illustrating how asynchronous data is transmitted. A start bit is defined as a transition from logical 1 to 0. The eight data bits are then transmitted with the least significant bit being transmitted first and the most significant bit being transmitted last. A parity bit is then sent followed by two stop bits. With the AY-5-1013, the parity bit can be omitted completely and there is a choice of one or two stop bits following the transmitted data.

the data available reset line is strobed. Actual transmission can include or exclude parity, have one or two stop bits, and data can be in 5 to 8 bit words. These options are pin selectable.

Table 1 is a pin function description for the AY-5-1013.

There are obviously many more functional inputs and outputs than are necessary for this limited application. We will purposely select only those which are absolutely necessary to minimize hardware and software logic. The keyboard has a 7 bit ASCII output code so a 7 bit word length is chosen by a binary 10 code on pins 37 and 38 respectively. Two stop bits provide for a more reliable transmission by allowing more time between transmitted words. Two stop bits are selected by tying pin 36 to +5 V. Parity is nice, but unless you are going to do something about it, it's a waste of time. At 110 bps, failures will be rare and in many hours of operation I have not yet received a bad character transmission. Parity is eliminated by tying pin 35 to +5 V.

Both transmitter and receiver interfaces utilize an NE555 oscillator to provide the clock frequency (see figures 3 and 4 for schematics). For a 110 bps serial rate, this frequency is set for 1760 Hz and must be maintained within 1%. For this reason only mylar or polycarbonate capacitors should be used. This transmission rate can be much higher, possibly reaching a rate of 20 or 30 thousand bits per second. But we must be realistic: 110 bps is 10 characters a second, which is beyond the typing capabilities of most sane individuals. Building a 9600 bit per second data link to a keyboard is absurd. The lower the data rate, the fewer problems you will encounter in the long run.

Construction of the receiver and transmitter boards is straightforward and wiring is not critical. The unit in the den requires a +5 V and -12 V power supply and an appropriate case. Most new keyboards require +5 V for operation and the interface power supply should be made large enough to accommodate both.

All my keyboards have cables with 11 pin "octal type" sockets *[electron tube sockets and plugs similar to those of the large*

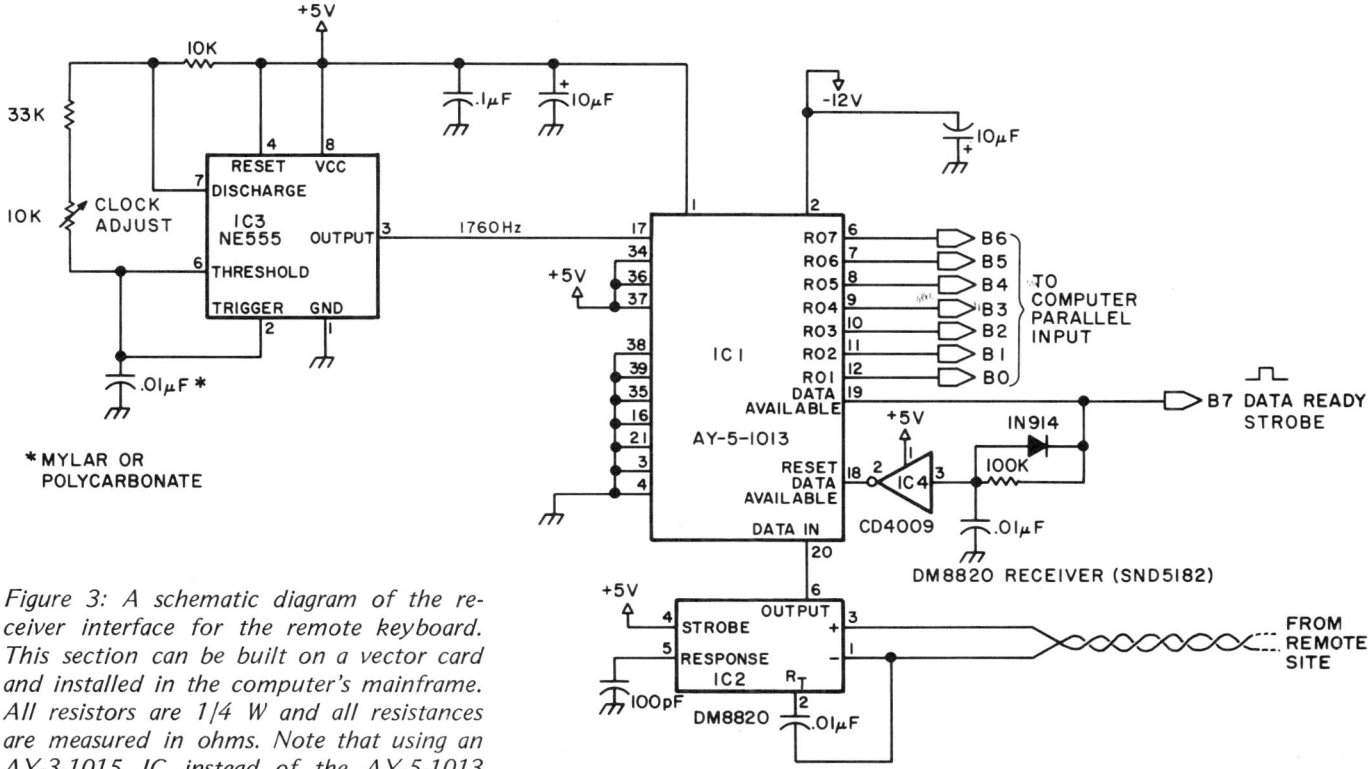

Figure 3: A schematic diagram of the receiver interface for the remote keyboard. This section can be built on a vector card and installed in the computer's mainframe. All resistors are 1/4 W and all resistances are measured in ohms. Note that using an AY-3-1015 IC instead of the AY-5-1013 would eliminate the need for the −12 V supply.

"octal" tubes], so I naturally used the same receptacle on this transmitter box. The cable and connector can be any convenient type, and the keyboard will probably pull less than 200 mA. The only other connection is the twisted pair wire to the receiver board and this should be some easy disconnect like an RCA jack or two banana jacks, as I used.

The receiver construction is equally simplistic and its proximity to the computer eliminates the necessity for building additional power supplies. When a character is

Table 1: A summary of the pins and function description of the AY-5-1013 universal asynchronous receiver and transmitter.

Pin Number	Name	Symbol	Function
1	VCC power supply	VCC	+5 V power supply.
2	VGG power supply	VGG	−12 V power supply.
3	VDD power supply	VDD	ground.
4	Received Data Enable	RDE	logic 0 places the received data onto the output lines.
5−12	Received Data Bits	RD8-RD1	eight data output lines. Received characters are right justified; the least significant bit always appears on RD1. These lines have three state drivers enabled by a low level on the RDE line.
13	Parity Error	PE	goes to logic 1 if received character parity does not agree with selected parity. Three state output enabled by SWE.
14	Framing Error	FE	goes to logic 1 if the received character has no valid stop bit. Three state output enabled by SWE.
15	Over Run	OR	goes to logic 1 if previously received character was not read before present character is transferred to receiver holding register. Three state output enabled by SWE.
16	Status Word Enable	SWE	logic 0 on this line places status word bits PE,FE,OR,DAV,TBMT onto the output lines. Three state outputs.
17	Receiver Clock	RCP	contains clock whose frequency is 16 times the desired receiver data rate.
18	Reset Data Available	RDAV	logic 0 will reset the data available line.
19	Data Available	DAV	goes to logic 1 when an entire character has been received and transferred to the receiver holding register. Three state output.
20	Serial Input	SI	accepts the serial bit input stream. A logic 1 to logic 0 transition is required for initiation of data reception.
21	External Reset	XR	resets shift registers. Sets SO,EOC,TBMT to logic 1. Resets DAV and error flags to logic 0. Clears input data buffer. Tied to logic 0 when not in use.
22	Transmitter Buffer Empty	TBMT	transmitter buffer empty flag goes to logic 1 when data bits holding register may be loaded with another character. Three state output enabled by SWE.
23	Data Strobe	DS	strobe on this line will enter data bits into the data bits holding register. Initial data transmission is initiated by the rising edge of DS. Data must be stable during entire strobe.
24	End of Character	EOC	goes to logic 1 each time a full character is transmitted. It remains at this level until the start of transmission of the next character.
25	Serial Output	SO	serially, by bit, provides the entire transmitted character. It will remain at logic 1 when no data is being transmitted.
26−33	Data Bit Inputs	BD1-BD8	eight data bit input lines.
34	Control Strobe	CS	logic 1 enters the control bits EPS, NB1, NB2, TSB, NP into control bits holding register. Line can be strobed or hard wired to logic 1 level.
35	No parity	NP	logic 1 will eliminate the parity bit from the transmitted and received character. Stop bits immediately follow the last data bit. If not used, must be tied to logic 0.
36	Number of Stop Bits	TSB	selects the number of stop bits, 1 or 2, to be appended immediately after the parity bit. A logic 0 will insert one stop bit and a logic 1 will insert two stop bits.
37−38	Number of bits per character	NB2,NB1	two leads internally decoded to select five, six, seven, eight data bits per character. NB2 NB1 Bits per character 0 0 5 0 1 6 1 0 7 1 1 8
39	Odd or even parity select	EPS	determines type of parity appended immediately after data bits. Logic 0 inserts odd parity, logic 1 inserts even parity.
40	Transmitter Clock	TCP	contains a clock whose frequency is 16 times the desired transmitter data rate.

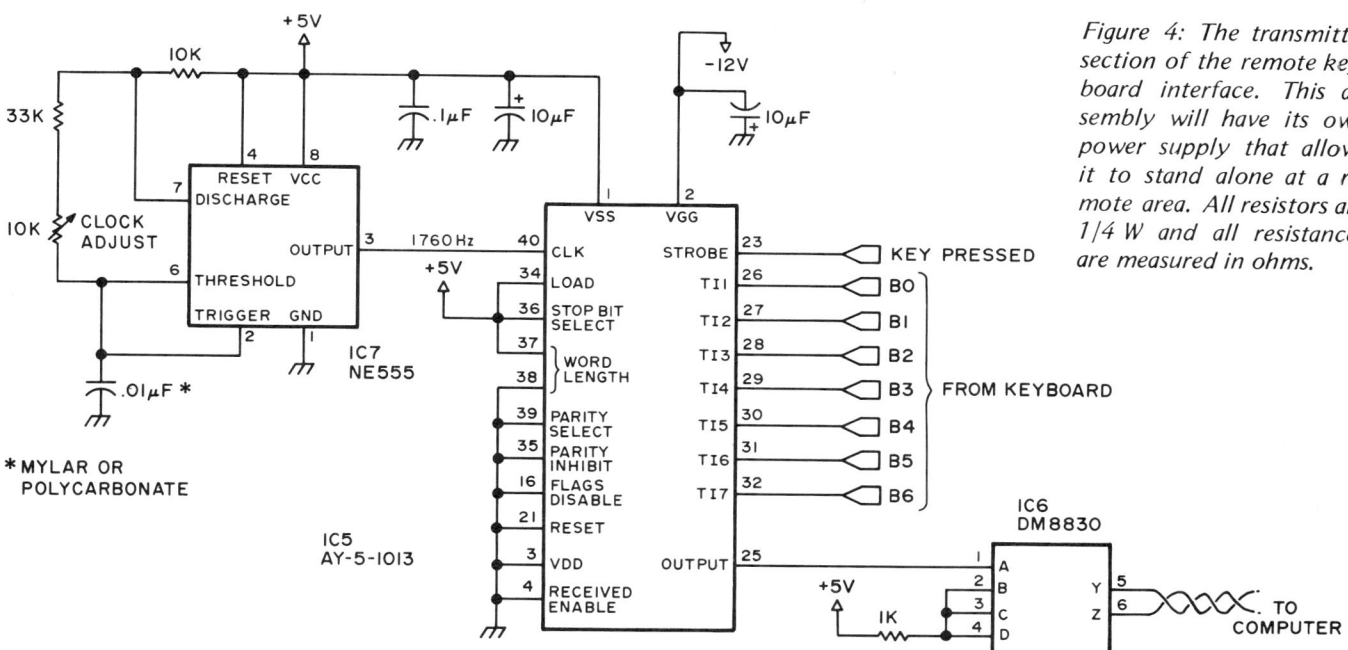

Figure 4: The transmitter section of the remote keyboard interface. This assembly will have its own power supply that allows it to stand alone at a remote area. All resistors are 1/4 W and all resistances are measured in ohms.

received, the data available line goes high. This signal is delayed and inverted and used to reset the data available line. The result of this circuitry is that the data available line will remain high only for the duration of the time delay set by the resistor and capacitor at the input of the CMOS inverter. If your system will not accept a 10 ms data ready strobe, then dispose of the CMOS gate and reset pin 18 via a computer output strobe or some other synchronized means.

The last point of discussion is the line driver and receiver. RS232C seems to be the standard, but this would require a plus and minus 12 to 15 V power supply for the drivers and receivers. The limits of most microprocessor power supplies are usually within +12 V and -12 V. Let's be practical for a moment. We aren't stretching a 1 mile cable along an arc welding line at an automobile plant (as occasionally happens when working with industrial automation as I do for a living). What we have is 100 to 200 feet of twisted pair in a relatively low noise environment. RS232C is for industrial environments, and is not necessary for this application. 5 V line drivers are quite acceptable in this application, and a 7440 NAND gate could be used as an appropriate driver. A somewhat preferred approach is to use 5 V differential drivers and receivers such as the DM8820 and DM8830. These National Semiconductor (or their Texas Instruments equivalents SW75182 and SW75183) devices may not be available everywhere. A Texas Instruments 75107 and 75110 combination with the appropriate pin numbers changed can be used instead.

IC Number	Type	+5 V	GND	-12 V
1	AY-5-1013	1	3	2
2	DM8820	14	7	
3	NE555	8	1	
4	4009	16	8	
5	AY-5-1013	1	3	2
6	DM8830	14	7	
7	NE555	8	1	

Table 2: Power pin assignments for the receiver and transmitter of figures 3 and 4.

Construction is straightforward, and checkout is a simple go or no go test. Make sure that all voltages are correct and that the keyboard inputs to the interface operate correctly. It is a good idea to use a frequency counter to set the 1760 Hz on both the transmitter and receiver cards. If the frequencies are not within a few percent of each other, it will not work.

Attach a 1 or 2 foot twisted pair lead between the two units, plug in the keyboard, and remove the CMOS inverter from the receiver card. To display the received data word, either connect the receiver output to a computer parallel input port and write a program to scan and display it, or attach some sort of LED buffer and driver kluge to display the output.

When a key is pressed on the keyboard, the ASCII code for that key should appear at the receiver output. Momentarily grounding the data available reset line will allow another character to be received. When this phase is accomplished, insert the 4009, string your 200 feet of twisted pair cable, hook your monitor up with 200 feet of coax, and start plinking away.■

Photo 1: A stepper motor controlled scanning sensor capable of detecting both infrared and visible light. A photo detector is mounted at the focal point of an inexpensive parabolic solar cigarette lighter. The computer controlled unit is capable of following a moving flashlight, detecting headlights in a driveway, and many other applications.

I've Got You in My Scanner

A Computer Controlled Stepper Motor Light Scanner

"Boy, sitting here is really relaxing, isn't it, Lloyd?" I leaned back in the recliner and looked out of my living room window at the dense forest no further than 30 feet from where we sat. The sliding glass doors were open and occasionally some furry little animals could be seen darting in and out through the underbrush feverishly searching for dinner. The setting midsummer sun created an orange and yellow background for the beautiful scene. I wondered why I had ever waited for five years before moving out of the city. All that noise and congestion. This was so peaceful.

"It's very nice up here, Steve. I especially like the big driveway. You have lots of room to park cars. When are you going to chop down all these trees and put in a lawn like everybody else?"

Although I was not actually far enough removed from such suburban beatitudes to scoff with impunity, I piped back, "Bah! We moved out here to get away from the rest of the world. The last thing I want to do is be reminded of civilization, whether that means people or grass." The alternative I much preferred was to turn into a leaf shrouded computer hermit. "Lloyd, if I could figure a way to put in a moat with alligators, I'd do it," I said, tongue in cheek.

Such was the tone of our conversation for the next few hours. Whenever Lloyd ventured into the Connecticut wilderness (as he called it) he would stop by and visit me. Because of Lloyd's practical knowledge of computer related subjects I often used him as a sounding board for article ideas. His diplomatic responses sometimes disguised his opinions so tactfully, though, that I wasn't always sure what he really thought.

Before we knew it the sun had set and we were enveloped in darkness. The moonlight cast a silvery glow across the tops of the trees but hardly penetrated to the underbrush. But the moonlight was of small consequence to us. Even with the additional dim light escaping from the next room there was barely enough illumination to discriminate facial expressions, but there was sufficient backlighting for the little night creatures to observe us. Having lived in my new house for two months I had finally become accustomed to the nocturnal sounds and no longer experienced heart failure whenever I detected a pair of eyeballs peering at me from between the tree limbs. It was, after all, the domain of the owl and deer and I was the intruder.

I was less sure of the effect on Lloyd. Far away from the accustomed roar of jets at JFK and the traffic jams on the Long Island Expressway, he was suddenly very quiet, almost subdued, as he stared out the window into the darkness. Suddenly his eyes became focused on something in the distance and, gripping the arms of the chair tightly enough to leave an impression, he craned his neck to get a closer look. Something had obviously attracted his interest.

"I saw something!" he said.

"It's probably some possum checking us out or some other small animal after the dinner scraps I put outside."

"No, it's no animal. At least no small one. I thought I saw a light too. How many possums glow in the dark?"

"Don't be an alarmist. There's nothing to worry about."

"Look, there it is again, Steve! I think someone's out there."

I, too, saw a form way off in the darkness. It was definitely an erect biped moving between the trees and making considerable noise as it went.

We jumped from our chairs and crouched together looking out through the screen. The same thought came to both of us: "Is it Bigfoot?!"

"Wait a minute," I said in a hushed tone. "This is Connecticut. That's absurd! How can it be Bigfoot? Besides, since when does Bigfoot carry a flashlight?"

The bright beam of a flashlight shot from the stranger's hand. The dim light revealed a large man in coveralls dragging a heavy sack and carrying something over his shoulder.

"He must have a gun!" Lloyd gulped, and we both dropped to floor level. "Quick! Call the police or something! Better yet turn on the outside flood lights. Maybe it will scare him away."

"Look, Lloyd, if you want to become a moving target walking across the room to the light switch go right ahead."

"How come your burglar alarm hasn't turned the lights on?"

I thought about the alarm system for a moment and then answered, "I've got sensors all over the driveway and the road leading to the house. I didn't put them out in the woods because it's more likely that someone would come down the road rather than hike through the woods."

"How come nobody told *him* that?"

"Look, it'll pick him up anyway if he comes within 50 feet of the house."

Before Lloyd could reply, the man in the woods stopped in a clear area. The object slung over his shoulder wasn't a gun, but a shovel. He started to dig.

"Steve, do you think he's burying a body?"

I gathered up what courage I could and decided to go out and confront the perpetrator before my front yard looked like the aftermath of Dunkirk. "Come on, let's find out what he's doing."

As we approached, the man ignored our presence and kept digging. Occasionally he pointed his flashlight into the hole, then dumped the contents of the shovel into the sack. Was there buried treasure on my property?

"Excuse me, sir? Excuse me?" I said softly but with resolve. When I did not receive a response I stepped closer and repeated a little louder, "Excuse me, sir?!"

"Shhhh, Sonny! Da ya wanna scare all these critters away? It's hard enough making a living these days without everyone getting into the act. This here is my mound, Sonny!"

Mound? Sonny? I listened to his voice closely now and examined his features as best as I could in the moonlight. His accent was definitely Maine — deep woods Maine, and I put his age conservatively at 70. He seemed harmless enough, but I still had some unanswered questions.

"Sir, do you mind telling me what you're digging?"

He swung the shovel up over his shoulder and turned toward me. His face was weather-beaten and aged, yet there was a youthful glint in his eyes. The gravity of the situation evaporated as he answered, "Worms."

"You're digging *what?*" Lloyd chimed in.

"Worms," he answered again. "This hea mound," he pointed at the area where he was digging," is one of the best night crawler mounds in the county. Youst to be a farm around here, few yease back. This was the compost heap. Worms love it, ya know." He chuckled as he explained the worm breeding business to us city slickers. "I been diggin' around here off an on for 30 yease. Then someone came along and put a house on it." He pointed a boney finger at my place.

"I had no idea . . . ," I said, somewhat embarrassed.

"No matter . . . them's still my worms! I got ten spots just like this one and I'm transplantin' my worms. You know what a night crawler like this is worth around here, Sonny?" He reached into the hole and suddenly I had a handful of worms held in my face. I took great care to take shallow breaths lest I accidentally gasp and inhale one of the squirmers.

"No sir. I don't fish."

"Well, they're worth plenty. And I got to

116

dig a lot of them durin summa cause there ain't no worms in winta, Sonny."

His logic was irrefutable. He obviously earned his living at this. I felt a bit sad for the old codger. His digging really wasn't an inconvenience as long as he only took the worms and left the dirt. I didn't know enough about night crawlers to know the best time of night for harvest but I was sure we could work something out. I held my hand out to his and said, "You don't have to transplant your worms. What's a few worms between friends?"

A Modification to the Alarm System

At the conclusion of this episode I couldn't help but be concerned about the detection logic of the sophisticated alarm I had installed. There were sensors across critical points in the driveway and the road leading to the house that could detect the presence of a car or person. But, because of the likelihood of false triggering by wild animals, I hesitated to place similar detectors in the woods surrounding the house. I had thought the woods were impassable, but I guess I was wrong. The common denominator for anyone trying to make it through those woods at night is the necessity of a light. It should seem easy in principle to just place a light activated switch out there and activate the sequence when it detects some light source. Unfortunately, since the sensitivity would have to be relatively high, it would no doubt be accidentally triggered from lightning bolts and wayward fireflies. Complex integration and delay logic could

Circuit Cellar experimental setup showing the parabolic scanner as it detects a light bulb and a candle.

117

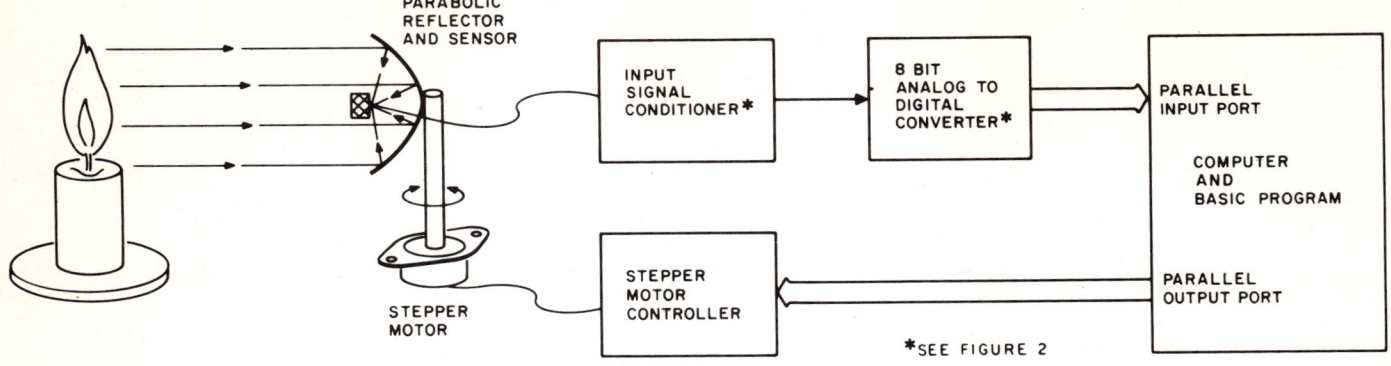

Figure 1: Block diagram of closed loop optical scanning system. The three main sections are the optics, consisting of a parabolic reflector and visible and infrared detector, the signal conditioner and input interface, and the stepper motor.

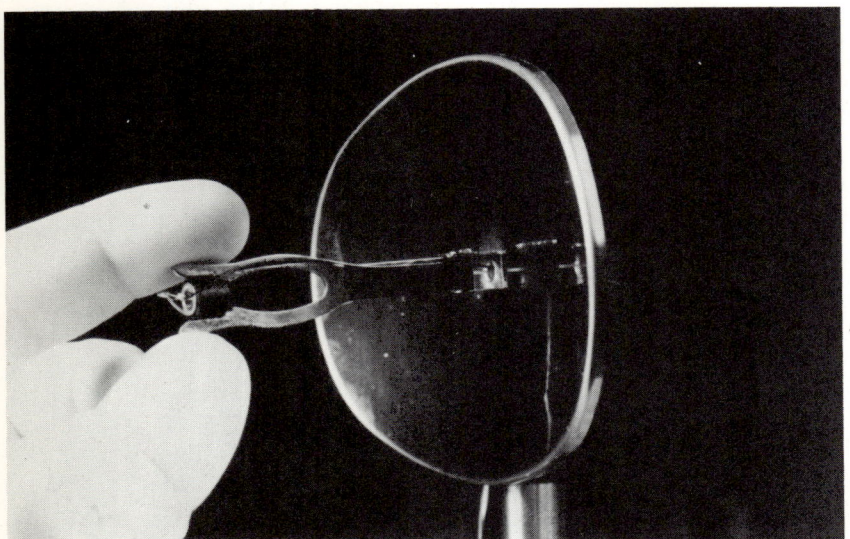

Photo 2: The parabolic reflector, used to gather light for detection by the photo detector.

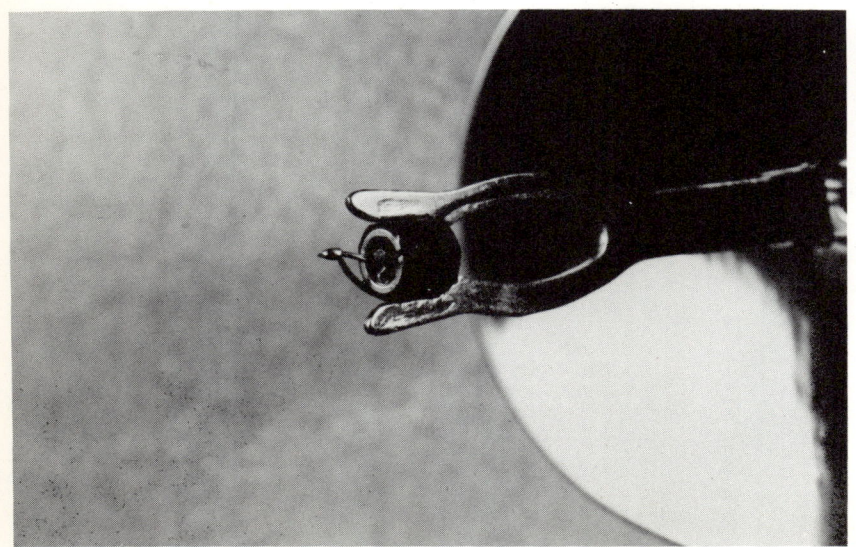

Photo 3: Closeup of the photo detector glued to the pronged holder.

be incorporated which would eliminate many false alarms but light level is still the only detection quantity.

Since a light source such as a flashlight or motor vehicle would have to move to approach the house, motion is another necessary parameter to consider. Most motion detection systems are passive beams whose sequential interruption triggers an appropriate response to a time and distance algorithm. Such a system of infrared or visible light beams, sufficient to protect four or five acres of property, would be prohibitively expensive if it incorporated a laser light source, and probably couldn't work reliably without one.

If we accept the premise that anyone coming through the woods on my property would need a flashlight or lantern, etc, then to detect the presence of an intruder requires a combination of light level and motion.

There are a number of methods that achieve the desired result. The most straightforward is to use a television camera, digitize the image, and after adjusting for ambient light changes, compare it to a previous digitized image. Many of the most sophisticated alarm systems incorporate this feature. While it is not beyond the capability of the more than modest home computer, it would be expensive in this application.

If You're Trying to Detect Motion — Move the Detector

Detecting motion with a light level sensor requires that a quantity of them be placed throughout the detection area. As the source moves, the relative light levels reaching all the sensors can be plugged into an equation and the location of the source computed. Tracking an object is simply a case of repeating this snapshot technique a number of times. Unfortunately, the concept is about

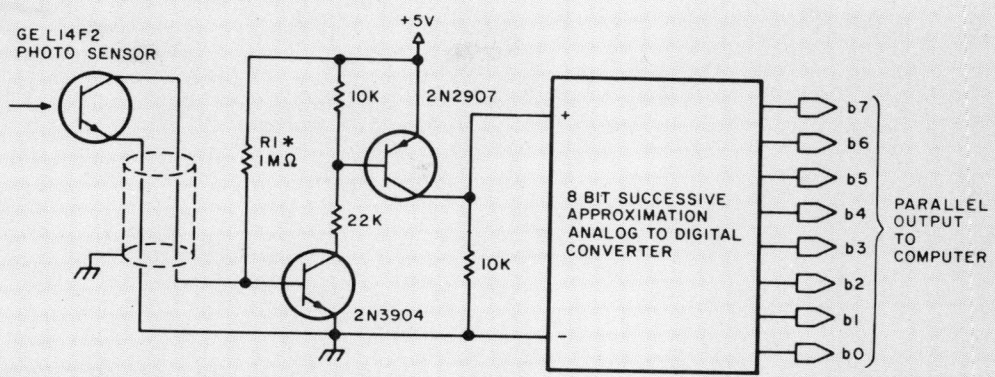

Figure 2: Optical signal conditioner and analog to digital converter that convert light input into a proportional digital output. The analog to digital converter shown was described in "Talk to Me: Add a Voice to Your Computer for $35" (page 77).

*Raising the value of this resistor will increase sensitivity. Lowering it will reduce sensitivity (range of resistor values is 4.7 k to 3.3 MΩ).

the only part that's simple.

An alternative approach is to point a light sensor at a source and then move the sensor to a new location. If eventually the source is again detected in this new position the source must have motion! This of course presumes that there aren't so many sources that placement of the sensor inadvertently coincides with a stationary source. Small but discrete steps of sensor displacement will increase the resolution of this method.

Build a Light Sensitive Scanning System

I wish to back off a bit at this point and explain that this design is not merely a motion detection system. That is one of its numerous applications and, as previously stated, it is the idea that prompted its development. The design is a simple, yet effective, light sensitive scanning system. A sort of passive radar (radio detecting and ranging system) if you will. It incorporates a sensitive visible and infrared light detector that is highly directional. In addition, it has the ability to accurately position itself on a rotational axis and sweep a wide area, much like a radar.

Figure 1 is a block diagram of the device. The scanning system consists of three prime components: optics, including sensor and reflector; signal conditioner and input interface; and finally, for closed loop control, a rotational positioning mechanism consisting of a 7.5° resolution stepper motor. The completed unit allows the computer to position its sensor in a known direction, read an analog value of the light level in that direction, and move to another point or track a moving source (more on this later).

The prime consideration in any light detection system is the optics. To take full advantage of any positioning mechanics, the light sensor must be highly directional. This is usually done with a series of lenses, the whole affair resembling a telescope. This technique is quite expensive and heavy. Instead of lenses, a highly polished parabolic reflector can be used to concentrate the light. One such device ideal for this application is an inexpensive parabolic mirror sold by Radio Shack for under $2 as a solar cigarette lighter. The unit, shown in photo 1, has a fork tipped hinged prong which extends from the center to hold the cigarette. Already designed to be at the focal point of the mirror, it serves as the perfect mounting bracket for the photo sensor. A GE L14F2

```
100 REM INFRARED SENSOR TEST PROGRAM
110 REM
120 REM
130 REM THIS PROGRAM CAUSES A SOUND SOURCE ATTACHED
140 REM TO LSB OF PORT 16 TO -BEEP- WITH   A PERIOD PROPORTIONAL
150 REM TO THE AMOUNT OF LIGHT SEEN BY THE LIGHT SENSOR
160 REM REV. 1.1     S.CIARCIA
170 REM
180 OUT 16,0
190 X=INP(16)
200 IF X<230 THEN GOSUB 220
210 GOTO 190
220 OUT 16,255
230 FOR T=0 TO X+5
240 NEXT T
250 OUT 16,0
260 RETURN
```

Listing 1: Program written in Micro Com 8 K Zapple BASIC that reads the light level from the analog to digital converter and converts it to a proportional pulse width on output port 16 (in my particular system configuration).

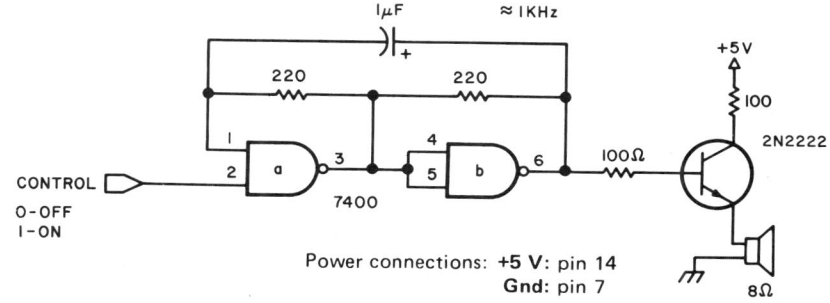

Figure 3: Sound source circuit (use with optical scanner test program above).

Photo 4: North American Phillips stepper motor, Model K82701-P2, and the SAA1027 controller circuit used to drive it.

infrared photo Darlington inserted into a phenolic sleeve is glued to the cigarette holder at the focal point as in photos 2 and 3. The lens of the photo sensor should face the reflector.

While the photo detector is infrared by design, it is highly sensitive to visible light as well. By choosing the infrared unit, a detection system can be designed that utilizes the best of both spectra.

The output of the photo sensor is essentially a current proportional to the light hitting it. The signal conditioner section of figure 2 converts this to an analog voltage level. The sensitivity of the photo detector is governed by resistor R1; changing this resistance value will affect both sensitivity and dynamic range. For the computer to read this voltage it must be converted to a digital quantity. While in theory any method, such as voltage to frequency, or voltage to pulse width, etc, could have been used, I'm a purist. The output of the signal conditioner is fed to an 8 bit successive approximation analog to digital converter. The details of this design were outlined in the June 1978 Ciarcia's Circuit Cellar in an article entitled "Talk to Me!" (page 77). Two slight modifications were made to the circuit for this application. The sample rate was reduced by placing a 0.01 µF capacitor in parallel with the 150 pF component already between pins 1 and 6 of IC1, and the offset potentiometer was readjusted to allow full scale unipolar operation (ie: 0 V input would give hexadecimal 00 output and +5 V input would give hexadecimal FF output).

The parallel output of the analog to digital converter is attached to an 8 bit parallel input port. Either an assembly language or a BASIC program can be used to read and display this quantity by querying the input port (input port 16 in my examples).

Exercising the device with a BASIC program is relatively straightforward. Listing 1 is a program written in Micro Com 8 K Zapple BASIC which reads the light level from the analog to digital converter and converts it to a proportional pulse width on output port 16. If a Sonalert or the circuit of figure 3 is attached to the least significant bit of port 16, it will beep. The beep rate will change as the reflector is pointed toward various light intensities. Printing out the analog to digital conversion value will give an accurate account of the sensitivity and dynamic range.

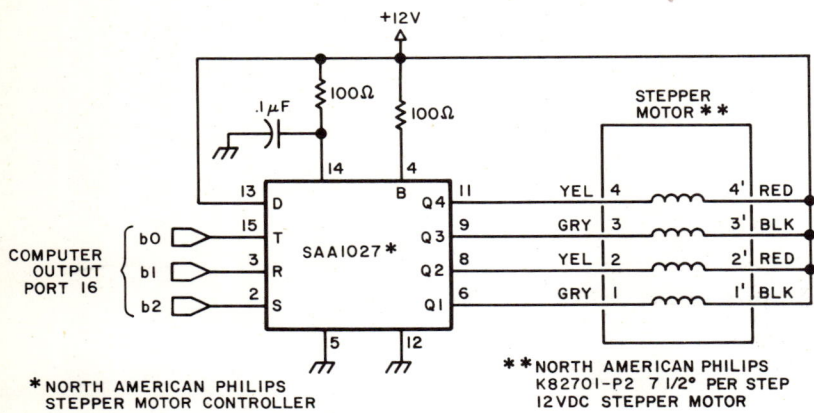

Figure 4: Connecting the stepper motor to the integrated circuit controller.

```
100 REM THIS PROGRAM DRIVES THE STEPPER MOTOR IN A BACK AND FORTH MOTION
110 OUT 16,1 :OUT 16,255 :REM PRESET STEPPER CONTROLLER
120 REM
130 REM
140 REM GO 25 STEPS CLOCKWISE
150 FOR D=0 TO 24
160 REM BIT 2 IS SET HIGH AND BIT 0 IS TOGGLED TO GO CLOCKWISE
170 OUT 16,5
180 GOSUB 390
190 OUT 16,4
200 NEXT D
210 REM
220 REM RETURN SCAN DELAY
230 FOR S1=0 TO 10
240 GOSUB 390
250 NEXT S1
260 OUT 16,1 :OUT 16,255
270 REM GO 25 STEPS COUNTERCLOCKWISE
280 FOR D=0 TO 24
290 REM BITS 1 AND 2 ARE HELD HIGH AND BIT 0 IS TOGGLED TO
300 REM GO COUNTERCLOCKWISE
310 OUT 16,7
320 GOSUB 390
330 OUT 16,6
340 NEXT D
350 GOTO 110
360 REM
370 REM IN BETWEEN STEP DELAY TIMER
380 REM DELAY TIME SET BY VALUE OF T1
390 FOR T=0 TO 5
400 NEXT T
410 RETURN
```

Listing 2: A BASIC program that drives the stepper motor and demonstrates the sweep action. It initializes the stepper motor, drives 25 steps clockwise, waits a short period, and then returns to its initial position.

Add a Stepper Motor for Positioning

Now that we have an effective light sensor, we must add rotational mechanics to provide *sweep*. The simplest method for rotating this relatively lightweight reflector is to mount it directly on the shaft of a stepper motor.

An inexpensive stepper motor is available from North American Philips. This unit (shown in photo 4) is relatively small, and a single integrated circuit controller is all that is needed to interface it to a computer. The particular unit in this article is a 12 VDC 7.5° stepper motor. This means that there are 48 steps per revolution, and, if one were trying to scan a 180° field of view, the stepper should oscillate between 24 clockwise and counterclockwise steps. This would give the impression of "sweep."

The electronics of the stepper are outlined in figure 4. Three bits of a parallel output port are necessary to control the direction and speed of the motor. The three signals are S, R and T, for set, rotation and trigger. When first engaging the motor it should be set to a known condition by pulsing the set input low while keeping the trigger input high. Once initialized, the direction of rotation must be chosen. This is done by setting the R input low if clockwise rotation is desired and high for counterclockwise rotation. An actual step is initiated by simultaneously making a 0 to 1 logic transition on trigger input T. By repeatedly toggling this bit, continuous motion will result. The stepper motor in this article is capable of 200 steps per second.

A BASIC program which drives the stepper motor and demonstrates the sweep action is outlined in listing 2. It initializes the stepper, drives 25 steps clockwise, waits a short period, and then returns to its initial position.

Making a Scanning System

To produce a closed loop controlled scanning system, the reflector and photo sensor are attached to the stepper motor shaft by any convenient means. I glued the reflector to a sleeve which attached to the shaft of the motor. The concept of closed loop control comes from the ability of this unit to position itself, take a light reading, and perform some further action as a result. This could be to step to a new location or to stop and remain stationary on any source above a certain light level.

Listing 3 is the BASIC program of such an exerciser which seeks out and points at a light source. As the parabolic reflector steps through its sweep, it checks the reading of the analog to digital converter and compares it to a set point. If the set point is exceeded, the program will stop stepping and point at this source. Should the light be extinguished or obstructed, the sweep resumes until it finds another source of sufficient intensity.

```
100 REM THIS PROGRAM SIMULATES A CLOSED LOOP -RADAR-
110 REM IT SCANS BACK AND FORTH 25 STEPS IN EACH DIRECTION
120 REM LOOKING FOR A PRESET LIGHT LEVEL EITHER PRODUCED BY
130 REM OR REFLECTED FROM SOME OBJECT IN ITS SCAN PATH
140 REM IT WILL STOP SCANNING AND REMAING POINTING AT ANY SUCH
150 REM OBJECT IT FINDS. IF THE OBJECT MOVES, THE SCANNER WILL FOLLOW
160 REM
170 REM
180 OUT 16,1 :OUT 16,255 :REM PRESET STEPPER CONTROLLER
190 FOR D=0 TO 24
200 OUT 16,5
210 REM TAKE ONE CLOCKWISE STEP
220 GOSUB 550
230 OUT 16,4
240 GOSUB 480 :REM READ SENSOR
250 NEXT D
260 REM
270 REM RETURN SCAN DELAY
280 FOR S1=0 TO 10
290 GOSUB 550
300 NEXT S1
310 REM
320 REM
330 OUT 16,1 :OUT 16,255 :REM PRESET STEPPER CONTROLLER
340 FOR D=0 TO 24
350 OUT 16,7
360 REM TAKE ONE COUNTERCLOCKWISE STEP
370 GOSUB 550
380 OUT 16,6
390 GOSUB 480 :REM READ SENSOR
400 NEXT D
410 FOR D=0 TO 25
420 NEXT D
430 GOTO 180
440 REM -RADAR- SENSOR READ ROUTINE
450 REM A/D INPUT IS ATTACHED TO INPUT PORT 16
460 REM LOW LIGHT LEVEL IS A VALUE OF 255 AND HIGH INTENSITY
470 REM IS AN INPUT VALUE OF 0
480 X=INP(16) :REM READ A/D CONVERTER
490 L=10 :REM PRESET LEVEL SET ....THIS WOULD BE A BRIGHT LIGHT
500 IF X<L THEN GOTO 480
510 RETURN
520 REM
530 REM
540 REM DELAY TIMER TO COMPLETE MECHANICAL MOTION BEFORE READING SENSOR
550 FOR T=0 TO 25
560 NEXT T
570 RETURN
```

Listing 3: A BASIC program that causes the scanner system to seek out and point to a light source. The scanner tracks the light source as it moves. If the light source is extinguished or obstructed, the sweep resumes until another source of sufficient intensity is found.

This is a rather rudimentary program but it incorporates all the basic structure to which enhancements such as motion detection and tracking can be added. It will, as now written, follow a flashlight as someone walks across a room. It is left as an exercise for the reader to drop a net over the perpetrator.

There are a few other little things you can try after you've built this gadget. The sketch on page 117 shows the portion of my basement (the "Circuit Cellar") immediately adjacent to the computer system. After modifying the BASIC program of listing 3 to print out a number on a scale of 1 to 9 (a period is 0) indicating relative intensity, and turning on a light and lighting a candle, I initiated a single scan across the room. Listing 4 is a printout of that scan. The sensitivity of the device had to be set very high to pick up the candle, and the result was rather interesting. The scan allowed the computer to "see" around the room in front of it.

```
. . . . . . . . . . 1 . . . 1 6 9 7 3 1 . . . .
```

Listing 4: A single scan of the room containing the light bulb and candle. A modification of the program in listing 3 to print numbers on a scale of 1 to 9 (a period is 0) indicating relative intensity.

```
. . . . . . . . . . . . . . . . . . . . . . . . .
. . . . . . . . . . . . . . . . . . . . . . . . .
. . . . . . . . . . . . . . . * . . . . . . . . .
. . . . . . . . . . . . . . * * . . . . . . . . .
. . . . . . . . . . . . . . * * * . . . . . . . .
. . . . . . . . . . . . . . * * * . . . . . . . .
. . . . . . . . . * . . . . * . . . . . . . . . .
. . . . . . . . . . . . . . . . . . . . . . . . .
. . . . . . . . . . . . . . . . . . . . . . . . .
. . . . . . . . . . . . . . . . . . . . . . . . .
```

Listing 5: Ten sweeps of the room. The relatively large size of the light used in the experiment accounts for the large number of asterisks at the right.

NOTE: The K82701-P2 stepper motor and SAA1027 are available singly or in quantities. For details contact:
Sales Dept.
North American Phillips
Cheshire CT 06410
(203) 272-0301

There is an intense light source to the left and a rather low level one to the right. By incorporating gain selection (changing the 1 MΩ resistor in the signal conditioner) under program control the computer could reduce the gain selectively to determine the origin of each light.

One further experiment entailed taking numerous sweeps and combining them to form a digitized computer picture. First the program was changed back to a threshold detector again. As it scanned the 25 steps it would print out an asterisk (*) for anything that exceeded this threshold and a period (.) otherwise. A protractor was attached to the arm of the tripod so that the angle of the reflector could be adjusted by a known increment each time the computer stopped between scans. The result was as illustrated in listing 5. The ten scans form a computer's eye picture of the wall. Again, because of the dynamic range differences between the candle and the light, the incandescent bulb appears much larger than it actually is.

Conclusion

Here's a simple device that can detect and track infrared and visible light sources. See what you can do with it. I don't want to leave anyone with the impression that I'm waiting for a burglar with a million candlepower flashlight to come tripping through the woods. This is but one sensor in a larger system, and the infrared capabilities, which I neglected to discuss in detail, are its primary application.

There have been numerous articles on light seeking robots. With this detector it is quite possible that the mechanics and software could be reduced considerably. I've often thought about building a robot, but my mechanical talent is nonexistent. When I can build one with a screwdriver and a soldering iron only, I'll write about it. (My thanks to Lloyd Kishinsky for graphics ideas used in this article.)■

About the Author

In my travels through the personal computer field, I have on occasion mentioned the fact that I work with Steve Ciarcia. The response to this statement is a barrage of questions that would take a week to answer. It seems that a number of people have read Steve's articles but have not had the chance to meet him. For the latter group, the following description may help acquaint you with the man who writes that intelligent, humorous, and popular column in BYTE magazine called "Ciarcia's Circuit Cellar."

Although Steve's full time job of computer consultant commands a great deal of his attention, he devotes a lot of time to other interests and hobbies. Steve's private side is just as colorful as his professional side. He and his lovely wife Joyce recently purchased a beautiful home on a hilltop outside of Hartford, Connecticut. Steve gave his lawnmower away years ago, but fortunately his front lawn is composed of cedar chips and wild flowers and requires no upkeep. In addition, the house is made of redwood so it doesn't have to be painted; the home is capable of taking care of itself, leaving the Ciarcias free for other activities. Upon entering the house one discovers a large kitchen filled with spice racks, cookbooks, a coffee grinder, wok and other cooking utensils. Steve is not only a whiz with Zapple but with apple strudel and chicken cacciatore as well. He enjoys fine food and rates Tangueray martinis and freshly ground coffee high on his list of beverages. Many of Steve's readers may be surprised to discover that some of his greatest creations come out of the oven. His talents extend equally well to hardware, software, silverware, and Tupperware.

The living room is the focal point of the main level. It is hexagonal shaped with glass extending from the floor to the 12 foot ceiling on three sides. The woodland view is beautiful and comes complete with ferns and furry creatures. The carpeting is plush and mossy green, and the huge fireplace in the center of the room is surrounded by a conversation pit. Soft guitar music floats from the large speakers in the corners of the room. If ever there was a spot suited for peaceful contemplation, this is it.

A description of the Ciarcia residence would not be complete without mentioning two of the friskiest inhabitants, Brenda and Whiskey. These two black Scottish terriers spend most of their free time running in the woods, chasing rabbits and butterflies. It's obvious from their behavior that they're delighted with their new home. In addition, the dogs (they will surely be offended when they read this) are ham actors who spend hours posing for Steve's photographs.

The lower level (alias the Circuit Cellar) is a world unto itself. After all, how many people have to buy a new house because they've outgrown their old basement? Yet even with all the room Steve has provided for himself, the sheer volume of the electronic gear cluttering the shelves and counters means that the bulk of his work is usually done on less than two feet of bench space.

What does Steve look like? For those of you who have pictured Steve as a small, spectacled, balding individual, forget it! Dressed in jeans, workboots and a flannel shirt, Steve resembles a bearded lumberjack from Oregon. Upon closer inspection, his rugged appearance is tempered by twinkling eyes and a friendly voice, more like a teddy bear than an outdoorsman.

But don't make the mistake of assuming that Steve is a country bumpkin, either. He is an Electrical Engineer with over 10 years of experience. His current position is Director of Marketing for an electronics and computer science consulting company. His experience includes nuclear instrumentation, process control, digital design, and product development.

Trying to keep up with Steve is like trying to outrun the 5:15 express. He manages to hold down a full time job, write a monthly article for BYTE, put together two books and even go to Mexico for two weeks to babysit for a computer at the Miss Universe Pageant. One person even asked me if Steve and a twin brother work together 24 hours a day in order to complete his projects. (Steve doesn't have a twin, but I suspect that he writes with a pen in each hand.)

Any computer enthusiast visiting the Circuit Cellar will feel like a child in a candy store. If it had a few more flashing lights and video screens the place could pass for the control tower at the local airport. Some of the units act almost as if they have minds of their own. One little box on the shelf has something like a miniature radar antenna on top. Although Steve says that it is just a "simple infrared light detector," I suspect the thing is alive; it tracks the movements of anyone in the room! (The gadget is described in "I've Got You in My Scanner!", contained herein.)

At times it feels as though the Force is lurking just around the corner. One night as I went to load Startrek to impress a friend, it spoke back in a stern tone, "Please not tonight, I have a headache." The second attempt to load Startrek generated the response, "This is the second and final warning. Keep your cotton picking fingers off me. Turn me off and go play somewhere else." As of that moment I have been on the wagon. Pink elephants, maybe, but talking computers? Never!

The equipment is constantly changing and expanding. At present Steve has a Z-80 system with 64 K of memory, dual floppies, a Votrax speech synthesis board, touch input video display terminal, Selectric printer, Decwriter II and a second Z-80 system with 26 K of memory. Many of the interface circuits described in Steve's articles are connected to these two systems. Also sitting on the shelf are a 4 K Scelbi 8008, DG8080, and an 8085-based SDK-85. There are several video displays surrounding the systems including a graphics terminal of Steve's own design.

After seeing some of the circuits Steve has developed, one would think he must have a laboratory with all the latest test equipment. Steve does have a lot of nice equipment, but doesn't need as much as one would expect. Often he simply develops a circuit to fill a gap in his collection of equipment. According to Steve, "If I don't have what I need, I build it." Many times the circuit he develops performs the job of equipment costing many times the price.

It would take a month for most computer enthusiasts to come up with some of his ideas. With Steve, however, it is another story. One Friday afternoon he casually mentioned that he was thinking about putting together a circuit that would allow a person to touch the video screen and select desired information instead of typing on the keyboard. Early Monday morning in walked Steve with a box under his arm and a smile on his face. "It needs a few refinements, but it works," he reported. "I was pressed for time so I did the software in BASIC." Five minutes later a sensor frame had been placed around the video screen and the system was turned on. On the screen appeared the command, "SCRATCH ME I ITCH." As Steve touched the screen it uttered what could have passed for a sigh and "THANK YOU I NEEDED THAT" materialized on the screen. Several other equally remarkable demonstrations followed. The resulting circuit is described in this book.

Working with Steve is truly an experience. Occasionally members of the local computer group will get together for lunch to talk shop and solve problems that crop up. Yesterday as we sat down for lunch the waitress rushed over with an extra supply of napkins for our table. No, it was not because computer enthusiasts are reportedly sloppy eaters! Steve just likes to solve problems and design circuits on napkins over lunch. I haven't decided whether the waitress is building her own home computer or selling Steve's ideas on the side.

Rumor has it that Steve uses a Post Office box because they would have to add an extra team just to provide home delivery for his mail. A close examination of his mail reveals a box from Denver, a padded envelope from Florida marked "Do Not Fold or X-Ray, Magnetic Recording," letters from Peterborough NH, postcards and letters from all over the U.S., Germany, Russia, Norway, Japan, India, and even the South Pole!

For those of you wondering about Steve's friend Ralph (April 1977 BYTE) he's alive and well. Lately he has been deep in thought, planning his next project: a set of modems to access Steve's super system via phone. After some of the past experiences it is very likely that Ralph will hear a perpetual busy signal when he tries to call.

Raymond Archer
Debbi Kishinsky
September 1, 1978

BYTE Books

Edmond Kelly, Jr., publisher
Blaise W. Liffick, technical editor
William H. Hurlin, production editor
Patricia Curran, production editor
Risa Swanson, production artist
E. S. Associates, production art
Techart Associates, drafting
George Banta Company, printing
Dawson Advertising Agency, cover design